find
me
unafraid

love, loss, and hope in an african slum

kennedy odede
and jessica posner

An Imprint of HarperCollins*Publishers*

FIND ME UNAFRAID. Copyright © 2015 by Kennedy Odede and Jessica Posner. Foreword © 2015 by Nicholas Kristof. All rights reserved. Printed in the United States of America. No part of this book may be used or reproduced in any manner whatsoever without written permission except in the case of brief quotations embodied in critical articles and reviews. For information address HarperCollins Publishers, 195 Broadway, New York, NY 10007.

HarperCollins books may be purchased for educational, business, or sales promotional use. For information please e-mail the Special Markets Department at SPsales@harpercollins.com.

FIRST EDITION

Designed by Suet Yee Chong

Library of Congress Cataloging-in-Publication Data has been applied for.

ISBN 978-0-06-229285-8

15 16 17 18 19   OV/RRD   10 9 8 7 6 5 4 3 2 1

To our families, and the SHOFCO movement

In the fell clutch of circumstance
I have not winced nor cried aloud.
Under the bludgeonings of chance
My head is bloody, but unbowed.

Beyond this place of wrath and tears
Looms but the Horror of the shade,
And yet the menace of the years
Finds and shall find me unafraid.

—From "Invictus"
  by William Earnest Henley

contents

foreword

by nicholas kristof

I've seen lots of unlikely sights in my travels as a journalist and author, but one of the most remarkable is deep within the Kibera slum in Kenya's capital, Nairobi. Kibera is not at first glance—how can I say this politely?—an uplifting place. It's a warren of tiny shacks on dirt paths that turn into mud and muck when it rains. Crime, joblessness, and sexual violence are common. The Kenyan authorities have offered little help, and Western aid projects haven't done much to create opportunity either.

Yet you amble down one of these tiny dirt paths, turn a corner, and there it is, a modern, cheerful school full of bubbly elementary school girls in neat uniforms, and a large sign: KIBERA SCHOOL FOR GIRLS.

What girls these are! They're chattering away in English (for many of them, it's their third language after Swahili and a tribal language), while brimming with poise and self-confidence. In class, they ace standardized exams and do better than wealthier students at much more privileged schools. The contrast between the hopefulness of these schoolgirls and their sometimes grim surroundings is striking—and it's pretty clear that these girls are change-makers who will build a better Kibera, and a better Kenya.

Yet the Kibera School for Girls isn't just an education story; it's also a love story. The school is the brainchild of Kennedy Odede, who grew up in the slum, and Jessica Posner, a Colorado girl who took a junior year abroad to work on street theater with Kennedy in Kibera. Jessica insisted on staying with Kennedy and his family, horrifying them all—"No white person has ever stayed in Kibera!"—but she browbeat them and then, when she saw the rats and toilets and was privately aghast, was too stubborn to back down. Kennedy and Jessica learned from each other, she helped him get into Wesleyan University on a full scholarship (even though he had no SAT score or high school transcript), and together by force of will they built the Kibera School for Girls and a broader development effort called SHOFCO, or Shining Hope for Communities. It includes a clinic, a water source, economic empowerment programs, a community newspaper, a women's empowerment group, an effort to fight rape, and so much more, and is now expanding this model across Kenya's slums.

SHOFCO is a love story, but it's also a lesson in development. The organization succeeded in part because it had someone with local knowledge and charisma to lead the way, and in part because it had a policy wonk foreigner who could help open overseas wallets. That's a potent partnership. If it's just foreigners, there's a risk that locals will see them as cows to be milked, or that a project won't have the necessary buy-in from local people. Indeed, SHOFCO is successful partly because it didn't begin as an aid program at all but as a local empowerment movement, with Kennedy and his buddies organizing soccer games and street performances decrying rape. Only after it was well established did it take on a more structured dimension, building effective partnerships.

Kennedy's life underscores one of my favorite aphorisms: *Tal-*

ent is universal, but opportunity is not. Everyone who encounters Ken can see his prodigious gifts of leadership and enthusiasm, but even he could have easily gone in a wrong direction. He tried his hand at thievery but fortunately he turned out to be a wretched mango thief and was so scared when he was caught that he mostly stayed honest after that. He did fall in with a gang, though, and sometimes his anger and frustration boiled over and led him on a path toward violence. But, ultimately, he applied his talents to building and creating, not to destroying, and aspiration trumped frustration. So many people helped him, from childhood buddies to an Italian priest to Wesleyan admissions officers, and in the end it all came together. But to see Kennedy, or to see the brilliant and self-confident girls at the Kibera School for Girls, is to know that there are many other outstanding young children who won't get the opportunities they need. They lose, and so does the world.

There's a theory that cycles of poverty perpetuate and self-replicate in part because of despair. People feel hopeless, and then engage in self-destructive behaviors that make that hopelessness self-fulfilling. The implication, and there's a fair amount of evidence emerging for this, is that the way to break cycles of poverty is to give people hope—and in the largest sense, that's what Kennedy and Jess are doing. They provide education, water, medicine, and more, but above all they provide a vision of hope, a trajectory toward a better life, a reassurance that maybe Kibera and indeed the world's slums can become better places. That's why my wife, Sheryl WuDunn, and I wrote about Ken and Jess in our own book *A Path Appears* as an example of how a cross-country partnership can fight poverty and spread opportunity—with hope!

Too often, humanitarians and journalists alike depict global poverty as uniformly bleak and grim. Aid groups do that because they think the way to raise money is to say how awful things are; journalists do it because we're in the business of covering planes that crash, not those that take off. But the unrelenting focus on troubles masks the progress and risks turning the public off. The remarkable story of Kennedy and Jess makes a fine antidote to that gloom. Sure, they faced enormous obstacles, but ultimately their personal and professional saga is uplifting, hopeful, and thrilling. And I hope you have the chance someday not only to read their incredible tale but also to see their life's work, taking a winding mud path through Kibera, only to turn a corner and find—something close to a miracle.

part
one

prologue

kennedy

december 2007

The wall of discarded milk cartons is the only barrier between me and the gunfire outside. On a normal night, the noises of Kibera drift easily through these walls: reggae music, women selling vegetables by candlelight, drunken men shouting insults, dogs barking, a couple making love in their nearby shack. But now Kibera is frozen. The entire slum is holding its breath, praying for this rain of bullets to pass, like any other storm.

I'm shivering under the bed. It's so dark and breathing is difficult. I can feel spiders crawling over my back and rats poking my toes, but I stay still, afraid that any movement will draw the uniformed men. I hear a high-pitched scream, like that of a young girl. The uniformed men are spraying bullets, and they hit anyone or anything unlucky enough to cross their path. I close my eyes and pray that the girl will survive. They didn't come to Kibera for her. They came for me.

I haven't eaten since yesterday when the raids began; I'm

starving for both water and food. In my pocket I have two dollars, which could ordinarily sustain me for at least a week. But even if I came out of hiding, there would be nowhere to get food. All the shops in the neighborhood have been closed or looted. The road going into Kibera has been shut by the mobs and men in uniforms—paramilitary police. Nothing and nobody comes in and out without a struggle. They are sealing us in to die.

I hear gunfire, round after round in quick succession. The quiet afterward is almost as startling as the noise. I jump, and my head hits the underside of the bed hanging so low and close to the ground. My dog, Cheetah, barks outside the door. *Please be quiet,* I pray. *Don't call them here.* I lie frozen, anticipating the footsteps, but there is only blissful silence. Thirty minutes pass, and I do not hear any shots. Slowly I drag my body out from underneath the bed. My legs are stiff, and I dance back and forth to rid myself of the pins and needles. I gingerly open my front door, pat Cheetah on his head, and say firmly, quietly, "Stay." He isn't trained, just another nearly feral street dog, but I know he senses my urgency.

I knock on the rusting sheet metal door of my neighbor, Mama Akinyi. No one answers.

"Please, Mama Akinyi, it's me, Ken," I whisper.

Slowly, she comes to open the door and hastily sneaks me in. Her young face is gaunt. She is holding her little five-year-old girl, Akinyi. The same terror I feel is visible on Akinyi's face. I'm hungry and weak, and by good luck Mama Akinyi notices my dry lips. She offers me some of the porridge that she has saved for her daughter. I ask for only a sip, just enough.

We tune the radio to a local station, keeping the volume hushed. She has not seen her husband for the last two days. Many people have been shot in Kibera.

"The bullets are close," I say.

Mama Akinyi looks at me through a veil of tears. Her husband might be among the dead. While we listen to the radio we hear some men murmuring outside—with tin and cardboard walls, sounds easily trickle in and out. I perk my ears and hear from the murmurs that it's not just twenty or thirty people dead, but more than they can count. I don't need to listen any further. I thank Mama Akinyi and quickly go back to my house before endangering her family.

Several hours later there is still quiet, which now seems more eerie than the noise. Then someone is knocking, quietly but urgently at the door.

"Ken, Ken, are you there? Wake up! It's me, Chris."

Chris is just a few years younger than I am; I have known him his whole life. I open the door and see that he's frantic with terror. He is out of breath, panting, and I know what he will say before the words come out of his mouth.

"Leave, Ken, please. One of the men—he is showing people your picture, asking if they've seen you, if they know where you live."

I tell him to leave now, and he nods, knowing that any minute they might make their way here, using their guns and their money to get the information they need. I look at how skinny Chris is, and I thank him from the bottom of my heart for not selling me out. Even with this place turned to total chaos, I am reminded of how good people can be.

Cheetah begins to bark and won't stop. Then I hear the footsteps. Heavy footsteps. The men still have to make their way around the treacherously narrow corner. I calculate I have less than a minute to escape.

All I want to do is write her a letter, tell her how much I love her, and tell her that I should have listened, I should have left. Tell her how sorry I am for all the things we will never get to do and see together.

But maybe it's just as well. Probably none of it would have come true, our late-night plans to build a life together probably just an adolescent romance. She so sweetly believes anything is possible and my heart would break watching her come to know what I know—that no matter how you try or believe, everything can end at the cry of a bullet, the sound of soldier's footsteps, the breaking of a heart. Eventually she'd tire of the challenges of living in my world, and I'd grow tired too, living in hers.

I have my own dreams here, in Kibera.

Gunshot! Followed by a howl. Cheetah! They must have shot him in the alleyway, but I cannot risk going to look. Shaken from my thoughts, I run from the house. My heart beating, feet moving, I take precious extra seconds to lock the padlock on my door. I run blindly, looking for any cranny where I can hide. There is a sheet of metal that covers the opening to a small alley near my door. I crawl behind it and will myself not to breathe, praying my shaking body won't bump the metal sheet and give away my hiding spot. Through a crack I can see my door. The men materialize, weapons slung over their shoulders, dressed in fatigues, threatening in their uniformity.

Upon reaching my house, the men find the door is locked by my small padlock. Thank God I took the extra time to do that—with my door locked it looks like I am not home. Kicking the door hard, their warning clear, the intruders storm off. I wait in my hiding spot for countless hours to make sure the scene wasn't staged, and then I emerge panting and shaking, racked by both fear and relief.

I crawl on my stomach to the fence behind my house, climb over, and fall hard on the other side. My torso hits the ground like a sack of maize, but I feel no pain, as if my body has reached its saturation point. I begin running, hiding in the secret shadows of the shanties. I have no destination in mind, only the desperate desire to get away, to reach some elusive safety. I have to step over bodies still lying where they fell—the mortuary sweep has not yet begun, and everyone's afraid to venture out to claim the fallen. Kibera is a city of the dead. I am not scared of the dead, but of the living.

When I am finally far enough away, I stop to take a breath and pull out my cell phone. I swallow hard and dial.

one

jessica

september 2007

Even at four P.M. the relentless Kenyan sun pelts down. I look at
my phone, willing it to ring. I've been waiting at this makeshift
bus stop for more than an hour and a half. Old minibuses, called
matatus, pull up, packed to the brim with people. The haphazard, battered public vehicles are in sad shape, their bumpers ir-
reparably bent or about to fall off. The people crammed within
look at me with barely veiled questions in their eyes. I feel suddenly self-conscious, obtrusive.

Where is he? More buses and *matatus* come and go—but still
no sign of Kennedy. How many times is too many to call someone I've never met? My family always says I'm way too pushy.
I take a deep breath, but I just can't help myself, I dial again. I
ask if he is still coming. He replies, "Almost there." I hang up
unsatisfied—he said the same thing when I'd called more than
thirty minutes ago. I survey the landscape, looking for a place to
settle in. I'd had to ask where the "Adams Arcade bus stop" is—

and an old man wordlessly pointed to an unmarked curb. There is a gas station, what looks like a strip mall called Adams Arcade, a kiosk painted bright Coca-Cola red, and the curb where the buses swing in and out in loose coordination. Another *matatu* screeches by and I feel the Nairobi dust seeping into my pores. I wish there was a way to fix myself up a bit, but there's nothing to do but stand here and wait.

It is my fifth day in Africa. And my first time outside of the United States as an adult. When I told my parents that I wanted to go to Kenya for a semester abroad, they'd looked at me as though I were speaking another language. Wasn't Europe "abroad" enough? What happened to the daughter who hated camping, disdained dirt, and overpacked for a weekend trip to the mountains? My grandparents warned my parents it would be crazy to allow me to go to Kenya. While my parents might have wished they could forbid me to go, they knew better. Once I set my mind to something I am doggedly determined.

I hadn't originally planned to go abroad. I'd come from a public high school in Denver, and Wesleyan University woke me up to the possibility of all there was to learn. I didn't want to waste a second. But my best friend, Daphne, decided she was going to spend the fall of junior year in Italy, and I didn't want to be left at Wesleyan without her.

Daphne is tall, athletic, and beautiful, with a Canadian father and Greek mother. She grew up traveling, and she kept telling me that there was more to learn than what I would find in books and papers—there were foods to eat, the musical lilt of languages I wouldn't need to understand to be moved by, late summer nights to spend sharing stolen kisses. The world was a big place, and she encouraged me to go out and see it.

I was scared to find out just how big the world might be. I lived under tremendous, self-imposed pressure, determined to make every minute count, terrified that time would somehow run out before I became "great" or realized my purpose. I'd set myself on a narrow path when, at seven, I fell in love with the theater. I decided then that I wanted to be a professional actress and was obsessed with putting myself on this route toward "success." At Wesleyan I pushed the limit of what I could fit into a day; I didn't sleep or eat very much. I'd become so numbed by my need for perfection I didn't feel much of anything at all, always scared that enjoying something too much would pull me off my path. To distract myself from this tension, I started to date Joe, and I tried hard to convince myself I could love him. One day I took a study break that was not in my meticulous daily plan to sit with Joe on the floor of the library stacks and talk. Joe looked at me and said, "I wish I could be you. You've always known what you want."

I realized that was exactly my problem. At twenty years old, I'd never seriously rethought the plan I'd made at seven.

I went to the study abroad office and spent an afternoon lost in the binders describing all the programs approved for Wesleyan credit abroad. Unfamiliar places roused my curiosity: a program in Ghana about culture and music, a theater program in Russia, and a program in Nairobi, Kenya, about health and development—two things I blissfully knew nothing about.

It was only after I decided to go to Nairobi that I heard about Kennedy. Two friends from Denver had visited Kenya for the World Social Forum—a big activist gathering. Kennedy had spoken at the forum, and his organization, called Shining Hope for Communities (SHOFCO), performed a piece of theater. Upon hearing I was going to study in Kenya, my friends Bonnie and Becca gave me Kennedy's e-mail, suggesting I try to collaborate with his organization on a theater project. Kennedy and I spent the summer exchanging short e-mails, with his always ending "welcome to mother land and peace be with you!" Kennedy exuded a confidence, an honesty, that was disarming. When I'd first said I wanted to do a theater project with his group, he'd replied, "Here in SHOFCO we do miracles by the power of nature, but we'd love to learn more." But he didn't just agree to my participation—he'd asked me to send over my résumé. I was so nervous, I spent hours working on that résumé, hopeful that Kennedy would allow me to come and work with him.

I'd been so excited to finally find out just how big the world was, how far I could go. Yet as I wait alone at this bus stop, I wonder if maybe Kenya is just a little *too far*. At my homestay this morning, breakfast was a sour millet porridge, which I couldn't even fake eating. For the past two days Odoch, the academic director of my program, has been briefing us about cultural differences, safety, and expectations. He's from Uganda and fled during Idi Amin's rule. In his late sixties, he has a commanding presence, but there is a wisdom, a gentleness, and a youthful energy about him.

Odoch says that Kenyans will lie to foreigners all the time: they don't see it as lying; the truth is just slightly more malleable. He warns us that Nairobi is nicknamed Nairobbery because of the frequency of bank robberies and carjackings, but that we will probably be fine if we just hide should one happen, and that men here think that when they ask you out and you say no, really you're saying yes. According to Odoch, Kenyans invented the game of playing hard to get.

Donna, Odoch's American wife who has lived in Kenya for forty years, often interrupts him. She is a force of nature: a tall, outspoken, fast-moving, fast-thinking, muumuu-sporting, white ex-Catholic New Yorker. She is an anthropologist who wrote her dissertation on Maasai beadwork and now paints multicolored zebras, makes black Christmas tree angels out of yarn, jewelry of her own design, and recently took up experimental glasswork—in addition to writing and teaching.

Donna has been married to Odoch for the past twenty or so years, and a more unlikely and in-love couple I have never seen. Donna moves fast and talks even faster. Odoch moves with deliberate meditation and chooses his words very carefully. He can tell you no in such a diplomatic way that you are never sure if he really said no or not—and he is so kind about it that you just can't hold it against him.

"Do NOT get married while you are here. There is always a student who ends up married. Don't be that student," warns Donna.

I roll my eyes.

Odoch brings the conversation back from Donna's tangent to talk about the frequent, often violent university riots. In his youth, he used to be a ringleader of such riots. In a few months, Kenya will hold hotly anticipated presidential elections, and Odoch warns us to stay away from political rallies or demonstrations of any kind.

Only a few weeks before my arrival, an infamous underground gang called *Mungiki* beheaded many people in the Nairobi slum of Mathare. My dad heard the story on NPR. I'd loftily told him that one incident doesn't define a country and that, anyhow, the media was hungry for stories that fulfill white stereotypes about the violent Other. My dad told me to save the smart-ass theories for my Wesleyan classes.

Another bus pulls up, a bright blue KBS bus—more expensive and better regulated than the *matatu*s. He's the last person to step off, but without any words I instinctively know it's him: Kennedy Odede. He barely greets me, says only, "Let's go." He walks fast. I have to run to keep stride. Unsure how to navigate the busy traffic and skinny curbs too thin to be called sidewalks, I teeter dangerously close to the tarmac road. Kennedy takes me by the shoulders and places me on the inside, away from the traffic, so that a reckless driver would hit him instead.

As we walk, the big skyscrapers of downtown Nairobi, several miles to the northeast of us, melt into the distance. We weave through markets with everything from chickens to chairs displayed for sale. Abruptly the paved road stops, and the buildings seem to shrink and huddle closer together. We continue on a dirt path. There are people everywhere. I have to push my way through the dense crowd, trying my best not to fall in the mud. There are so many people I can hardly make out individuals—people are going every which way, with determined strides.

Before us sprawls Kibera, one of Africa's largest slums. Separated by a set of train tracks from the nearby lower-middle-class areas that enjoy formal provision of electricity and water, Kibera gives new meaning to the saying "the other side of the tracks."* In Kibera, hundreds of thousands of houses made from sheets of corrugated metal and other recycled materials are piled nearly on top of one another. Garbage-lined paths thread the neighborhood instead of roads, and the terrain consists of hilly slopes and steep inclines that without paving are uneven, making it difficult to maintain balance. With its own markets and shops, Kibera is almost a city unto itself, except that inside of the slum there are no government schools or health services, running water or legal power services. No one knows how many people live inside the slum—estimates range up to one million people in a space about the size of Central Park, entirely marginalized.†

I can't believe this exists just minutes away from the beautiful houses, roads, grocery stores, and shopping malls. The Kibera slum goes on for as far as my eyes can see—the sheer magnitude of it incapacitating. I can't go on, can't just keep walking as if this were a sight I see every day. I've never imagined that something like this could exist.

It takes Kennedy a few moments to realize that I am no lon-

---

* In this book, "Kibera" references the vast slums, not the surrounding lower-middle-class areas such as Olympic, Ayany, Karanja, etc., technically included in the area now designated as the "Kibera constituency."
† Population estimates of Kibera are highly contested and politicized. They vary widely from 170,070 (2009 Government of Kenya census) up to 1 million ("Kenya: The Unseen Majority: Nairobi's Two Million Slum-Dwellers," *Amnesty International*, 2009).

ger keeping stride. My face flushes with embarrassment at my transparent shock. Kennedy just stands next to me, and for a moment we stand on a hill looking at it together, through entirely different eyes. When my legs finally work again, we continue.

There are piles of trash that look as though they've been collecting for years. Puddles of rank, standing water often block our way. Reggae music drifts through the air. Women line the roadside with their makeshift businesses; cardboard trays filled with cooking rest in their laps.

A group of about eight little boys, who can't be older than six, walk past us, heading home alone from a local informal school. In their ragged uniform shorts and pullover sweaters, they gather around one woman cooking something that looks like french fries. One little boy proudly presents his money to the woman and buys one fry each for his friends, keeping only one for himself. I'm transfixed by this little brigade as they eat their treats, savoring each bite of their single fry. The selflessness, the generosity of that little boy cuts me to the core. I try to picture the same scene in America. Here, one child has precious pocket money and instead of buying a snack for himself, and eating it as his friends watch wistfully, this child takes obvious pride in his ability to provide for his pals. The boys run off along the crowded pathway until the bright red of their uniforms becomes a series of tiny dots.

Everyone greets Kennedy as we walk by with affectionate exclamations of "Mayor, Mayor!" I look at him quizzically and he just smiles—not offering any explanations. I guess he's practically a legend in these parts. I don't know much about him, but it's clear from the greetings as we pass that at only twenty-three, he inspires enthusiasm in this desperate place. It feels a little like walking with a celebrity.

To me, children shout out "How are you? How are you?," the one English phrase they apparently all know to use when they spot a *mzungu,* a white person. We turn off the main road, jump over an open sewer, and weave through several narrow alleyways, carefully avoiding the jagged, protruding corners of renegade iron sheets, to arrive at Kennedy's house.

The house can't be more than ten feet by six feet. It has a single plastic window and a door made from repurposed wood that barely closes. The walls are made out of corrugated metal and colorful cardboard milk boxes. A sheet hangs down the middle, separating the "living room"—a small table, battered couch, and metal chair—from the "kitchen"—a corner with big yellow jugs and a small camping stove—and the "bedroom." There's no power. The only source of water is the group of beat-up yellow jerricans stacked in the corner. There is a photograph of Marcus Garvey on the wall wearing an ornate feather hat. Hanging next to him, incongruously, is a poster for the movie *Titanic.* Kennedy has so few possessions—what there seems to be the most of is books: *Siddhartha,* Mandela's *Long Walk to Freedom, Mandela: The Authorized Biography, Negro with a Hat: The Rise and Fall of Marcus Garvey,* and *A Testament of Hope: The Essential Writings and Speeches of Martin Luther King.*

He says softly, "Welcome to my home."

My eyes stay transfixed on the books. He notices my gaze.

"There are two ways of escaping your poverty," he offers quietly. "One, you can use drugs, get drunk—escape. Or you can escape into the world of books; that can be your refuge."

I nod; books have often been my refuge, too.

"Do you want to know why I was late to meet you?" he asks with a gleam of mischief in his eyes, his tone shifting from serious to playful. His gleeful giggle would stand out anywhere.

I want to know.

"I had to walk!" He tells me that he had ended his shift at his current janitorial job in the city center, only to realize that, as so often happened, he wouldn't be able to buy dinner if he spent his fifteen cents for the *matatu.* So he walked more than an hour to meet me. When he was getting close, he convinced a sympathetic conductor to let him ride the last five minutes, just so I would see him stepping off the bus—with the dignity of a paying customer. He laughs.

I'm not sure how to respond—taken aback by his ingenuity, his pride, and the fact that if he used fifteen cents for bus fare he wouldn't be able to afford food. I'm stricken by a sudden understanding of what it would mean to him to have the thirty dollars I casually put in my pocket this morning.

We sit in silence for a moment, and I sense that my inability to laugh at circumstance the way he does—my obvious discomfort with my own privilege—has somehow let him down. Until now our conversation has flown with deceptive ease, and this moment reminds us that we are little more than strangers, from entirely different worlds.

"Do you want to see the SHOFCO office?" he asks, shifting the awkward energy.

"Of course."

We make our way back through the paths of Kibera to the iron-sheet SHOFCO office that stands precariously on the edge of the slum next to the railroad. This humble shack is SHOFCO's very first office, Kennedy tells me with pride. They still use it for meetings, theater rehearsals, and community forums and I hear laughter echoing from inside. Not wanting to interrupt, we go on to the second SHOFCO office in Olympic, a few rented rooms in the lower-middle-class estate that borders the slums of Kibera. A bunch of young people are hanging out, drinking tea, using a computer, and tending to the chickens and the small garden out back. As soon as I step through the gate, the energy of this place washes over me. These young people clearly love being here—it is their space. Kennedy's organization is much more than just a theater group. SHOFCO also operates a slumwide sanitation and cleanup program, and a women's empowerment program that educates and distributes sanitary pads in schools. There are also departments dedicated to communications, sports, and income-generating activities.

Kennedy introduces me to Anne, his childhood friend who runs SHOFCO's women's empowerment program, called SWEP. Her family owns the plot of houses where Kennedy lives and she lives kitty-corner to him. In a logbook, Anne records the number of beaded bracelets that the SWEP women have made this week. She explains the group is for women living with HIV, and they make bracelets to earn enough to feed themselves and their children. I learn that Kennedy started the SWEP project before SHOFCO, when he was only sixteen.

"I saw how these women were suffering. I used to buy them food with anything I earned. I guess that is how the group started."

"The women all call Kennedy their husband!" Anne laughs and elbows Kennedy. "He takes care of them."

Kennedy fends her off, chuckling, and says *"Kuenda uko"*—jokingly telling her to get back to work.

Next Kennedy introduces me to Joseph Kibara, nicknamed "Chair" because he has just been elected chairman of SHOFCO in their annual elections. Chair can't be older than twenty-six, but something about him makes him seem like a regal old man. He is clearly proud of his distinguished title and sits drinking a cup of tea as he participates in a small meeting. He rises slowly to ceremoniously shake my hand in welcome. Another young man with a shy smile stands and introduces himself as Nicholas Masivu, the treasurer. They get back to their meeting, excitedly writing plans down on a large calendar.

As we walk out back to see the garden where the group grows vegetables to sell, I ask Kennedy, "If he's the chairman, what does that make you?"

"I'm an adviser," he says mischievously.

Kennedy's best friend, Antony, hears this and laughs. "Don't let him fool you. Kennedy knows how to make sure everyone feels like SHOFCO belongs to them. He makes departments and then everyone votes on the leaders. I'm the head of communica-

tions. Then there is theater, SWEP, sanitation, girls' empowerment, soccer, and economics."

Kennedy feeds the chickens, whose eggs are another income
generator that supports SHOFCO's activities. I can't help but
marvel at the carefully thought out structures he's put in place,
and I say so.

Antony tells me that Kennedy has helped to start more than
a hundred small businesses with a philosophy he calls "pass it
forward." He gives out small loans from his meager earnings and
then requires that instead of paying the loan back, the recipient
designate a new person to receive a loan. The chain of loans has
launched barbershops, water stands, vegetable stalls, and many
other small enterprises.

"It was the great Jamaican leader Marcus Garvey who taught
me that for a people to rise up they must be economically independent. He started many black-run businesses. The idea that
SHOFCO and our community must be self-reliant is inspired by
him," Kennedy says, his conviction effusive.

A tall, skinny young man opens the gate. Kennedy jumps
boyishly in the air and shouts, "Coaches!"

They shake hands and fist-bump and then come over so Kennedy can introduce us. "His name is also Kennedy, so we call him
Coaches. He coaches the soccer teams—and they always win!"

I stand on the side, watching Kennedy talk with many of the
SHOFCO young people. It isn't hard to see why people call him
Mayor. A girl named Mary comes over to me and confidently
introduces herself as the person in charge of sanitation and girls'
empowerment. She goes right up to Kennedy and loudly starts
giving him a hard time about something, which everyone clearly
enjoys. I feel an immediate desire to become friends with these
young people—to share in their sense of purpose.

Suddenly Kennedy sees the sun setting and jumps.

"Where did the time go?" he exclaims. "We better get you
back to your homestay before dark."

No! I think to myself—*I'd rather stay here.*

Again, I have to work to keep up with Kennedy. As we cross a busy street, Kennedy reaches for my hand—holding on to it well after we are safely across. I look down at my hand and then up at his face quizzically—and he quickly lets go.

"Sorry!" he exclaims. "In my culture, it is customary to hold hands. It is a symbol of respect and friendship."

My mind spins from all I've seen as the day's last beams of sunlight smile down.

I head back to Woodley Estate, the comparatively leafy middle-class gated community where my homestay mother, Mama Rose, lives. Now that I've seen Kibera, which is, unfathomably, only a fifteen-minute walk away, I'm discomforted by the discrepancies between the two places. Mama Rose's place is a two-story house with running water, power, and a television. I realize that compared to Kibera, Mama Rose's house is a palace. Yet just days ago, when I was first dropped off here, I felt very much in the middle of "Africa." The house is small and outdated, with furniture and a feel from the seventies. Outside the community's high black gate is a market with handcrafted stalls lining an unpaved road. From there a narrow alleyway runs into a bigger market called Toi, which merges with a part of Kibera called Makina. The part of Toi Market near my homestay is casually referred to as *mzungu Toi* because its prices cater to the middle class and are much higher than "real Toi," which lies just a few meters farther away.

During the summer before embarking on my trip, I'd e-mailed Kennedy to ask if in addition to working with him at SHOFCO, I could live with him and his family in Kibera. I'd told him that I could pay him, as was standard for my program to cover the costs of host families. I'd told him he wouldn't even notice I was there.

He'd replied saying, unequivocally, absolutely not. Foreigners never live inside Kibera. He couldn't imagine my surviving without running water or electricity. *You are an American,* he'd written, *and I live a very simple life.*

I'd e-mailed back, saying, *I'm a simple American. If you can live there, I can too.*

Immediately upon arriving, I asked for a moment with my program director, Odoch, to discuss my living arrangement idea. Odoch gave his consent, noting that we probably shouldn't inform the study abroad program, since its administrators likely wouldn't approve. Later, another student asked if she could live in Olympic, the middle-class area just outside Kibera, and Odoch said no—it was too dangerous to live so close to Kibera with the upcoming elections. Instead of making me nervous, Odoch's inexplicable consent made me feel special.

Ever since I was a child my reaction to the forbidden has been a stubborn desire to keep pushing: obstacles make something uncontrollably and deeply necessary. The words *you can't* unleash a determination so intense that at times it even startles me. I want to know *why—why can't I? Because we said so!*—an obviously insufficient reason—my parents would say when I was little. While they may have thought that this impulse would abate with time and maturity, they are still waiting.

That night, sleeping in a comfortable bed, the TV on quietly in the background, the contrast between this and Kennedy's life in Nairobi is laid bare. My resolve to live in Kibera strengthens as this seems like the only way to even begin to break through the barriers that exist between me and the young people I'll be working with.

A few days later, I meet Kennedy for lunch at the Nairobi Java House. Kennedy spends a long time considering the menu. I order a sandwich and salad, and after a calculated pause, Kennedy orders the exact same things. He eats awkwardly, the fork held incorrectly. We discuss details about the theater project and his efforts to recruit young people to participate, and the scheduled hours for rehearsals.

Finally, we get around to talking about my e-mail—when I bring it up.

Kennedy emphatically repeats that no white person has lived deep inside of the slums of Kibera for more than a few nights—a few weeks tops. It's just not possible. Instead he suggests that I move into the SHOFCO office in Olympic.

I'm determined to prove him wrong, to show him that the differences between us aren't as vast as he might think.

two

kennedy

At six, I found my first gray hair. It was on the top of my head, right in the center, and when my mother saw it, she hugged me close and told me it was a sign of wisdom—a prophecy about my future. Exuberant with pride, she ran to tell anyone who would listen that there was a light at the end of our suffocating tunnel of poverty: the prophecy of greatness foreseen by my gray hair. But I knew better. By the age of six I had already lived through more than many people have at sixty—and my one gray hair was all I had to show for it.

I was born in the middle of a terrible drought. My mother was fifteen, unmarried, and terrified—ostracized by all in the rural village except her own mother, my grandmother Esther. To be conceived out of wedlock was dangerous for an unborn child, and especially for a boy. In the village, it was common for the mother's male relatives to kill baby boys born out of wedlock, or to take them to the woods and leave them to die. Such a boy was seen as a threat to the mother's family's ancestral land. Without a marriage to tie the child to a father, a boy might one day demand to inherit a piece of the relatives' land. So my mom prayed for a girl.

In the village, there are elders who see and know things. They have a sensitivity to secrets and prophecies that we may not be able to see ourselves, and their powers are revered. One day, in the middle of the drought, a powerful seer had a vision. She came to my grandmother Esther's hut and told my mother that a baby would be born on that exact night. To have a seer predict a birth was no small thing in my community, and the village was abuzz that entire day over the prophecy.

Indeed, I was born that night. My mother gave birth, at fifteen, in my grandmother Esther's tiny hut, with no skilled birth attendants present. No one in the village wanted to help; even the traditional midwives were afraid of becoming tainted by my mother's bad reputation. My grandmother's hand was all my mother had to squeeze when she could no longer bear the pain. And then my feet came first. When my grandmother saw the feet, she knew why the seer had made her prediction. This was not a normal birth. It was the end. Esther feared she would perhaps lose both her daughter and her new grandchild, too—it was unheard of for a woman and baby both to survive a breech birth in my village with absolutely no medical assistance. My grandmother prayed that the passing would be easy while she sat holding her daughter's hand for what she was sure would be the last time. But this was a night of many miracles. Both of us lived, and the story goes that at the sound of my first cry, the rains came. Odede—it means "after the drought." It rained for days and days.

Following my birth, the village elders called a special meeting to discuss the fate of this baby boy. They considered how the mother was unmarried, and as such the boy would likely be a problem later. Maybe they should take the baby out in the woods, leaving him for the dogs as they had done many times before. Still, the elders gave pause because this baby was born feet first. In our Luo tribe's lore, only kings and tribal leaders survive a breech birth. And then the rain—how could they explain the rain? Luos take signs very seriously. My mother always said her heart refused to beat on that day as she waited for them to decide my fate.

Many villagers assembled for the announcement. The village seer, Ojimbo Maloko, an old man, stood and decreed for all to hear that I was a blessing—my birth had brought the rains. My grandmother also told me how in this moment she burst into tears; the words *"Nyasaye duong,"* which mean "God is great," floated from her lips up to the heavens. This seer decreed I was a baby not just for the village, but for the world; I needed the name of a leader.

The villagers spent the next several days coming up with names. They proposed Ramogi, the name of another great Luo seer, or Luanda Magere, a famous warrior. Maloko was not satisfied and continued to insist that, no, this baby needed a name of the world. Then my grandmother suggested the name of the American president whose "airlifting" program had taken so many bright young people from our area to study in America. When I was born, these young people were returning home to become the great doctors, lawyers, and leaders of Kenya—one of them was Barack Obama's father—and because of them, everyone in Luo land knew of John F. Kennedy. And so I became Kennedy Odede.

Before I was two, my mother married Babi and moved with him to Nairobi, a place where he had heard whispers that work was plentiful and problems melted away. They left me in the village with my grandmother Esther.

I was the apple of Esther's eye and, even as a toddler, I knew it. She always fed me first, saying I was a small boy who needed to grow big. She would play with me and hold me, tickle me, and carry me everywhere, because I could not walk long after the age

I should have. I will never forget Esther's gentle hands scooping me into her arms and gingerly setting me down, always within her sight. To everyone else, I was a burden.

Then, when I was three, a rabid dog bit Esther. She suffered greatly before she died. Not understanding the gravity of her situation, I climbed into bed with her and asked when we would go to the market again. I was with her at the end—tears came from her eyes as she told me that I should never forget, no matter what, that I had a place in the world. My uncles in the village didn't want me, so my mother was forced to come take me with her to the city. My middle name, Owiti, means "unwanted or thrown-away child."

In Kibera, there were no more soft hands. Just from the way people touched me, I knew I was a burden, another mouth they couldn't feed. When they carried me from place to place, I could feel my own heft, could feel their disdain as they tossed me down. When I was nearly four years old my family had given up hope that I would ever walk. My lameness brought my family even more shame than our poverty. Then, one day, I took my first steps in Kibera. I stood near the river of sewage and actually walked across a makeshift bridge. The news traveled fast: the child of the people who brought their lice with them wherever they went, at least that child could finally walk.

At five, I had one pair of shorts—no shirts, no shoes. My sister Jackie, two years younger, had two pieces of clothing because she had inherited the shirt I had outgrown. Babi could not afford a belt, so he used a string. The women in our neighborhood often said that insects could not survive in the conditions in which we lived. The water sold by the vendors in Kibera was too expensive for us, so we filled our jerricans in the running sewage, which my mother tried to filter with sand.

At night none of us could sleep. We itched and tossed and turned—red marks appearing on our bodies—infected with lice and fleas. One day my mom was lucky and able to afford a small piece of soap, only the size of a coin, from a neighborhood shop. She woke us up early that morning and we each took a bath, using as little water and soap as possible. The unfamiliar lather from the soap made my body tingle, and Jackie cried. Then my mom washed our clothes and spread them out in the little space between our house and our neighbors' to dry in the sun. I sat inside on the floor, shivering and clean, when I heard a commotion outside.

"You want to spread your diseases to us! Remove these dirty clothes from here!" It was one of our neighbors, Mama Omondi, shouting.

I looked at my mom's face. She is a woman of great pride, and to look at her it was as if she didn't hear. She didn't move, didn't dignify Mama Omondi with a response—she just kept slowly and deliberately boiling water for tea in our only pot, taking care to use as little *mafuta* (cooking oil) as possible to boil the water. Mama Omondi didn't stop, continuing to hurl insults about our poverty, until we heard a flurry of activity. She had taken our newly washed clothes and thrown them onto the ground, stomping on them for emphasis. When I saw our clean clothes covered in dirt, I burst into tears. I knew we'd probably never have soap again. My mother came over to me and wiped my tears. She shushed me gently and told me that no matter what happened in life, I shouldn't give up so easily. She winked and pulled another quarter-size piece of soap from her pocket—she had saved it for another day! She was my hero. It broke my five-year-old heart to see the neighbors treat her like that, but she taught me early that it didn't pay to care.

My mother is the strongest, most courageous person I know. When I was a child, the sense of joy and strength she drew from defying expectations, or standing up for what she believed in, no matter how many people she alienated, often made me afraid for her. I didn't understand why she was always willing to risk so much. Later, I grew to respect and admire her conviction.

My mother, Jane Achieng, or Ajey as we call her, was born a rebel. The eighth of twelve children born in remote and rural Kenya, she never got the chance to go to school because as a girl, her place in the world was to marry and have children. She was forced to spend her days toiling over housework, walking hours to fetch water, and preparing food, usually porridge, for her brothers' return from school each day. When she could, my mom would sit with their books and try to teach herself to read. She kept it secret—a girl reading was rebellion—but she desperately wanted to understand this secret code of words.

By the time Ajey was twelve, most of her age-mates were already married to older men from nearby villages. Rarely did a girl protest—when she did, she was kidnapped and forced into marriage. One of Ajey's friends went to fetch water and never came back—the next news was that her family had received a handsome dowry, and this was a cause not for grief, but for celebration. My mother didn't want an arranged marriage for herself. Despite her poverty, she had unrealistic desires of marrying someone she might choose. I can imagine that like any blooming adolescent girl, my mother longed to be touched, to be treated for a moment like the beautiful and spirited woman she was becoming.

When she was thirteen, the village council of elders, called a *baraza,* arranged for her to become the sixth wife of an older man from a neighboring village. Most of the villagers were dumbstruck—this man was far too wealthy for the likes of Jane Achieng. To have more than two wives was a sign of riches. The entire village was so proud—my mom had brought blessings on them through this prosperous match. Her bride-price was to be seven cows and ten goats, a sum the village had not seen in many years.

My mom saw it differently. She didn't want to be married off to a man old enough to be her grandfather. But what choice did she have? My grandmother Esther sympathized—she loved my mom, and despite the fact that Esther was never educated herself, she was a progressive woman who didn't want to see her daughter consigned to a life of misery. She was my grandfather's second wife—his first wife, Alice, could not bear children. But Esther and Alice were best friends, like sisters. Although she could not bear children herself, Alice delivered all twelve of Esther's.

Unable to directly challenge the elders' decision regarding Ajey's betrothal, Esther helped my mom escape in the dead of night. Esther sent Ajey to live with Esther's sister in a village far enough away that my mom's whereabouts would be unknown. Ajey stayed in hiding in my aunt's village for many months, but when my mother's father died, she had to return home for the burial. When Ajey arrived back in the village, no one besides Esther would speak to her. Ajey was cursed—even blamed for causing an oppressive drought. No parents wanted their daughters to associate with my mother; no one wanted to be around her lest she pass her terrible luck onto them. After she deliberately flouted the ruling of the elders, and the desires of a powerful man, she had no place in the society. The villagers tried to make her life miserable as an example to others, so that no girl would ever behave in the same fashion.

When Ajey was fourteen, the elders came to her hut and told her this was her final warning—get married; she was setting a bad example for the girls in the village. There was no one who could go against the elders, and my mom knew that any minute a match would be made against her will. After a few days, another man, old enough to be her grandfather, was found. This man hailed from another village called Sakwa. He had four wives, and my mom was going to be the fifth wife.

The old man came in a convoy of bicycles to inspect my mother. My mom sat quietly, frozen. Next, the old man sat with my uncles to negotiate the bride-price while drinking local brew together. Each side appointed its chief negotiator. My uncle touted my mother's accomplishments—young, a good cook, and strong enough to do hard work. The old man did not bargain back. Instead he doubled the dowry in a show of great pride—he was also a man of wealth and wanted everyone to know this.

The agreement made, my mom was called from the kitchen to come and pay respects to her future husband. She would leave that very day to become his wife. My uncles handed Ajey over, knowing that the dowry would soon follow. In our culture the girl is taken first, and the cows come next. When she shook his hand, it was papery with signs of aging. My mom seethed and asked if she was allowed to finish her cooking before leaving for her new home. She went back into the kitchen and started to make porridge. When it was ready, hot and steaming, she poured it into a calabash and walked back to her brothers and the old man, everyone smiling at the show of respect that Jane Achieng was—finally—showing in the face of her marital obligations.

Instead of handing him the calabash, she threw the steaming hot porridge at his face.

The old man made a noise like a child, and everyone else went running. The elders and Ajey's brothers fell over themselves in their efforts to get away from her, their faces flushed with embarrassment and anger. My mom ran away from the village, away from her fate. Word traveled to all the villages in the area. Something like this had never happened before. Her brothers made a vow to teach her a lesson, promising to tie her up and beat her in front of the entire village.

My mother stayed in hiding with another aunt for a year. So it was that Ajey escaped not one, but two, arranged marriages. Sometimes I wonder what for. No matter where she ran, Ajey would need to marry—there was no place for an unmarried woman in our society. And then came my conception followed by Ajey consenting to marry Babi. The only boy in his family, Babi had dropped out of high school because of drugs. As a young man, Babi was already an alcoholic with a reputation for violence. He was considered an appropriate match for the monstrous Jane

Achieng. Ajey married Babi to help provide for me, and so I too became a part of her suffering.

Babi I liked best when he was just a little bit drunk, since that was the only time he would laugh or make jokes with us.

"Sometimes being poor is the best thing in life. You kids know how rich people live their life getting worried all the time? We can be poor and happy!"

I interrupted him. "Babi, we are not happy. I want food, soda, toys, and TV. Rich kids have all those things and their parents also take them to school. How can we be happy?"

Babi turned to me and said, "I know that, but listen. I see the rich people in the city and hear about how they live; they are always scared that someone will steal their property, they can't sleep content as you sleep, and their kids are not like you and your sister Jackie. Their kids are spoiled."

Jackie and I giggled in superiority. I didn't know what being spoiled meant, but I knew it wasn't good, and like any child, I loved when my parents said something nice about me, which Babi rarely did. Especially to me: he always singled me out. He beat me even more than he beat my mother, his blows knocking the wind out of me. He took special delight in beating me while he forced her to watch, helpless. I learned early to stay out of his way.

I liked Babi okay when he was medium drunk, too. Medium drunk made him tired. He'd still hurl insults at all of us, but they seemed halfhearted. Sometimes he'd throw a few things, or push my mom a bit, but soon he'd fall asleep, and we'd all breathe a sigh of relief.

When he was really seriously drunk, we knew trouble was coming, and fast. Once when I was only five, he beat me so hard that feces escaped from my body—my only crime was asking my mom for another spoonful of rice. Babi hated to see me eat. Sometimes Ajey would try to feed me something before he got home, just in case. Once, he found her doing this, and he poured the hot water she was boiling for tea over her head. I screamed, knowing I was the cause of her pain.

In our Kibera neighborhood, it was easy to know if people had food or not. You had to light your charcoal stove, a *jiko,* outside in the open air for the charcoals to catch fire. If you did not bring your stove outside to cook, you showed the neighborhood the depth of your suffering. The women in our neighborhood liked to show off, especially our neighbor Mama Omondi. When they cooked meat, everyone knew. My mom would sometimes pretend that we were cooking, too, by lighting the charcoal stove outside, even if we had no food to put on it. She would tell us to rub our lips with oil so that they looked shiny, as if we had eaten something, in case a neighbor came to visit. She didn't allow us to eat at the neighbors' houses, warning us that the neighbors would "backbite" us.

"You don't show your nakedness in public" was how she put it.

At night we sat on the floor of our single-room home and prayed in our native language, each secretly asking God in our hearts to hear us—this time—and grant us even a momentary reprieve from this suffocating poverty. My mom never went to school, but she could read and write in *Dholuo* (her native language). She loved reading the proverbs from the Bible, the one book in our home. After reading, we all sang hymns until it was bedtime. Many nights my stomach made noises so loudly, it was as if it wanted to sing along.

For a time, Jackie and I would sneak away during lunchtime to go to Mama Omondi's house to eat, even though we knew my mom would especially hate our eating at this neighbor's house. Then one day when my mom and Mama Omondi were fighting, Mama Omondi shouted, "Woman, do not argue with me when you can't even feed your own kids! I always feed your kids for you. Why do you give birth to an army of kids and yet you cannot afford to feed them?"

My mom was furious. Jackie and I tried to deny it, to no avail.

I was afraid to go back into our house. My mom, when she is mad is enough, could scare away even hunger.

That night, it rained. Wet and hungry, I sat in an alleyway near our house, hidden by the evening shadows as I passed time by drawing in the mud. I didn't mind being outside. I hated our house when it rained. Our roof, cobbled together from cardboard and old iron sheets, allowed the water to pour down, drenching the cardboard boxes we used as mattresses.

"Here," said a voice, as an outstretched arm appeared offering a precious piece of bread.

Omondi. My dear friend and playmate, son of Mama Omondi. I hesitated before accepting his deeply generous offer.

"Don't worry, I won't tell," he said.

Omondi and I sat in the rain together as I ate, slowly savoring each morsel. Then we looked at each other and exchanged mischievous smiles—our favorite thing to do was to play in the rain together! We ran through the alleyways, sliding in the mud and laughing with glee. We found the torn-up remains of a black plastic bag on the roadside and strutted down the street imagining we were rich and holding a dignified black umbrella.

Omondi and I made our own toys. We made a soccer ball using discarded plastic bags and string. We made buses and cars out of cans. Other kids admired our handiwork, and sometimes, when another kid wanted to play with our ball, we would trade time with the ball for food. My aunt Atieno called me Ogwanjo, which means a sportsman who is brilliant and brave, because I liked to play soccer and made these soccer balls from trash and string.

One day I saw something very strange, people walking around who looked like they had come directly from the grave, their skin was so pale. *Mzungu*s. They carried a black machine that flashed bright when they pointed it at me. I screamed. I thought the machine was going to harm me, and so I fled. Later I learned it was a camera. Its flash and their voices terrified me. We didn't see them often, less than once in a year. But whenever I saw them, I ran and hid.

I had many ideas about them; first, I did not expect them to be smart, because they loved to take pictures of silly things like chickens on the street, shanties, and other things that were not interesting. Second, since I had seen a kid touching their skin and shouting, "How are you?," for many years I believed the name for all white people was "How are you?" I touched their skin as well and found it soft, but I was surprised and a bit disappointed because I thought touching it would leave a mark on my skin too.

Omondi attended an informal local school because his family could afford the fee of about five dollars per month. Of course my family could not afford even the minimal fees, but Omondi shared his lessons with me. When he did his homework, I would do it with him. He'd teach me what he was learning, and I would trace letters with his one precious pencil, writing mine first and then erasing so he could write his.

But then, out of the blue, Omondi started feeling sick and weak, no longer strong enough to play. I sat for hours on the floor of his home, watching him lie there motionless. No one knew what he had—maybe measles, maybe malaria, maybe just poverty. My mom told me not to go to their house, because I might get whatever he had, but I didn't care. He always disobeyed his mom to help me; I wasn't going to leave him when he needed me.

Then one day, he was dead—at eight years old. His family could not afford to take little Omondi's body to the mortuary. So he lay on the floor of their house, and after a week, his body actually became taller and started to smell. Children were not allowed to see the dead, but I would sneak in to see him because I wanted to know if he would come back. No one explained what was going on; I was lonely and scared. Every night the community would come together and play loud music, pray, and collect money to take Omondi to the mortuary until they had raised enough. I saw Omondi as he was carried away. *My friend is not the same,* I thought. *He is sleeping but it seems he is just gone.*

After that I woke in the middle of the night, sweating and screaming with bad dreams. I wanted my friend Omondi back. I realized how much he had helped me, how generous he had been at such a young age. I couldn't sleep for fear that I would dream of him again. I refused to walk in the dark, for fear that I would see him.

Only weeks later another neighbor died, a girl in her early twenties. Her death caused much fear. In those days, no one really knew about HIV/AIDS, and so when people got sick and died from the disease, their bodies covered with sores, everyone was afraid. The bodies were wrapped in cloth until the family could afford a coffin, and the house was shunned. Everyone was always afraid that the ugly deaths people died would affect them too. I was seeing how harsh the world could be; those with the most misfortune are always afraid of how quickly, how unexplainably, it can always get worse.

One night, our door was kicked open and two policemen stormed inside our house. They were tall, wearing big boots and touting even bigger guns. There was a flurry of confusion. My sister Jackie clung to Babi's leg, and the new baby, Liz, began to wail. I jumped up from the cardboard box I was sleeping on, shielding my nakedness by hiding, doubled over, in the corner.

"Him." They pointed at Babi.

Babi had been lucky enough to get a job welding that day, but as the police kicked him, the story came out. Apparently, some things had been stolen at the site that day, and they blamed him. My mom screamed as one of the policemen savagely threw his boot into Babi's rib. In our house, Babi was always the aggressor, never the victim, and so I didn't know what to think as I watched him get beaten. I silently prayed for Liz to be quiet—she was like my baby, as I spent my days looking after her. The other policeman tore through our house, breaking one of our plates and damaging our few other belongings as he looked for the stolen goods.

"They aren't here, I don't see nothing," he said to his comrade.

Babi lay shaking, holding his broken ribs, his eye banged up and his nose bleeding. I felt bile brewing in my mouth. I was going to be sick if I looked at him; seeing him vulnerable was both thrilling and terrifying.

"Take him anyway," the other policeman barked. "Maybe he hid them or sold them. We better give them something."

"No—please! I am pregnant! I have three children! Please! We have to eat!" my mom sobbed hysterically, throwing herself at Babi and displaying the most outward affection I'd ever seen between them. The police roughly shoved her out of their way, dragging Babi out of the house.

As my mom lay on the floor holding her belly, crying and broken, I promised myself that I'd become an *ogwanjo,* a warrior, for her. I knew deep down how much my mom loved and always helped me, even though she was often scared to show it because of what Babi might do to her, and I wanted so badly to help her. I scooped up baby Liz and held her in my arms, rocking her gently. Looking back, I was just a child comforting another child, but that night it didn't feel that way. It felt like the entire world rested on my shoulders.

With Babi in jail and not bringing home the occasional money he earned—what little bit remained after he drank most of it away—we were desperate. There was no one to help. Our household was infamous for causing a lot of noise and chaos in the neighborhood, and my parents' frequent fights and this latest encounter with the police didn't help.

But then, my mom had an idea. That next Saturday morning, my mom called a group of women to meet at the church. She left

Jackie in charge of Liz and told me to come along.

"Kennedy, I need you to help me write."

I hadn't been formally taught to write, but I had learned from Omondi and another friend, Boniface. Boniface was the neatest boy in the 'hood; his clothes fit him perfectly, and he went to informal school. Kids were often told to stay away from me so that I didn't influence them, given my family's bad reputation. But Boniface was brave and did not care what other people thought.

Boniface and I made a deal that we would both learn how to read and write so that we could write letters to each other when we were older and lived in different and far-off places. I would eagerly wait for his return home each afternoon, hungry for the knowledge he carried in his scrappy notebooks. While Boniface was in school, I looked for old newspapers on the street and in the garbage. I struggled through them, highlighting with pencil the difficult words, which Boniface then wrote down and took to his teacher. Every day, Boniface went to his teacher with this long list of words that we could not read. Even though I was not the one in school, I became better and faster than Boniface. But at some point, Boniface's teacher tired of our curiosity and told him to stop compiling extracurricular words and to focus on schoolwork instead.

So I kept compiling my words and waited for Sundays at church when Father Francis held the service at St. Michael's. After the mass, I asked him to help me read those words. Still in his gown, he'd look at me. "Kennedy, how can I help you?" he would say jovially.

"Father, please help me read these words."

"Can you try first, then we can work it out."

I struggled. He took the paper from my hands and started reading them to me. He suggested that I repeat after him. I did, and he was impressed. "Kennedy, can you now read them by yourself?"

"Yes," I said.

I read for him, and he told me that I have what is called a "sharp brain"; I didn't see any blade but I just nodded in confusion. I asked him if I could bring some more words for him again. He suggested that we should always do it on Saturdays, and so it became our routine. As I went to leave he asked me, "Where did you even get this vocabulary?"

"From the old newspapers I found on the streets, in the garbage."

He looked at me and, nodding his head, said that was impressive. He promised to bring me magazines next Saturday.

I improved my English so that even Boniface was amazed. I was much better than the kids who were going to school. I kept disturbing Father Francis with requests for definitions, and I could see he too was tiring of me. He could not keep up with me and said my vocabulary was getting hard even for him. Finally, he gave me my own guide to the world of words: a dictionary.

Now what did my mom need me to write? Why? She always refused to tell me until she was ready.

When we reached the small iron-sheet church, there were twenty women gathered. I don't know what my mom said to get them to come because I knew for a fact that many of them didn't like her. But my mom could have been a professional political strategist; she always knows how to get people to follow her.

Ajey got straight to the point. Without pleasantries or pretense, she addressed the women, commanding the room like she was born to make speeches like this:

"We can be as proud as we want, but we all know we have problems with money. When we get it, our husbands take control of it, and we never have enough for what we need. I have an idea for how we can get our own money."

Now she had the attention of the women in the room! I watched my mom, captivated by both her bravery and her ingenuity, as she continued.

"Every week we meet, and each of us brings fifty shillings to each meeting. We combine the money, so fifty shillings becomes one thousand, which each week goes to a different person. With this money we could start our own businesses, we could make more money, and we could even save some for emergencies. We keep rotating until everyone has gotten the one thousand, and then we can start over again, with each person contributing one hundred shillings per week."

"We could survive," Ajey added softly. She sounded like a preacher or a fighter.

For a moment the room was quiet, and then suddenly everyone was talking at once. My mom had struck a chord.

"We must all sign our names and make a promise to attend every week and to contribute without fail. If one of us fails, then we will all fail. Can anyone here write?"

No one raised her hand; my mom made eye contact with me and winked. Now I understood. At ten years of age, I became the official secretary for the women's lending circle.

"Can we start tomorrow?" one woman asked urgently.

I saw my mom's breath catch in her throat; it was the question on her mind too. Chaos broke loose again as everyone began to talk about whether they could gather fifty shillings today. Everyone was determined to try.

The next evening all the women met back at the church, and all but two people had managed to get fifty shillings. My mom had removed our last fifty shillings from her secret hiding place below her cardboard "mattress." She had planned this all along. The group held official elections, declaring my mom the chairwoman and me the secretary. I helped all the women sign their names or initials onto a piece of paper, feeling myself swell with pride. Then it came time to decide who would get the first week's collection of money. My mom selected Mama Otieno as the first beneficiary.

As soon as I saw Ajey handing over all that money, panic rose within me and I elbowed her and hissed, "Ajey! What are you doing? That was our last fifty bob; without it we will have nothing! We needed that money most!"

She glared at me. "Kennedy, sometimes trust demands sacrifice."

I didn't talk to her the entire walk home; her big words would leave us hungry for a week.

Three weeks later it was our turn for the money, and I did a little dance on the street! After the meeting, Ajey and I went straight to the market and she doubled the stock of her tomato business, buying onions and *sukuma* (kale) too. We sold the entire stock in one night. For the first time in weeks my mom could proudly make dinner outside in the open for all the neighbors to see.

My mom shared some wisdom as we ate: "You have to know in this world that we live in, there are two things: God and small gods. You see, there is one God, but he is very, very busy. He has the problems of everyone in the world to worry about so don't expect that he will get to yours anytime soon. Then, there are the people we meet. These people become our small gods, able to help us in our daily lives as we struggle along on our journeys."

three

jessica

I'm moving in.

On the phone this morning Kennedy insisted on meeting me at Prestige Nakumatt, one of the last landmarks in the city, before getting on the *matatu* to Kibera. I indignantly informed him that I'd find my way alone, not only into Kibera by *matatu* (which might have been adventure enough) but also to his house on foot. I told Kennedy it was silly and even insulting that he suggest otherwise. I didn't mean to argue with him as much as I did—it usually takes me longer to fight with a near stranger.

Now I am alone on a *matatu*, route number eight to Kibera, thrilled and a bit terrified. Celine Dion's "Because You Loved Me" blasts from the speaker. As Celine hits her crescendo, the *matatu* driver suddenly pulls over. There is a throng of people waiting to board at this unmarked but widely acknowledged stop. The conductor gets out and shouts, "Kibera, Kibera, *kumi, kumi,*" banging the sides of the vehicle for emphasis and ushering inside as many clients as physically possible. *Kumi.* I make a mental note to find out what this word means.

My lips make the shape of the lyrics to the song almost out of habit, "I'm everything I am [*dramatic pause*] because you loved me." In the States I'd laugh or even shudder with disdain if I heard this song, but here I find something reassuring in its stale familiarity. I'm not the only one jamming to Celine. The two older Kenyan men sitting in the row in front of me are halfheart-edly singing off-key. No one pays much attention. This song, their singing, the crazy weaving of the vehicle as the driver cuts ruthlessly around anyone in his way with little regard for the cars coming at us from the other direction—this is all commonplace to the other passengers.

I clutch the exposed metal of the seat so tightly that my hand turns white; below my feet there is a hole and I can see the rough tarmac exposed. We careen down the road that goes into Kibera, past the worn-down shacks, mosques, and restaurants. A small blue metal shack has a sign that says CYBER CAFÉ, and a bright yellow structure's sign reads SENATOR PUB. Behind a group of men shining shoes, another hand-painted sign reads THE BEST HUS-TLERS IN THE WORLD.

At what feel like random intervals we pull over to let passen-gers out—the door creaks open and everyone pushes to get off. The conductor barely waits for people to step out before reaching out of the door to pound the roof—what I take as the signal for the driver to go—and the vehicle lurches onward before the door has even closed.

I'm not sure where to get out, and I scan the surroundings for something that looks familiar, a landmark that I might have passed when Kennedy and I came on foot before. Everything looks alarmingly similar, unquestionably foreign. I ruefully re-member my conversation with Kennedy this morning. I can now see that Kennedy's insistence that he meet me was a kindness—a quiet acceptance that the world I come from is just a very differ-ent place—and not a judgment.

Panic rises in me as the *matatu* driver slams on the brakes and comes dangerously close to hitting a much bigger bus. The drivers yell out the windows at each other and although my Swahili is limited at best, I get the gist. The bus driver refuses to move, and the road is too narrow for us to maneuver around him, although our driver tries, and for a few moments both are stuck.

I remember the week before when Patrick, my tall, deep-voiced Swahili teacher from school, led our orientation and explained how the whole *matatu* system works. He told us that our program would greatly prefer it if we took city buses—either bright green and yellow labeled CITY HOPPER, or the blue ones labeled KBS—instead of the *matatus*. He explained that *matatus* were unregulated and in various states of disrepair, with dangerous drivers. They were also crowded and prone to thieves.

With Patrick our group went to test out a city bus. When none appeared after a fifteen-minute wait, Patrick grudgingly ushered us into a *matatu* instead. I asked Patrick if the corner where we got on was the "stop."

"Yes. For this *matatu*."

"So there are different *matatus*?"

"Yes. Each *matatu* has a number, and each number goes to a different place."

"So where do you get each number and how do you know where it stops? Is it like a taxi? Will they stop where you tell it?"

"No. It's a *matatu*. They all have specific routes."

"So . . . is there like a route map?"

"A what?"

"A route map. Something that says which numbers go where and where they stop and how frequently?"

Patrick just looked at me for a moment, truly perplexed by my question, as if trying to picture what it is I was asking.

"No, there is nothing like that," he said with a dismissive wave.

"So how do you know?

"You just know."

Similarly, Odoch had prepared us for how Kenyans give directions: "They will tell you to go, and to go, and to GO—until finally you will reach."

I realize how wedded we are in America to knowing all the details. Directions given without specifics, buses with no route map make me deeply anxious. I decide not to panic and to try to see this as an invitation to freedom. To really look and have to pay attention instead of clinging to the false security provided by detailed directions, my face buried in a map.

I'd decided immediately that I prefer the excitement, the thrill of adventure that comes with a *matatu* ride to the expected organization of a bus. There is something renegade about such a ride—the blaring music, the vehicles long past retirement age still whizzing by on their routes, all the people crammed together, united by their desire to get somewhere—that makes me feel deliriously alive.

The *matatu* to Kibera eventually starts moving again, after our driver finally decides to sacrifice his pride and move to the side so that the other bus can pass. I see a Coca-Cola mural that looks vaguely familiar—but I hesitate because Coke seems to be painted across this entire country. The conductor is about to close the door when, acting on impulse alone, I jump out. There are men gathered on the corner reading the newspaper—they glance at me but quickly return to discussing the politics of the day. I rest my thumbs on the straps of my backpack, trying to appear cool and calm, as though I do this every day.

Starting to walk along the outer road, I search for the path Kennedy and I followed the other day that cuts through the lower-middle-class houses and shops and leads to the railway line and start of the slum. The shops are busy. I stop to watch as a butcher cuts pieces of meat from a raw carcass suspended from the ceiling, displayed prominently through his makeshift windows. I've never seen anyone cut meat from what looks like a whole raw cow. The smell isn't putrid exactly—it's sweet and at the same time leathery. For a moment I just stand, smelling.

I continue onward and soon the run-down, but comparatively well-off area of Olympic starts to melt away. The landscape begins to look more like the slums of Kibera—congested and informal. Everything looks so unfamiliar, so foreign to me: the windy paths, the makeshift houses, the enterprises sprinkling the road. Even stranger is my realization that to the many people who live here—this is just what life looks like. To them, there is nothing unusual about it. It's impossible to imagine that so much of the world lives this way until you see it for yourself. Even seeing it, it's impossible to fathom: the garbage, the chickens, and the children toddling alone through the street. I'm overcome by a desire to know everything about this place, its corners, crannies, and secrets.

The farther I go, the more lost I become. There are a million tiny pathways that lead off this main path—which I'm not even sure *is* the main path. Without signs or any familiar place markers, I feel like I'm in the middle of a maze. I already have a terrible sense of direction—my dad's birthday present to me on my sixteenth birthday was a GPS. Why on earth did I think that my instincts would give me some clue, that some inner voice would point me in the general direction?

I look at my phone. Five o'clock. Soon the sun will set, and then I have no idea what I will do. I can't call Kennedy and tell him I'm lost, because then I lose, and I have a feeling he keeps score. So I try to pretend that I belong, which only makes me stick out more. I walk up to a woman selling vegetables, squeeze a tomato to see if it's ripe, and ask how much—as if I am simply in the market for some fresh tomatoes. She raises her eyebrows but plays along, the edges of a knowing smile at the corners of her mouth.

For a fleeting moment I wonder if I should be scared. I've

naively told myself that nothing truly bad could happen to me, because I've managed fine up until now. I've never before been lost in the middle of an African slum. Yet when I look around me, into the eyes of the old woman selling tomatoes, or as I walk past a group of young men playing a version of checkers, I don't perceive any hint of a threat. In their eyes I only see their own curiosity staring straight back at mine: *What is this white girl doing here?*

If my mother could only see me now—she would probably kill me. Picturing her outraged face, I can't help but release a breath of laughter. A group of young men walk by and I hear words I recognize, "*Mzungu amepotea.*" I laugh to myself—that white girl is lost—absolutely true.

Out of nowhere Kennedy appears.

"Someone came to my house," he offers sheepishly. "They said, 'Mayor, there is a *mzungu* walking around lost, she must be here to see you.'"

"Mayor?" I say with a raised eyebrow, remembering hearing everyone call him this last time I was in Kibera.

He laughs in his full-throated way and we start to walk home. "Informal mayor! If *mzungu*s come here, it's often because of SHOFCO, so they just assumed. Good thing they told me, too. You might have wandered back to America before you found it," he says with a taunting smile.

"Americans—are you all this stubborn? Insisting you can walk through a strange slum alone, insisting on moving in with a man you don't know even after he says no—that place must be a difficult country." He shakes his head.

Now it is my turn to smile. "I think I might be slightly more stubborn than most."

He shakes his head. "My mother thinks you are crazy," he says, as we arrive at his house. "You know it isn't too late to change your mind. No one has ever seen a *mzungu* living this deep inside of the slum."

"Are you saying yes?"

"Do I really have a choice?" He looks pointedly at my huge backpack.

"Just one thing," he says. "People have been telling me that if anything happens to you, the U.S. Embassy and power of America will come after me. I am just a poor boy. I don't want to put myself or my family in trouble."

I have to bite my lip to keep from laughing, but when I look at Kennedy's face I'm surprised to see that he is genuinely afraid. Fear looks strange on his features; I can instantly see fright isn't an emotion he often shares. To me, it's absurd to think of the U.S. Embassy bringing its wrath down upon Kennedy, but I see just how real this possibility seems to him. For a second I wonder if I *am* putting him somehow at risk, if there is something I should also be afraid of too.

Since nothing truly bad has ever happened to me, I can't imagine that it could.

"I promise that I will protect you from the U.S. Embassy," I say, unable to keep myself from smiling a little. "I'll tell them how much you resisted!"

I want to convince Kennedy that letting me into his world won't be yet another problem he has to face.

"Where can I put my stuff?" I squeeze my backpack off and put it in the corner of the room, next to a stack of duffel bags that seem to serve as Kennedy's closet. I stretch my arms up and twist side to side—the pack was heavy—and the room is so small my arms almost reach the walls.

We sit down, and out of nowhere I start to tell Kennedy that several of my friends think that my desire to live in Kibera is some sort of cultural tourism, a fascination with the Other. He cocks his head to the side, looking decidedly unaffected by my statement, and asks without wavering, "Is it?"

"No, I don't think so," and I go on to tell him that maybe there is probably always some element of that, but that's not it. I will never even begin to understand this place unless I live here, unless I see what it looks like at night and what its daily rituals are. I want to work with SHOFCO's program that uses theater as a tool for activism. It feels like viewing this place from the outside will compromise that.

I keep talking. I honestly never knew the world looked like this, I tell him. I naively thought it mostly looked like some version of my life. Sure, I've seen pictures of places like this, but they seemed so far away that I was able to keep them on the fringe of my reality, able to live like those worlds didn't intersect with mine. It would be easy to come into Kibera every day and volunteer, then to go home to a nice homestay or hotel, to still live in another world—to minimize the intersect.

He nods, and I see that he knows what I mean. But of course, I know that even if I live inside of this slum, I have a privilege that no one else here has: I can always leave.

"There is an expectation that when white people come to a place like this, it's to help or to teach," I say earnestly. "I don't have anything to teach; I think I have much more to learn. Maybe by doing something different and living here, for some stretch of time, people might see that I really want to get to know them without the barriers that are so hard to tear down, to simply see the human beings on the other side. Otherwise if I show up to teach theater, everyone will tell me what they think it is I want to hear, and that will be it. The terms of engagement will never change—"

Kennedy interrupts me: "Do you always talk this much? You Americans make everything so complicated." He shakes his head and continues, "You can live here, as my friend. It's simple. Of course there may still be barriers—living here won't change that—but you don't have to represent every other white person, or those cultural tourists, or whatever things you were talking about." His smile is gently mocking, yet compassionate.

"Just one question," he says with a very serious look. "Do

you tell your parents that you e-mail strange African men living in slums, whom you've never met, and ask to move in with them?"

I burst into laughter, and we just sit there laughing for a few minutes before I finally get it together enough to speak.

"No! And I'm not sure I will them until after I get home either! I've always found it easier to get forgiveness than permission!"

"Come on," he says, laughing. "I will show you around; you didn't see everything last time."

In the area surrounding Kennedy's home is a tiny strip of cement that forms a small alleyway, the cement itself worn with little holes from continuous scrubbing. There are more than a hundred tiny one-room homes right on top of each other in rows. Children play noisily outside, and women wash their clothes in the makeshift alley between the houses.

Kennedy shows me the toilets. There are two pit latrines next to each other, each a tiny, crudely constructed room walled in with metal sheets and repurposed wood. One is used by everyone in the entire plot: more than a hundred families sharing this little hole. As Kennedy opens the door, several rats scurry out, and I almost pass out from the smell. The one next to it has a lock, although the door barely closes all the way, and, with spaces gaping in the shoddy walls, there is no real privacy.

When I ask Kennedy about the lock, he looks at me, debating if he wants to answer before he says, "No one but the landlord and I have the key. The toilet belongs to the owner of this plot. I didn't have the key either, until you decided to stay here." He adds dryly, "Watch out for the rats."

The look he gives me couldn't be any clearer; he still doesn't think I will make it long here. For the first time, I feel a shadow of doubt creeping up my spine. Maybe he is right. Maybe I am in way over my head.

There have been obvious efforts made to keep the area as

clean as possible, but in the corner there is a dumping site for trash, and the smell carries. Chickens walk around picking at the trash. Nearby, there is a big steel tank that holds water; a family who runs a small shop at the corner sells the water, and people line up to fill their containers.

For my first night, Kennedy cooks a delicious spicy beef stew with rice for dinner. Months later, I learn that he had saved for weeks to be able to afford meat on my first night. Kennedy's younger siblings, five-year-old Shadrack and six-year-old Collins, join us for dinner. There are eight children all together. Kennedy is the oldest, and many of his siblings often sleep in his room at night. The boys eat ravenously, and I notice that Kennedy eats little meat—giving them most of his share.

During dinner, Kennedy firmly declares, "There is one other thing. You can't pay me."

In my study abroad program, host families are paid for the expenses they incur in hosting. I had already proposed that arrangement to Kennedy. I open my mouth to protest.

"Please," he says before I can speak. "We're friends. If you were just working with SHOFCO—okay. But I can't take money from a friend. In Africa—men provide," he jokes.

I insist that I will at least buy groceries if he won't let me pay him directly, but he closes the conversation, saying we'll discuss it later.

After dinner, shyly at first, and then with increased bravery, Kennedy's little brothers begin to ask questions about America. They want to know if we have dogs and cats in America, and if they are fed every day and get to visit the doctor. I confirm this.

After thinking about this for a moment, Shadrack says, "I wish I were a cat in America."

I am caught off guard, and Kennedy avoids my gaze. I have an uncomfortable sense that he doesn't want me to see all the ways that he and his family suffer. I see how much pride he has, and while he's agreed to let me live with him, there is a professionalism and a distance he's maintained. I get the sense that were I to trespass too close, he'd make me leave.

"Bedtime," he says to the little ones, breaking the silence.

His siblings clear their places and then run out the door— tonight they will sleep nearby in another place that belongs to Kennedy's mom. Usually, they share Kennedy's room; tonight there will be nine people sleeping at his mom's.

"You know, they don't have to leave because of me, it's totally fine if they sleep here too."

"They make a lot of noise."

"Where do they sleep anyway, when they are here?" I blurt out, unaware of how insensitive my words sound until they hit the air. In a neutral tone, without apology, Kennedy says they sleep on cardboard boxes on the floor. Suddenly I wonder where I will sleep. Gingerly, looking at Kennedy for permission, I peel back the sheet strung up like a curtain to see what is hidden behind: one single bed. *What have I gotten myself into?*

————

The next morning I'm jolted awake by unfamiliar sounds. There is fierce knocking on the door. For a moment I'm not sure where I am—I don't remember falling asleep. I look down and see I am still fully dressed in yesterday's clothes lying on the single bed on top of the only paper-thin blanket. My body is hugging the edge so closely I feel like I might fall. Only an inch away, Kennedy is out cold, facing the other side. We must have fallen asleep! I feel like I'm trespassing. I lie absolutely still for a moment, trying to piece together the end of last night, how we got here, and what I should do next. Kennedy, groggy from sleep, wakes up and goes to the door to see what all the pounding is about. He becomes engrossed in an animated conversation that he seems to find very amusing.

"What was that all about?" I ask when he closes the door.

"Well, they all came to ask if you are still alive! You see, they think that white people like you will immediately die if they live in the same conditions as us." He shakes his head.

I open Kennedy's door to go to the bathroom, and sure enough, there is a line of people gathered outside. I awkwardly wave on my way to the bathroom, as if to say *Don't worry, I'm still alive!* An old grandmother with leathery skin, missing teeth, and both kindness and confusion in her eyes waves back. I put on a lightweight scarf, and once I'm inside the latrine, away from prying eyes, I wrap it around my nose to block out the stench—and try not to breathe much. When I squat, I notice holes in the iron sheet and shudder to think that someone might be able to see.

Getting out of there as quickly as possible, I look for a place where I can have a moment of privacy before facing Kennedy, but there isn't any to be found. I draw too much attention. I lean against the wall to think, before I realize everyone is just standing around, watching me. I guess I will have to learn to process my most private thoughts with a gaggle of women and children staring at me as if I'm a ghost. A bombastic radio voice carries the news in Swahili through the thin walls. In the house next door, someone is rustling around, cooking breakfast. Outside, women are washing clothes and calling out to their children. A few houses down I overhear raised voices—an argument. Here the intimacies of daily routines have no place to hide.

So, under scrutiny now, I wonder, *How did we both fall asleep on the bed?* I remember arguing about who would sleep on the small wire sofa. I had insisted it be me, since I'd promised in my initial wheedling to just curl up into a ball so small he'd barely notice I was there! A true gentleman, he was adamant that since it was my first night I should take the bed—and after that the sofa would be fine. *Sofa* might be an overly generous word. It is a metal two-seater with thin fabric draped over its tough wire frame.

Kennedy comes out, toothbrush in hand, and laughs when he sees me leaning against the wall facing a growing audience. "Did you greet your fans?"

He's friendly but distracted, just going about the business of his day. I sigh, relieved. If he isn't going to say anything about the bed, neither am I. He's changed into the green DENVER T-shirt that I brought him as a thank-you gift. He offers to fill my Nalgene bottle with water, and I clean it using the ultraviolet light wand I bought at REI with my dad, guaranteed to make any water drinkable. Looking at the brown-tinged water, I grimly hope it works. I shake the bottle up and down and the stick lights up. All the children are absolutely enthralled by this—they gather round to watch and insist I repeat the feat again. I have to admit it does seem like magic that this seemingly simple technology can somehow make even this water drinkable.

I copy the way Kennedy brushes his teeth—putting paste on my brush and using a sip of my newly cleaned water—before spitting in a little hole underneath the fence that flows into the sewage just on the other side.

"Now I'll show you how to shower," Kennedy says. He clears the table from the middle of the room and puts it on the bed. He takes out two plastic basins and places them on the ground. He pours water from a jerrican into one of the basins.

"So you stand in one basin, the empty one, to start," he explains, stepping in to demonstrate. "And then, you use your hands to scoop water from the other basin over you." The basins are not very big and don't provide a very generous perimeter.

"How do you keep the water from going everywhere?" I ask, incredulous.

"You aim so it falls into the basin you're standing in. Get it?" he asks—as if it's the simplest thing in the world.

"My hands aren't very good cups. I'll splash the water everywhere," I say ruefully. "You'll regret you invited me here."

He hands me a plastic cup, one of only three, from his kitchen, and says, "I didn't."

"Didn't what?"

"Invite you here. And don't mix that cup up with the others, once you've used it for bathing. That's why we use our hands instead."

He wants to go buy some milk for tea, and he tells me that I can lock the door from inside while I shower. He leaves and I lock the door behind him, shaking my head. Great. Now I've desanctified one of Kennedy's few cups and disappointed him with my inability to cup water in my hands. I dig through my backpack for my travel soap, shampoo, and conditioner and quickly strip, not wanting to take too much time because my need to shower in privacy has barred Kennedy from his own house.

I stand in the first basin, shivering. I take the cup, fill it with water, and pour it over my head, trying not to splash. It's cold! Unprepared for the temperature, I jump, and only a third of the water lands in the basin. I laugh to myself, wondering why on earth I would have expected the water to be heated. Bracing myself for the chill this time, I pour the water over my head again, trying to get my hair wet enough so that the shampoo will lather. It only half works. My hair feels dry and hard rubbing against itself, and I still need to get the shampoo out. My aim doesn't improve, the basin isn't much assistance in catching the runoff, and pretty soon the floor is covered with water. There isn't enough water left in the basin to mess with conditioner, so tangled dry hair will have to do. I reach for my fast-drying towel. After that, I try to comb my thick, knotted hair but soon give up and just throw it back. I say a silent thank-you that there is no mirror in Kennedy's house and glance apologetically at the puddle I've created on the floor. I try, unsuccessfully, to mop it up.

Ruffling through my backpack and longing for a closet, I can't imagine living like this all the time. It's hard to see my clothing options with everything stuffed inside the backpack. I know this is not worthy of a complaint, given the hardship that surrounds us, but all I can think is that I really wish I had brought the dress.

When I'd packed, my mom and I laid everything out on the

floor of my bedroom. We'd argued fiercely about what to include and what to leave out. The program was insistent that you had to be able to carry everything you brought. My mother and I had a heated argument, with her saying how impractical I was and my saying how uninspired her practicality was. My mom tried to make me take a hat with a protective mosquito veil around it.

"Do you want me to look like a beekeeper?!" I asked my mother indignantly.

I am always willing to sacrifice convenience for fashion. My mother couldn't understand why I so desperately needed to bring my new sundress. How could she be so dense? I. Just. Needed. It. In that dress, I felt ready for anything. In the end, her sense had won out.

I miss my bedroom in Denver with its clean beige-colored carpet, its orderly layout. Kennedy's house is so small. The smell of cooking kerosene has coated the walls. Now that I'm alone, I wrinkle my nose and shudder at the smell.

I dress in shirt and pants and again try to brush my hair. But without a mirror I can't tell if I've been successful.

Kennedy knocks on the door and peers inside, holding a plastic packet of milk. I've never seen milk packaged like this. He uses his teeth to tear off the corner and pours the packet into a pot—a *sufuria*. He takes out his camping stove and lights it with a match, his fingers skillfully retreating from the flame. I try not to wince at the fresh wave of kerosene, smelling like earth and rubber combined. Kennedy sparingly measures out tea leaves and mixes them into the hot milk, bringing the liquid to a gentle boil.

The next day, Kennedy invites me to spend time with him and his best friend, Antony, whom I met when I first saw SHOFCO. I invite Kyla, a new American friend who is also studying abroad on my program. Kyla is funny and adventurous, always ready with a sarcastic remark. She is studying African health and politics at George Washington University, and her knowledge makes it even more obvious how little I know. It's Kyla's first time in Kibera, and I feel a secret thrill at being the one to introduce her—although I'm very aware that it's not mine to introduce.

"Let's get sodas and hang out at my house," Kennedy suggests, grabbing my hand.

As we walk down the winding road, Kyla pulls me aside and asks, "Why are you guys holding hands? Is something going on?"

"In Kenyan culture, it's just a sign of friendship," I respond, echoing what Kennedy told me the first day we met, proud that I've learned a local custom before Kyla.

We go to Kennedy's house and hang out for the rest of the afternoon. Kennedy turns on his small battery-powered radio, and we take turns showing each other our "culture's" dance moves. Kyla and I do the "sprinkler," "lawn mower," and "swimming." Everyone howls at how bad we are. Then it is Antony's turn—and we laugh even harder because he is just as bad, if not worse! Neighborhood kids crowd into the doorway to watch the show, and we quickly become the afternoon's entertainment. Kennedy can seriously dance and he knows it. He pushes the table aside and moves his hips, knees, and shoulders in dazzling synchronicity. The neighborhood kids whoop and dance around in the alleyway outside like victorious warriors, imitating his moves and chanting "Ken, Ken, Ken!"

It feels like we could be anywhere in the world—just a group of silly young people having a really good time.

Later that night, after everyone's left and Kennedy and I are settling into our places at the edges of his single bed, a chaste space left modestly between us, my phone beeps. It's a text message from Kyla: "My host sister says it is *not* Kenyan custom to hold hands!" My face flushes.

On the narrow pathway outside of Kennedy's house I see a woman with a baby strapped to her back carrying a huge bucket of water on her head and balancing another full jerrican on her hip. Thinking of a lecture I had in school this week about the status of women in Kenya, I shake my head.

"Women have a hard life here."

Without a moment's hesitation, Kennedy nods his head.

"It's true—women work so hard. When I was a little boy, it was always my mother struggling so that our family could survive."

"In a lecture, we learned that traditionally before marriage, everything a Kenyan woman has belongs to her father. And that traditionally it is not culturally acceptable for women to live alone single, so women move from their father's to their husband's home and transfer all belongings to the husband!" I say indignantly.

"Yes." Kennedy sighs. "Especially for the poor. For the upper class it is different. It is unfair. This is why I wanted to create SWEP, the women's empowerment program at SHOFCO. There is much work to be done." He pauses. "But in some ways we revere women in a way that your culture does not. In African culture, women are sacred—seen as the givers of life."

"It seems very confining to me that a woman's sole worth depends on having children. And I heard on the radio that people believe that to rape in marriage is actually impossible."

"Many people here still think that," he says, nodding. "But it never used to be even debated. The fact that you heard it on the radio is a sign that things are changing in Kenya."

"At a lecture I also learned that in Swahili culture, when a man wants to marry, he tells the girl's father that he is interested in acquiring a kitchen. If the father has more than one daughter, he might say—which kitchen? That feels so wrong."

Kennedy is quiet for a moment, and his brows come together deep in thought. "I see what you mean, but I also see those pictures of what America expects of women. They are supposed to look like tiny toothpicks."

I burst out laughing.

"It's true, we suffer under a different kind of unfair expectations."

I begin to wonder if it is indeed more complicated than it seems. Many of the women I have met here exhibit such strength; they radiate a grounded power that I find myself seeking.

We wind our way through the narrow path, careful to avoid getting caught on the jagged, iron edges of the houses.

"I need to do laundry," I say.

"Me too," Kennedy smiles. "I'll show you how."

"You do your own?" I have seen that this is very rare. Most single men have their sisters help them with their laundry—washing here is a difficult task as it's all done by hand.

"I do my own, and I'll do yours too. You have to scrub hard without machines." Registering the surprise on my face he adds, "I'm a different type of Kibera man."

four

kennedy

The day Babi got out of jail, I recognized his footsteps before he appeared, and dread filled my stomach. Almost immediately, he found the precious women's group money where my mother had hidden it at the bottom of the maize flour, stole it, and went out to get really, really drunk.

"Tonight, I'll beat that wife of mine who can't take care of her husband," he bellowed when he returned from the *changa* den, enjoying the angry vibrato of his voice and not caring who heard him.

Our door was only made out of flimsy wood scraps, almost like cardboard, but my mom tried to hold the frame to block the explosion we all knew was coming. I quickly threw water on the charcoal stove that my mom had lit to boil water, so that he couldn't use the hot coals as a weapon. I grabbed baby Liz and pulled Jackie with us into the corner. Babi slammed his entire weight against the flimsy door, knocking my mom, still holding the thin door flap, back to the floor. The mosquitoes and cool night air came rushing in.

"You stupid woman, where is the food?" he sneered.

Ajey tried to ignore him—since he'd stolen our money, we of course wouldn't have any food to eat! He was so drunk he smelled terribly, and soon he vomited on the floor, filling our home with the stench of sewage and stale liquor. He flailed and tried to steady himself on the slippery floor. He grabbed Ajey's neck, strangling her.

"Woman, I'll kill you today!"

Ajey started to stutter, struggling to breathe, and I looked over at Jackie, the panic clear in my eyes.

"Ken, don't," Jackie whispered, touching my arm and reading my mind. "You're so little—he'll kill you."

My parents continued to struggle. I tried to sneak toward the open door, carrying Liz, as I knew things would only get worse here. We needed help. Babi grabbed me by the back of my torn shirt, ripping it even more. I felt my body grow stiff with fear—however cruel he could be to my sisters, he would always be ten times worse to me. There was no escaping him. As he picked me up, Liz tumbled out of my arms. He swung me around by my shirt and bashed my head into the iron sheet wall, then flung me to the floor like I was a doll, not a human boy. I found myself on the floor, on top of his vomit. Often my mom was even too scared to stand up for me—but this time she had had enough.

"You can beat me, but don't you dare put your dirty hands on those kids, who because of you will be hungry for the next endless days!" she screamed wildly.

My mom is a large woman, rounder and as tall as Babi, but still she was no match for his strength. He tried to beat me, but my mom shielded me from his kicks and blows, receiving a brutal beating in my place. Jackie and I blamed ourselves, devastated as we hid in the corner watching this cruelty.

For the next month, my mom never had a moment of peace. The fights between Babi and her got worse and worse, and sometimes my mom just wouldn't come home, sleeping somewhere else to avoid him. Mama Otieno was in the women's group and so she offered Ajey protection. Despite Babi stealing our money, the group was still going strong. The women were all starting businesses, starting to save, and beginning to have power in their households The men didn't like this group, and so they banned it, saying it was giving their wives "horns." The group continued to meet, but now in secret. I was still the secretary, and I knew that I was taking a big risk by helping this underground women's movement. I shuddered when I thought about what Babi might do to me if he found out about my involvement, but it was worth it to see my mom leading each meeting, to be a part of it.

My mom had another idea. She and the women's group decided to start screaming at the top of their lungs whenever their husbands beat them at night. Once one heard a scream, she would start screaming too. The howl would travel all over the neighborhood, picked up house by house, causing a ruckus, making it so that no one could sleep. Eventually, the neighbors would tell the offenders to stop beating their wives, not because they wanted to end the violence, but because they wanted to sleep.

One day, when Ajey came home, Babi was waiting with a machete. My mom had to run and hide; as she ran Babi chased after her and promised that he would bring her death. When he said that, I felt chilled to the bone, terrified that one day he would make his threats real.

I woke Boniface very early in the morning two days after the machete incident. With all the chaos, I hadn't eaten, and I wanted to see if we could find anything to eat in the garbage of the rich area across the river, a middle-class neighborhood called Lang'ata Otiende. We had to go very early, before the street boys got to the garbage, to find anything. Still, Boniface and I had no luck that day. We decided to walk back to Kibera to Toi Market to see what we could find. We were desperate. Toi Market, a hodgepodge of stalls, was crowded as usual. In the distance, we spotted a woman selling mangoes on a makeshift wooden stall. Two little boys, we easily disappeared into the chaos of the market. Boniface and I put our small heads together, our eyes glued on the woman with the mangoes, many of them looking overripe. In whispers we plotted. Boniface would approach first and talk to the mama, trying to distract her. I was smaller and less noticeable. While he distracted her, I would steal two mangoes.

He approached slowly, casually.

"How much for a mango? One shilling?" Boniface asked her. "Your mangoes are not that nice. Some of them have ripened too much, others are still not yet ripe."

"We have the mediums." The woman bent down and reached around to find the mangoes she meant. "Young boy, this is good. How many do you want?"

"I want ten, but you have to give me a good price," Boniface bluffed.

"No, no, I can't sell these mangoes below ten shillings. So that means ten is one hundred. Maybe I'll add one extra."

I crept around the other side of the stall and began to crawl on all fours. Hearing Boniface had her engaged, I snaked my hand up the back of the cart and felt my fist clench around a precious mango. But just then the woman turned around to see my small hand appear and shouted the deadly word: "THIEF!"

I froze. I dropped the mango instantly; my heart was pounding. I had seen people burned to death by mob justice for stealing tiny things, like a mango. In this country, those who steal huge amounts of money, like from the government, don't get punished. But when you steal a mango in a crowded market from a poor woman, you know you're done.

People surrounded me, and I felt hands raining down on my flesh. They beat me, kicked me. Boniface ran; he had to. As my small body absorbed blow after blow, everything blurring, I hoped he was safe.

The mob came thick and fast. They didn't care that I was a kid, no more than ten years old. They didn't even know what I had stolen. I heard some people asking, "What did he steal?," and others responding, "He's a thief!" I felt my rib crack, searing pain all over my small frame. I tried to grit my teeth, the way I did when Babi beat me, but there was no escape, no bracing myself to withstand the blows from so many people at once.

Suddenly the crowd parted, and someone forced his way through. I couldn't see clearly—everything was spinning and blood was pouring from my nose—but I could vaguely make out that he was nicely dressed.

"I want to know what is going on here!" he shouted. Then he saw me, a curled-up ball of dirt and blood. "Wait, I think this is a little boy. Why are you doing this?" He stepped in front of me, forming a barrier between the pulsating crowd and me.

People threatened to beat him too. "You can't support a thief!"

Then he said, "Wait! I want to pay for this kid. What did he steal?"

Nobody answered. Then a young man behind me shouted with menace, "Mango." The man asked again, "How many mangoes did he steal?" Nobody answered.

He insisted, "Who did he steal the mango from?" People called for the vendor. She came over slowly from her spot on the sideline and he asked her how many mangoes I had stolen.

"One," came the answer.

"I'm paying. If I pay, can you let the boy go free?" he implored the crowd.

"No, no, no. He has to be taught. He has to be taught discipline. He will do it again and then he will become big thief," they shouted back.

I was shaking. I still could not speak. I looked into his eyes to say, *Please don't leave me. If you leave me, I am dead.*

"I will pay more than one mango. This boy is bleeding. He has already been taught a lesson. We have to stop this. He is a child. Look at him, he is so small. You don't treat kids like this."

The vendor held out her hand and I couldn't see how much money the man put in it with his clenched fist. He looked down at me and offered me his hand to pull myself up. The mob stepped back, and then everyone slowly began to return to whatever they had been doing, the excitement over, and my freedom bought.

Finally, I could speak and I said, "Thank you so much, thank you so much, may God bless you."

The man helped me up and we walked away together, his arm loosely over my shoulder to help me walk, my limping body still racked with pain. I was certain several ribs and my nose were broken. He asked me why I had done it and said that stealing was bad. I told him I had not eaten for the past two days and I was very hungry. He took me to a shop and bought three packets of maize flour and even gave me one hundred shillings.

"Who are you?" I asked him incredulously.

"I'm a man of God," he said, before sending me on my way.

I thought about my mom and her prayers. I had read the Bible, I had heard sermons in the church, and I had heard about the angels. Now for sure I believed in them.

The angel's food didn't last long, and one morning, I could not stand the hunger any longer—I was tired of hearing Jackie and Liz crying. I decided to cross the river and climb the hill to visit Lang'ata and its missionary home, Missionaries of Charity. I took responsibility for our welfare, despite the irony that often I might be forbidden to even eat the food I brought home. There was a long line of hungry women from the slum at the missionary home, waiting and pleading with the sisters for food. The sisters were so nice, but the line of too many people overwhelmed them. I was a little boy of ten, and the angry and hungry women clamoring for their place in line were squashing me. I could barely breathe. I was the only child who came to look for food for his family. The rest were grown women, mothers themselves.

The women fought one another, but they had sympathy for me as the only child in line. The sisters asked me about my family and gave me the desperately needed food. Some of the women neighbors went back home with nothing, while I carried my bag with triumph. My mom and my siblings were proud of me.

Begging for food from the missionaries became a routine that I did once a week. But I was not always lucky. I might come back empty-handed when the sister on duty was not the one who knew me. One morning, as usual, I went to the missionaries to beg for food, and by good luck my favorite sister was in charge. Anytime she was in charge, my bag was loaded with enough food to sustain my family for at least three days, if we only ate once a day. We never wasted food, we never had enough, and my belly rarely got filled with food—only with water.

One time I was on my way home with the food when five boys much older than me attacked. The boys ambushed me and struggled to take away my bounty. I cried, but there was no one nearby to help; it was almost dark and so no one came to rescue my food or me. I'll never forget how terrible it was for someone to snatch away what I considered as important as my life. I was left on the ground hopeless. I cursed my assailants; I wished them all sorts of bad luck. I went home crying and my mom was red-hot mad. All my siblings cried. My mom couldn't take it—she was so upset. We went back to look for those boys, as if they would be there waiting for us. But of course we didn't find them. That night we slept without anything in our bellies.

Babi blamed me for losing the food and accused me of selling it and then pretending that it was stolen. I swore in the name of God I was telling the truth, as in my family we all knew that you couldn't lie when using the holy name of God. Still, Babi beat me while my mom tried to shield me from his kicks and blows. Afterward, I thought of the story of Jesus's birth. Jesus was born into poverty, in the manger of a barn. The story in the Bible tells us that Jesus endured hardship and remained an honest and good person whom people began to worship. I was inspired by this story, and my faith gave me the strength to face another day. If Jesus could do it, so could I. I swore in the name of my mother and the name of Jesus Christ that no one would ever take food away from me again. I said, "They'll take it over my dead body." I trained one of the Kibera street dogs to accompany me to the missionaries, rewarding the dog with small scraps of food. The Kibera dogs were so tough that everyone was scared of them. My dog became my companion, accompanying me whenever I went to seek supplies. One day, I went to the missionaries to beg for food as usual and everyone expected that I would come home with my usual plastic bag of food. But, by very bad luck, the sister that I was close to had been transferred to another country.

When I went home with nothing, now for a second time, I found myself in a trouble. Babi looked tired, worn out by the weight of the world. He sat nursing a cup of tea without milk or sugar. I did not speak, because I knew from experience that when he was like this, it was better not to engage him. Babi looked straight into my eyes and I looked down again. We all knew that when Babi did that, there was gasoline inside him that would soon explode.

"Kennedy, you are silent? Why are you rude to me?"

"I'm here, Babi."

"Where is the food?"

"The sister who was my friend has been transferred to another country."

A cup went flying through the air and smashed against the wall, breaking into little pieces. If I had been two seconds slower, it would have hit my head. Unable to bear it around Babi any longer, I exploded. I left the house. I decided to run away permanently. It was for my own protection, and it was also to protect my mom. I was ten years old.

The first night I found a stall where women sold vegetables during the day, and I crawled underneath to use it as a shelter to sleep. I lay there crying, praying that nothing bad would happen to me. I thought of the stray dogs that could bite me, and of the thieves that could attack me. The night could mask so many terrible things. That night was long, the longest night I've ever experienced. Sleeping in the open air made me feel so alone. I asked God, *Why do I have to suffer? What have I done to deserve all of this?*

At that moment an idea about survival came to me. I knew a kid who was a few years older than me. He used to be our neighbor, but when his parents died, he became homeless. His name was Kamau. Parents warned their children to be careful with Kamau—being a street child, a *chokora,* was something to disdain. Kamau didn't really care; he never even bothered saying hello to anyone. Although we had grown up together, he never even said hi to me. Since joining the streets he had left our world and became part of something else entirely. Sleeping in the cold, I realized I needed to find Kamau.

There was a corner, a place called Gumo, that was infamous as the base of the street boys. I decided to make my way there.

"What are you doing here, are you a spy?" a kid shouted at me.

His words caught the attention of all the street kids. The energy changed, and I felt like I'd been thrown into the midst of wild animals—predators who had not made a kill for days. Before I could answer, a heavy slap landed on my face. I saw stars in the air, wobbled, and fell down. The group moved in on me.

"What do you want? Why do you came to stare at us?" voices shouted.

I could not find words. I had run away from violence in my family, and yet again I was met with violence. Kamau and I had been friends as little boys. I never made fun of him after he joined street life the way the other children had. Surely he would help me. As I lay on the ground, the street kids started tying me up with a rope.

"If you can't talk, we are going to make you talk," another voice shouted.

"We are going to teach him a lesson."

The kids tied my legs and hands and carried me to what they called the disciplinary center. They held sticks in their hands. I closed my eyes and heard them say they would beat me until I told the truth, until I told who had sent me here to spy on them. I didn't know what to say—I had come to the streets to find a new family. I had thought I might find acceptance, instead of just another hell on earth. The street boys began whipping me, ruthlessly. I bit my lip as I writhed and tried not to scream—Babi's abuse had taught me how. Between the blows and the searing pain I stammered, "Please . . . I'm a friend of Kamau . . . Kamau . . ."

"What did you say?" the leader—Commando—asked. He was much older than everybody in the group. He could have been in his early twenties. Everyone seemed to be scared of him and stopped beating me at his words.

"How do you know Kamau?" he asked in a soft voice. He seemed ready to talk with me. "How do you know Kamau?" he asked again. I tried to regain my voice.

"Kamau is my friend since we were babies," I answered.

"And what is your name?" He asked.

"My name is Kennedy," I answered, trembling.

"We will wait for Kamau to come back from fetching water. If you lied, you will experience what you have never seen in your life," he warned.

I sat, tied up, in breathless anticipation. What if Kamau ignored me? What if he pretended not to know me? In that case, I would die that very night on the street.

As I waited, I observed the street kids. They looked dirty, but I watched as some took improvised baths, washing their bodies and afterward putting on the same dirty clothes again. They surrounded the fire, cooking together. Some cut *sukuma,* others made *ugali.* It was a strange kind of family. They shared stories, laughing and trying to best one another. I wanted nothing more than to be part of their crowd.

Commando was much cleaner than anyone else. His eyes

were red. He drank something out of an old whiskey bottle, sipping slowly, sitting on a stone, presiding over the commotion. He didn't speak much, but when he did, he was taken seriously. The fire grew higher, and over the flames Commando's eyes met mine.

Kamau stumbled into the camp with water, a heavy load for a boy. Everyone gathered around him, preparing for a great drama.

"Kamau, do you know anyone called Kennedy?"

"No idea." Kamau responded.

"He claims he knows you?" Commando asked.

"I can't see his face," Kamau replied. Commando took out a bright flashlight and shone it on my face and I squinted, just praying. Kamau moved slowly toward me.

"Ken!" He shouted—he smelled of alcohol. "What are you doing here?"

Relief washed over me, its impact so overpowering that I almost lost control of my bladder.

"This is my boy from the 'hood," Kamau told Commando.

"Sorry, Kamau, we had to give your boy some dosses, before he said that he knew you," Commando said, explaining my sorry state. He ordered another boy to untie me. I stretched out my arms, rubbing the indents the ropes had made on my wrists.

I sat with Kamau by the fire, letting its warmth reach me all the way inside. Kamau asked me what I was doing there, and I recounted the sad story of Babi. Kamau wasn't surprised—the whole neighborhood knew the torments I endured.

The food smelled so wonderful it made me delirious. When it was ready, the boys invited me to eat with them. I had to pace myself, concealing how desperately hungry I was. Who knew where they had gotten the meat from, but it tasted salty and nearly melted in my mouth. We shared food in tin containers— five people to one tin. Commando was the only person who got his own. I picked at the food—trying to eat as little as possible.

"Ken, you have to eat. Here nobody will encourage you to eat. You will end up with nothing," Kamau whispered.

When we were done eating, Commando told me to wash the dishes. I didn't protest. Within ten minutes all the tins were clean.

Kamau asked me if I wanted to join the group. He said that being a part of the group was better than being a homeless kid on your own, because the boys protected one another. Kamau explained that things would be tough at first—I would have to earn the respect of the group. He also made me promise not to share the secrets of street life. I nodded, taking in everything Kamau said, knowing that learning the rules of this different world could mean survival.

Kamau left me for a few minutes to go talk to Commando, and I knew they were talking about me. I saw Commando shake his head, and I worried it wasn't going well.

Then Commando gestured to me, and I ran to his side.

"Ken, now you have to prove that you are a man, and Kamau will tell you details," he said. "We don't want kids here, and hopefully you are not a kid, so tomorrow you better prove it!"

We slept outside under the night sky, without blankets. I watched Kamau sniffing petroleum and glue. He offered the jar to me and said I wouldn't feel cold if I used the petroleum. I shook my head. It was cold, but somehow it felt safe like no other place before. As I drifted off to sleep, I thought about what Commando had said, how I was to prove I was a man.

I woke very early, and by about four A.M. I was hiding under a stall at Ngumo near the bus stop. All night, I'd asked myself how I was going to prove how tough I was, and finally I had an idea. I remembered when my mother used to come very early to buy vegetables from Kenyatta Market, not far from the street kids' base. The women put their money in traditional cloths tied around their waists. I had decided to wake up early and grab one of those cloths from a woman going to the market.

I heard people coming and got ready. Suddenly, what came

to my mind was an image of my mom walking to the market. I felt a pang of remorse and wondered if maybe it would be her I would see walking down the road. I shook those thoughts from my head. I peeked out. It was still dark and they couldn't see me, but I could see them, a group of women. As they approached, I felt myself freezing—should I do it or not? Then I thought of the other street boys still asleep: if I did it and succeeded, I would win their respect. I would not harm anyone, just snatch the cloth and run like a tiger.

Just as they passed, I leapt out, ripped the cloth from the woman on the left, and bolted away. Behind me I heard the cries of "Thief, thief!" I put my chest into my movement, willing my legs to carry me faster, exhilarated and at the same time sad for the poor woman. I made it back to the base panting and un-folded the fabric to find 150 shillings. I crinkled the paper be-tween my fingers to make sure it was real. I couldn't wait—I woke up Kamau.

Kamau laughed when I told him I planned to give all the money to Commando.

"Stupid," Kamau said, "after a successful mission, you don't hand everything over, but hide a little something and then hand over the rest. But never let Commando learn that you've hidden something."

Kamau told me to give him fifty, and to tell Commando that I got a hundred. Kamau promised to share the fifty to buy lunch for us all week. I handed over the fifty shillings and made my way over to Commando.

With pride I told him, "See, I am a man! I did my first mis-sion while everyone was asleep!"

Commando grinned and pulled me quickly to the side, whis-pering, "Don't let them hear how much. Now you are my boy, I will protect you. I want to hear how you did it. You tell everyone that you got fifty . . . okay? If anyone asks, you say you only got fifty," he repeated.

At breakfast, I told the story of my mission: "I hid under the stall, and I saw two men and a woman walking together. I learned some karate and boxing in the ghetto, so I was prepared to defend myself. I walked up to them and told them to stop, but one man withdrew his knife from his pants. I kicked his hand, the knife fell down, and I punched the other man in the teeth. He fell down. Pow! I warned them to stay on the ground as I searched their pockets. The guy stood again and knocked me down. I fought back by punching his nose. Blood spurted from his nose. He was like a giant, and the woman and the other man were frightened after I knocked him out and ran away."

Everyone was in awe of my skills and looked at me with deep respect. Commando put fifty shillings into the food fund, and the group cheered. I could see Kamau shaking his head at the fifty shillings, looking at me as if to say *I told you so*—he had taught me how the street works.

The next day, Kamau asked me to join him on a dangerous mission in the city center.

"We are going to steal parts of fancy cars and sell them. They have a hot market!"

Upon hearing the details of our mission, I felt panic rise in me. I realized Kamau was expecting me to use my supposed karate and boxing skills. If I told Kamau the truth, he would know that I was not a man, just a little scared boy who had lied.

"What will happen if they catch us?" I asked.

"Death," Kamau said—as if it were no big thing. "And if we are dead, no pain, no suffering, no stress. We are all equal in death." He laughed.

"Kamau, do you *want* to die?"

"I don't want to, but I'm not scared of it. Ken, look at our life, and how people treat us! We are unwanted. Who cares if the invisible disappear?" Kamau's voice was hot with anger.

"I would care if something happens to you."

As we approached Kenyatta Avenue, where the cars were

parked, Kamau told me which parts to look for. He warned me not to take anything off a Mercedes-Benz, as they didn't have a market.

"Toyotas are the best. But don't let a Benz go; you have to at least destroy the glass or puncture the tire. How can they have a good life and we are suffering; we better teach them a lesson. Ask these rich people for food or even money, they will just roll up their window. If the wealthy don't want to help us, let them pay for repairs!"

I suggested to Kamau that since he was the expert, maybe he should steal things, and my job should be to destroy the cars. He dismissed the idea.

Kamau was a pro. Within two minutes he had taken the side mirrors off three different cars, while I'd barely moved. I couldn't think which part to remove, what to do first, and before I knew it Kamau was yelling at me that it was time to go. As we walked back, Kamau was triumphant, but I knew I hadn't done my part. I wanted to try again the next day, but Kamau warned me to wait at least a month before trying the same place, as they would be watching.

On the other side of town we went into a shop that sold spare parts for cars. Kamau pulled out the side mirrors as if they were crown jewels. The owner, whom Kamau called Boss, offered only 120 shillings for all of them. They argued for more than twenty minutes, neither budging, until they reached a deal of two hundred shillings, and I knew Boss was taking advantage of us kids.

With the money in hand, Kamau suggested we go eat lunch. At a nearby kiosk we asked for *madondo,* which means beans and *chapati.* No one wanted to sit near us—people moved off in a huff. Kamau told me to get used to it; this was life as a street boy. I wanted to eat in a rush and leave the customers in peace, but Kamau said we should enjoy and take our time: we had paid.

"Tonight, I promise you will have the best night," Kamau said as he reached in his pocket and handed me a bottle. "Sniff slowly."

Petroleum. I held it in my hands, trying to sniff, but it made me dizzy. Kamau encouraged me not to give up. I began feeling as if I was not walking with my feet but just moving through the air.

"Kamau, are we flying?"

Kamau was laughing so hard. Just seeing him made me happy; he was my man in this new life. Although the street boys were one family, everyone had their friends—their allies. Mine was Kamau.

One time, Kamau and I snatched an old woman's purse. The woman screamed; she was old enough to be my grandmother. In Africa, we believe in curses and especially that old people can curse young people. Immediately after we snatched the bag, a moving bus grazed Kamau's shoulder.

Another time Kamau collected shit from a latrine in a bucket. We stood by Mbagathi Road, a major road that leads to the district hospital.

"This is the deal, you will ask for money. You be the nice one smiling at them. Whoever refuses to give us something, I will throw shit in their faces."

A lady came toward us, beautiful, wearing dark glasses, a pink skirt, and black shirt. She held a small bag. Kamau told me to get ready to ask for money.

"Kamau, that woman is so beautiful that I just want to admire her, please let her pass," I begged.

"Ken, we are at work. We didn't come to look at the women!" exclaimed an exasperated Kamau, as we let the pretty woman pass.

The next person was a middle-aged man wearing a blue suit, holding an envelope in his hands. As he approached I asked him to give something small. He pretended not to hear but gave me an evil eye. Kamau took two steps back, ready, and BAM! Poor man, his whole face was full of human waste. Kamau demanded that he give what money he had, unless he wanted more shit. The guy threw his entire wallet at Kamau and ran.

People had seen what happened to the man with the blue

suit. Suddenly the job was easy; everyone who passed gave money without even being asked. I couldn't believe how much we collected; it was like a Sunday service where everyone gives his or her tithes. The mission accomplished, we left the bucket half full of shit by the roadside. Kamau suggested we count the money before we reach the base.

"I can't believe this. It's 524 shillings!" Kamau shouted. I was speechless. We wouldn't have to endanger ourselves for another week.

We walked back as if we owned the streets, with no fear of anyone attacking us. We were the attackers. We were the souls tired of living. I walked slowly behind Kamau. Looking at him from behind, it felt like walking with a ghost. I saw an empty body, I saw someone who had given up totally on the world.

Back at the base, I walked over to Commando, who sat smoking a joint. I shared in a few mind-numbing puffs. Commando told me how lucky Kamau and I had been in our missions; he wanted me to know it wasn't always lucky. The group had lost more than fifteen kids in the past two years. Most of them lost their lives while on missions, to police with guns, or to the rage of a mob.

At night, high on petroleum, I looked up and saw the moon and the stars. There comes a time when nature is the only hope. Once I had asked my mom about the origin of the stars and their difference from the moon. She told me at night when God is asleep, he uses a huge blanket and the blanket has one huge hole and tiny holes. The huge hole is the moon, and the small tiny holes are the stars. Stars will always follow you wherever you go. With the stars I would never be alone. This consoled me, that no matter how far I went, I could still see the same stars.

On Saturdays we all went to the nearby river to wash our clothes and bathe. Even on the streets, the weekends brought with them a reprieve. One Saturday when I woke, Kamau was nowhere to be seen. I set out to find him, as I knew his usual places. I walked toward Kenyatta hospital. From afar, I saw a large group of people gathered near the bus stop, hundreds of people, some running away, others running toward. A few women passed me, pulling their children close, going in the opposite direction.

"What is going on there?" I asked them.

"People are beating a kid who stole a purse. Oh my God, I can't watch," the woman lamented.

My body was shaking, my blood boiling and at the same time freezing.

I moved closer and closer. The crowd grew. Men were throwing stones, using sticks and metal against a body on the ground. I couldn't make out who was being beaten, just that the clothes were soaked with blood.

"These kids have been terrorizing people for a long time. Now they have learned a lesson," someone said.

"Police . . . police," people began shouting, and everyone made way as the police approached the person lying on the ground.

"*Kufa,*" said one, meaning the person was already dead. They loaded the body onto the back of their truck. I moved closer to try to see if I could identify the body. As they turned the body over, I saw the face of my dear Kamau. It was Kamau being loaded onto the truck, Kamau killed so senselessly, not more than thirteen years old, Kamau who they were taking away from me.

I stood rod straight, watching as the police drove off. I couldn't move, looking at the blood of my friend still fresh on the ground. Was the crime worthy of such a punishment? Our lives were so close to death. Every day we were just a bad break away. I walked away, weightless.

At the base, the news had already arrived. Everyone knew it could have been any one of us. I asked Commando what we would do. He looked straight into my eyes.

"Ken, here we don't bury the dead. There is nothing we can do."

I pictured Kamau's body joining the piles of other unclaimed bodies in the city mortuary.

A few weeks passed, but nothing was the same on the streets without Kamau. Instead of doing missions during the day, I tried to look for odd jobs, but no one trusts a street boy. Sometimes, I got small jobs helping women from the market carry their vegetables to the bus stop, but it was time consuming and earned me little money. I had not contributed to the food fund for a while, and I felt guilty eating food from the street kids' base. But after what happened to Kamau, I was not going to engage in any more criminal activities. After he died, I was traumatized and so lonely. I was not close to anyone the way I had been with Kamau.

At the market I noticed a woman who always looked tired. She had a small food kiosk, but no one helped her with it. She played loud Kikuyu music and her restaurant was called Safi, therefore she was known in the market as Mama Safi. A street kid told me that he had already asked her for a job fetching water, and she refused. So I knew that she couldn't offer me any job. But I was tired of doing nothing and tired of begging, which also did not bring anything. Early one morning, I went to Mama Safi's restaurant before she arrived and just started sweeping and cleaning the compound. It felt good to do something.

She arrived to see me sweeping and screamed, "Stop, Stop! I don't want violence with street kids; we know how you start working without negotiation and then you demand to be paid."

"Mama Safi, I'm just helping," I responded.

"I'll pay you twenty shillings, but next time ask me before you do it, as I might not have the money, and then your people will attack my restaurant," she said.

I gritted my teeth, but I had made up my mind before coming, and so I told her I didn't want any money, I was doing it for free.

She stopped in shocked confusion and shook her head, asking how someone could work for no money. I told her I was just looking for anything constructive to do with my life and time. She was convinced that there was some trick. I took her four yellow twenty-liter jerricans to fetch water and hauled them back before she realized what I'd done. She protested loudly, confused, and I refused her money again—feeling clean of heart again for the first time in months.

The words of my mother came to my mind: *Ken, whatever you do, do it with one heart. If you're peeling an orange, peel it well. Whatever you put your hand on, you have to make sure you have done your best.* That had become the motor of my life, what drove me. Even when I joined the street gang, I was totally focused, because you can't be fifty-fifty.

Mama Safi didn't come too close to me. She could smell the petroleum and glue, and I could see she still didn't trust me. I spent the day standing outside her restaurant, telling her to just let me know if I could help. Finally, she called me to sit down before clients came so that I could have some food. It made me feel at least a little like a human being. I ate my lunch fast as people started pouring in. I helped her to clean dishes and cleaned the tables when each customer finished.

The following morning I did the same, and the one after that and after that. Then, after a week, Mama Safi came and she said, "By the way, what's your name?" All that time I had been an unknown person, invisible, just a *chokora*. A *chokora* can't be trusted, can't do any good. I felt so happy that she asked me my name.

"My name is Kennedy."

"Kennedy" she said, "*chokoras* don't behave like this. Are you really a street boy?"

"Not all of us are bad, but we are looking for things to do and nobody trusts us. I want to thank you so much for trusting me enough to give me this opportunity."

After that, at the end of the day she gave me the remaining food. As I headed back to the base as the sun went down, I watched birds flying overhead. The birds were going to their nests; they had a home where they could rest after a hard day's work. My heart asked: *What about me, where is my nest?* I saw a street dog also without a home sitting by the garbage, his tail between his legs, signaling his fear. I saw that there was no real difference between this street dog and me.

I took the food back to the base and shared it with other boys. Everyone was happy because I had brought food back. The sheet that I slept under was so black now you could never again call it white, and it was full of bugs that bit me, but I was cold without it. The best solution was to inhale more petroleum and glue and then I could sleep as if I were dead.

Mama Safi advised me to stop using drugs. Once in a while she gave me some clothes, and I started looking much nicer than the other street kids. After a time, she gave me the key so that I could sleep inside the restaurant. Eventually, she even gave me money. Mama Safi started to trust me enough that she allowed me to accept money from the clients, as I always passed it over to her. Sometimes she came early to cook and left me on my own to sell the food. I did not take even a single dollar that was due to her. The gang still accepted me, because at night I brought the remaining food.

Often, very early in the mornings, I saw a white man passing outside the restaurant. He walked holding his rosary and people parted on the road to give him space, acknowledging him with murmurs of "Father." He always waved at me and said *"Jambo."* I just loved his voice.

I pinched my nose to make my voice sound like a *mzungu* and said back to him, "Hello, how are you?"

Startled by my cheeky nasal voice, he laughed.

"I'm fine," he said surprised.

We repeated this routine for several days.

One day he stopped and asked me in Swahili, "What is your name?"

I held my nose as I replied: "My name is Kennedy. I'm speaking like a *mzungu,* like you!"

The father let out a whooping laugh, holding his belly.

"Like President Kennedy! My name is Father Alberto. So you know English?" he asked me.

"A little," I replied.

"Why do you want to speak like a white person?" he asks me.

"So I can own English the way they do!"

He laughed again. "Kennedy, do you go to school? Where are you from?" he asked gently, his kind eyes taking me in.

"I'm from Kibera. No food or money so I ran away. I've been living on these streets."

"Kennedy, would you like to go to school? To learn English?"

I felt my heart flying into my throat at his kindness.

"Father, there is nothing I would love more."

He placed his hand on my head, in blessing. As soon as he left, I rushed back to the street kids. I wanted to tell everyone the news.

"I'm going to go to school to learn to speak like a *mzungu!*"

No one even looked up, the disbelief and disinterest apparent on their faces.

Tall Simon only said, "Be careful. *Mzungu*s eat people."

"WHAT?!"

Another boy, Chege, said, "No, they won't eat you, they have a lot of money, they are very, very rich. That man will take you as his kid; you are going to ride a bike, you're going to have good food. Do me one favor, will you always bring food to us here?"

Chege told me white people have a private room in their houses. He told me I would never see inside that private room because it's locked. In that private room there's a tree and the leaves are money. The leaves just fall and that's why white people have money.

I gave away my sheet and my drugs because everyone said white people didn't like drugs and I would be arrested if I had them. I didn't tell Commando I was leaving because I knew I might not be welcomed again, and I decided to see if living with the priest worked out or not. If not, I might be back.

five

jessica

My foot slips. Black, thick mud—please, let it just be mud—coats the canvas of my shoe and I cringe as I feel it seeping through. A squeal envelops my throat, seeking a way out, but I push it back down, clenching every muscle to keep from shrieking "ew- wwwww!" Kennedy looks at me, one eyebrow raised, waiting. His look clinches my determination. I don't want to be what he expects, what I know I am. "Need help?" he asks—offering his hand to steady me as we cross this sewage river by skipping from stone to stone. The surface area of most of these stones is barely big enough to hold a footprint. "I'm fine," I mutter. When he turns his back to continue crossing, I desperately shake my foot. I say a quiet prayer to pull it together.

We ascend a steep hill; Kennedy is fast and nimble, and I struggle to keep up. We arrive at the top and turn back around in the direction we've come from. My breath catches; beneath this open hill lies all Kibera. I've never seen Kibera from a vantage point other than being in the middle of it, crushed by it. From up here, I can see its tight corners and weaving pathways. There are so many rows of houses they look almost miniature. I see clothing hanging on lines to dry. There is something intimate about trousers washed so many times by hand that the color and fabric has worn thin in the middle. I look away.

It seems surreal that this is now my temporary "home." I steal a glance at Kennedy. He is quiet, his eyes fixated on the landscape below. I follow his gaze and smile. It lands on his house, his own tiny world in the middle of all this chaos. I can't help but wonder what my mother would think.

We walk from the edge of the hill toward the soccer pitch—I've never seen earth so richly red before. "GOAL!" There is a blur of dust and commotion as team members run to congratulate the tall girl who scored. This whole area is an empty space, bordering Lang'ata, which has become the slum's soccer field. It's so open, I breathe in and out deeply, noticing the space my body takes up once outside of Kibera's tight confines.

"This is where the SHOFCO soccer teams practice," Kennedy explains.

I watch transfixed as they nimbly cross the field in bare feet.

"They are so good!"

"I used to be pretty good myself," Kennedy jokes. "And the SHOFCO teams—they are Kibera's champions!"

As the team sees Kennedy approaching, practice comes to a halt and the players swarm him. In the rush, I move off to the side and watch Kennedy high-five and fist-bump his admirers. He is clearly at home in the midst of this chaos as he calls out jokes and encouragement and mimics a soccer drill to much hooting and hollering. He then motions me back and tries to introduce me to forty players who haven't stopped shouting things they want Kennedy to hear.

Kennedy stands in front of the group, speaking in animated Swahili, gesturing and clapping his hands with laughter. I look at this group of boys and girls watching him with rapture. They are drinking in his words of encouragement and hope, laughing and exclaiming in what can only be described as gentle devotion. I watch him too, the ease with which he engages them, the genuine warmth in his smile, the determination in his eyes. It strikes me very suddenly that he was born for this; leadership comes to him as naturally as walking.

I talk to a few of the players as Kennedy takes the coach by the shoulder and walks away with him, deep in conversation. The players ask me where I am from, and what I'm doing here. When I say that I'm volunteering with SHOFCO, several shout their enthusiasm. Others ask me what the differences are between Kenya and America, but before I can answer, Kennedy comes up behind me and guides me away from the excited chaos.

"Come, I want to show you something," he says.

We walk along the perimeter of the bluff in silence. I can still feel the joy and exuberance from the soccer field.

We arrive at a place overlooking Kibera. There are trees and rocks, and we're beside a river.

"This is my private place," Kennedy says. "I come here to meditate, to think—to get away from it all. I used to bring books up here. Marcus Garvey when I was mad at how the world treated me. Nelson Mandela and Martin Luther King when I was searching for inspiration. This is where I had the idea to start SHOFCO."

There is a sense of peace up here, and I can easily picture Kennedy contemplating the challenges he left down below.

"I've never brought anyone here before."

Before I can respond, unsure if he even wants me to, Kennedy turns away and sits down on one of the rocks. He knits his eyebrows and grows serious, transported by his thoughts, and suddenly it's as though I'm no longer here. I sit down a bit of a distance away—I don't know how to read him, but something tells me that even though he brought me here, he's not inviting me to come too close. He is so mercurial. It's amazing how quickly he shifts from this jovial, larger-than-life visionary to closed and quiet, almost brooding. I don't want to overstep my yet-to-be-solidified welcome. He is quiet for such a long time, I start to wonder if I should leave, and if I can even make it back on my own.

"Do you want to know how I first knew I was different?" he suddenly asks, without meeting my gaze.

"Yes."

"My mother was pregnant with me for fourteen months."

I burst out in astonished laughter. "That's absolutely impossible!"

He looks at me, indignant.

"It's true. Even the village seer says it's true. I was a unique baby. I was in her womb for fourteen months! My mom always told me growing up that was the reason I was different. My brain had more time to cook."

I laugh again and look at Kennedy, shaking my head. He isn't joking but seems to be enjoying my amusement. I try to argue that this is scientifically impossible, how his mom would have died, but he dismisses me with a wave of his hand.

"Not everything works the way you *wazungu* think. In my tribe, we believe in things that you cannot see or understand. Not everything can be explained."

He will not hear my rational scientific arguments, so I have no choice but to compromise: "Well, I bet to her it did *feel* like a really long time."

"You know what else the village seer taught me? How to read messages written in the palms. Let me read yours," he says with a gleam in his eye. The warm, open Kennedy is back.

I scoot near enough to him to hold my hand out for his inspection. Apparently, I have interesting palms—instead of two broken lines I have one line that goes straight across, one long unbroken crease on both hands. Kennedy takes my outstretched palm. His thumb traces my line and he looks up in question. I explain that it's called a simian crease—and only 5 percent of the population has it on both hands.

When I was a child, I thought it made me unique. My brother retorted that it wasn't anything of the kind—it only made me more closely related to apes. My mother said that it can reflect a chromosomal abnormality. I always thought it could be associated with the circumstances around my dramatic birth. I was born full term, but weighed only four pounds and twelve ounces. My mom's placenta was unusually small—so I didn't get all the nutrition I needed. In delivery, my heart rate started dropping as the umbilical cord, wrapped three times around my neck, tightened. When doctors realized what was happening they rushed my mom in for an emergency C-section. Luckily, they got me out, untangling the cord in time.

I tell Kennedy all this and then stop abruptly, looking up to find him listening intently, his eyes still focused on my palm.

"So you could have died too," he whispers, as if this is significant.

"See anything there?"

Kennedy is fixated on one line that deviates from my crease, forming a v-shape in my palm.

"I'm looking, it takes time," he shushes me.

A nervous giggle escapes my lips, and Kennedy glares at me, impatient.

"Wait! There is something there. This one continues; the other goes another way. It means there is a choice in your future, and soon, the lines separate near the beginning. And whichever way you go, it won't only impact you, but many others."

I don't believe much in palm readings, or seers, or things that can't be explained, but it's clear to me that Kennedy does, so I try to keep from rolling my eyes.

I pull my hand back. "That sounds to me like a load of crap."

"Sometimes I see things when I am up here." His look is so direct, so unflinching, I feel my face flush.

"I'm going to spend the rest of my life with you," he says matter-of-factly and then, as if he's merely said he's going to the grocery store, he walks away with a spring in his step, down the edge of the hill, leaving me behind.

"You're out of your mind! You don't even know me!" I call after him, but he doesn't so much as turn.

———

Every Saturday morning, I sit frantically typing, trying to shape the scenes and exercises from the previous week of rehearsal into a cohesive play before my laptop battery runs out. The young people in the theater project amaze me. When we started working on the play, I asked each member to write down the five most important experiences in his or her life, as scenes for us to theatrically explore. I am blown away by what they share: being arrested for simply being poor, put in jail and forced to do hard labor until someone bailed them out, being tortured by the police, girls selling their bodies for money and getting pregnant. They talk about taking drugs to escape life, the death of parents, friends killing themselves (taking poison, burning themselves to death), hopelessness, joblessness, rape. We also talk about their hopes for the future—their dreams for equality, an end to tribalism, and the differences between the stereotypes of Kibera and the realities.

Kennedy interrupts my rhythmic striking of the keypad.

"Let's walk somewhere," he says. I push my notebooks and laptop to the side and scramble to find a sweater. He's so busy, time to just talk with him is precious. I hurry to catch up. Today, he doesn't seem in the mood for stories and so we walk in silence. It is easy to walk alongside him, each of us thinking our own thoughts and sharing the afternoon's glow. We pass Olympic, a big church on the outskirts of Kibera, and a car wash run by some enterprising young men, until we arrive at an iron-sheet structure bigger than any inside the slum.

"This is a local favorite," he says, and I read a sign that says GARAGE PUB.

"Have you ever had *nyama choma*?" Kennedy asks.

"What's that?"

"It's roast meat, a very good Kenyan specialty."

Inside we sit down at a plastic table on the back patio. He calls the waiter over and places an order for the *nyama choma,* adding two Tuskers, a Kenyan beer. His phone rings, and with an apologetic look he picks up. The tone of his voice shifts, and I immediately get the feeling that it's a girl on the other end. I study his voice, looking for a sign of who she is to him, suddenly realizing how little I know about him. His charm is so compelling; he's skilled at making people feel like he's letting them in more than he really is. Underneath there are many closely protected layers.

He excuses himself, walking to the back of the restaurant, phone clutched to his ear. I study his posture, his gestures, hoping to glean something from them. When he starts to walk back to our table, I pretend to be very interested in the label on my Tusker.

"My boyfriend, he's been in the Peace Corps in Zambia," I say. The lie just rolls off my tongue. I want to put a barrier between us, something that makes it safe for me, given what a mystery he is. I look in his eyes, and I can see he knows what I'm doing.

"When you were a child, what did you want to be when you grew up?" he asks.

"An actress, or director. To be successful in the theater. What about you?"

"A priest," he says with total seriousness. "That changed later on. But I saw the priests living what looked to me like a nice life; they were the ones who had food to eat, driving in cars."

I am learning so much about his world, while he knows nothing of mine. I feel a perplexing desire for him to be able to see my world too. I want him to grasp how different it looks and to help me map my place in all of this.

I tell him about where I grew up in Denver, the inviting family homes with garages and swings outside, with a hulking tree in the center of our lawn like an anchor. In our driveway, my brother, Max, and I imprinted our handprints into the cement when we were five. We'd moved from a small house on a bad block that I don't remember, except the green dinosaur cookies we used to get from the nearby bakery. At Christmastime the neighborhood came alive with lights, and one year my parents put funky household reading lamps in flower planters outside our house—"Solstice chandeliers," they called them.

Kennedy nods politely, but I can see with disappointment that he can't picture these scenes. While we are so comfortable together, I realize that we may never truly be able to understand each other's worlds. That might be too much to expect. I have pictures with me of my house, my dogs, my family, in a small pink photo album my mom put together, but I don't think I will show him.

My childhood was surrounded by all the comforts of upper-middle-class life in the Rocky Mountain West, and I never knew, until I came here, that my background could be something to apologize for. That these privileges were so randomly given to me, while other people were just as randomly denied. I'd always known my family was lucky; it wasn't until college that I understood that in fact I was privileged. Privilege has begun to feel like an inescapable infection. I carry its implications with me, and my desire to understand how it works only seems to underscore it.

He abruptly changes the subject, interrupting my thoughts: "How old do you want to be when you get married?"

"I'm not sure I ever want to get married. Since I was a little girl I've never really believed in the idea of it. I want a career, a life of my own. Love is a distraction; you get so tangled up in someone else that you forget what you want for yourself."

"In my culture, I'm old not to be married. Twenty-three is old enough that my mom has stopped asking me; she's given up."

"Are you going to get married?" I ask carefully.

"Not anytime soon. I still feel like I am young. I have other things I'm focused on. My work takes a lot of energy. A lot of la-dies and even their parents have tried to get me to say *kuisha,* 'the end.'" He laughs. "A Kamba girl even made me a love potion. Kambas are famous for their love charms."

"Have you ever been in love? Not charm induced?" I ask, joining in his laughter.

"No," he says, his tone suddenly serious. "I want a partner. In Kibera, women defer to their husbands. They wash the clothes, cook, and don't argue. That's not what I want."

"So you want someone to fight with?" I tease, enjoying the slow, confident smile that spreads across his face.

"Not fight—challenge," he teases back. "Have you ever been in love?" he asks.

"I don't know. I've said I was before, but really, who knows what that is?"

"I think it's being able to 'spend' for someone. Being able to give to the world outside because of them."

The sincerity in his reply shifts the balance. I can't think of a clever retort.

"I always think I'm too young for anything like that. I feel like there is so much left to live and see, and I plan to make the most of it. No strings attached." I meet his gaze and hold it for a moment before looking away.

"Me too," he replies. "I have much to do in this world. Except for you. I'd say *kuisha* for you in a second." I can't tell if he is serious or joking—and the prospect both excites and terrifies me.

"*Haraka haraka haina baraka*," I reply—a Swahili proverb I picked up from Kennedy a few days ago that means "hurry, hurry has no blessing."

He cheekily replies, "*Chelewa chelewa uta pata mwana si wako!*"

"What does that one mean?"

" 'Delay, delay, and the child will no longer be yours,' " he says with a mischievous grin. We both dissolve into laughter.

In the SHOFCO rehearsals, things are moving slowly. Some of the girls still don't say much. I've tried everything I can think of to make them feel comfortable, safe. But the only progress we've made is that now instead of one-word answers I get two. Isaac, Zadock, and of course Kennedy have each brought in two stories to share—each day we brainstorm and everyone goes home to draft something to bring in the next day. After Isaac finishes his first sharing, I look at Sadie, Amina, Regina, Deb, and Dorothy and ask so hopefully that it's pathetic: "Anyone else want to say anything? Someone new for a change?"

They avoid my gaze. Isaac finishes his second sharing, and as Zadock is about to stand for his turn, I make one more plea. "Hold on for a moment, Zadock—anyone else who hasn't tried yet?" Silence.

Dalton offers, "You know we all made the contract together."

He points to the big piece of paper posted on the wall that lists the agreement everyone has made. Most of it is ordinary— *Don't come late* (no one seems to follow that), *Be respectful*. One is unique, which Dalton himself, a very articulate and poetic young man, contributed.

"See—it says *Try to be private in public.*"

"You came up with that line, Dalton," Isaac teases.

"No one has to speak if they don't want," I say, resigned. "Zadock?"

"Wait." A small voice.

I spin around and see that Deb has her hand in the air.

"I wrote a story. I'll tell it," she says quietly. Deb is stocky and beautiful, her features very sweet and open.

"Great, great, great, okay, um, great, Deb, everyone."

"Well, this is a true story about my cousin. Last week she killed herself by taking five sachets of rat poison. I wrote this kind of short play from my imagination about her perspective. Do I just stand here and say it?"

"You can do whatever feels comfortable: sit, stand, whatever you like," I say quietly.

"I'll read it."

I nod encouragingly.

"So I'm pretending that I am cooking over the stove. Okay." She takes a deep breath, and we all nod.

"When I was a child, I never imagined that married life would be like this. I imagined it differently. Happy. This is my husband's home, but I do not live in it with him. He has been away for years. I must take care of the home, my four children, and make do on the little he sends. I wake each day feeling the shame of not being able to provide for my children, so some time ago I began to sell my body. Still, there is never enough for clothes, food, school. How I long for the days when I was a child. I used to go hunting for birds of the air with my friends, and so I thought of myself like a god, and I know that the birds also thought so about me because whenever I saw one of their kind I would release stones to bring them down for a game popular among the kids called *cha mama na cha baba kalongolongo*. I know that even though I am taking the lives of birds away from them, some giant or someone higher than me is also hunting me, but luckily he misses the target every time. Not anymore. My life is too overwhelming to live. Five sachets of rat poison. That should be enough."*

The sound of children screaming in play outside seeps into the small room through the tin walls. The noise outside only amplifies the silence inside.

"Thank you, Deb, so much, for trusting us," I say quietly, barely trusting that my voice will work. "That's it for today. See you all tomorrow. As always, if anyone has any questions, feel free to ask."

---

* Taken from script created in the fall of 2007 by an ensemble of SHOFCO youth.

Usually this offer does not have many takers. But today Regina lingers as everyone else filters out the door. Regina has yet to say more than one word. She is thin and dark, her lips full and eyelashes beautiful. She wears a black headscarf every day. Once, the first week, when I asked her if she had enjoyed the day, she said yes and has not spoken since. She comes every day and sits silently with her knees drawn up to her chest, looking off to the side. Once everyone has gone she says, "Can I talk to you?"

"Of course," I say, surprised. Kennedy catches my gaze, and I indicate that I'll meet him outside.

"Not here; tonight. I will come to your place."

"Okay. Do you know where Kennedy lives?" I ask hesitantly. She nods.

Kennedy and I walk down the path toward his house, both wrapped deep in our own thoughts. I trip over a few rocks, but we just keep walking past all the little shops with people gathered outside, the children playing in the garbage, and past the women cooking *chapati* on the side of the road. After a while he says: "You know what? No one says '*mzungu, mzungu*' anymore. Look, no kids are even saying, 'How are you? How are you?' Have you noticed?"

I look around, and it's true, no one is staring back. Kennedy and I are walking home, through the heart of Kibera, as if this is normal. Our eyes meet and we smile. As we approach the little cranny of mud and rocks that leads to our compound one little boy runs up to me chanting, "How are you? How are you?"

Kennedy shakes his head. "He must be new."

I laugh so hard I have to stop walking.

Later as I am cooking the *ugali* to go with the meat that Kennedy has prepared, Regina knocks on our door. Kennedy signals to me that he will take over, I take off the *kanga* that I have tied around my waist as an apron and go outside. Regina takes my hand and leads me to some rocks outside of our compound, next to the river filled with garbage and polluted by waste. We sit across from each other, each gathering our skirts tightly to keep them out of the mud.

"I don't have anyone to talk to," she says with her eyes fixed on her feet.

"I'm a pretty good listener," I offer slowly.

I wait for her to continue, and when she doesn't, I gently touch her arm. She flinches. I let my fingers softly settle.

"My parents never got along. They separated before I can remember; we don't divorce here like I hear you can in America. When I was twelve, I found a sponsor to help pay for my school. He paid my fees, and each month he would give me some little money for clothes and pads. I would hide them, but my two older sisters would beat me and take them. My mother abused me. She would refuse to let me go to school, telling me that I had to do the work. One day I came home from school and she was burning my things, so I went to my father to live with him."

She pauses, and I don't say anything, just nod, waiting for her to continue.

"When I moved in with my father, he began to sexually take advantage of me. When I was thirteen, I became pregnant with his child. I left, and with no place to go, I lived on the streets. I had the baby, a little boy, and my mama came and said that she would take my child but that she never wanted to see me again. When I tried to go and visit my son, they beat me until I went away. I stopped trying to visit. He's five now. I can't do anything to take him away from there because I can't support him."

A tear has stealthily leaked out of the corner of Regina's eye. She swipes it away in a deft, practiced touch.

"I got involved with the wrong people to make ends meet. I had a boyfriend who was a thief, a gangster, but I didn't know. I was at his house one night waiting for him when a mob came. They thought that because I was there, I must be a thief too. They burned down the house, took me outside, and stripped me naked."

The words become choppy, stuck. She squeezes my hand and continues.

"They walked me naked around the slum and then beat me very badly with machetes. They burned my boyfriend to death in front of me. He was screaming, 'Regina, Regina, you betrayed me.' I was taken to the hospital, but they kicked me out after two days because no one would pay my bill. My mother came and told me that she wished that I had died. I wished so too. I became desperate and so became, became . . ."

"It's okay," I whisper, even though I know that it isn't, that it might not ever be.

"I became a prostitute. Now I have three boyfriends, but none of them know. They give me some tiny money for food sometimes and places to stay. But they won't use condoms. I'm afraid, I'm afraid that I have HIV. My breast hurts and look"—she takes my pointer and middle finger and touches them to her breast forcefully—"there is a lump. One of these men, he wants to take me to his place for three days and then he says that he will marry me. I don't want to go, but I don't know what to do." She begins to shake, something deeper than a sob taking control of her body. "I don't know what to do."

"Shhh. Shhh." I wrap my arms over her, awkwardly at first but then she folds crying onto my lap. "Shhh, shhh, it's okay, it's okay. We'll figure it out. It's going to be okay, it has to be okay."

But really, I have no idea if it is or will be.

"What can I do to help? What is the first thing to do? What about your own place to stay that doesn't depend on men, would that help?"

She nods.

"Okay, okay. If it's okay with you, I need to talk to Kennedy."

She nods quickly. "You can tell him all of it. I think I want to tell my story to the group."

"You want to tell it to the group?"

"Yes. If I tell them, then I make it my story. I want to tell them, and I want them to turn around with their backs to me while I speak."

"Okay, sure. We can do that. When?"

"Tomorrow."

"Okay. What will you do tonight? If I give you a little money, can you stay with a friend and maybe bring food?" She nods again.

"Thank you, thank you for listening."

I think that perhaps she has told me this, trusted me with this, so that I can tell Kennedy, so that he will know what to do. I hope he will know what to do. I go back inside and sit quietly for a while, picking at my food. Slowly, I begin to share with him, until it all comes spilling out.

"She's eighteen. I cannot believe that she is only eighteen," I finish.

He makes a phone call to another girl in the theater group—Amina. She says that Regina can stay at her place. That she will go find her now and Regina will be safe. Kennedy and I talk late into the night about starting a sewing group for young mothers to earn a living making school uniforms, dresses, and doing other odd tailoring jobs. Eventually he falls asleep, but I can't. Regina's words keep running through my head, the memory of the lump I felt in her breast on my fingertips.

The next day, Regina stands in front of the group and tells her story. We all face the wall away from her, but I can hear her determination not to let her words be beaten by the tears. Afterward, in the silence Hadija stands up and without speaking switches places with Regina. She tells her story, which is all too similar and at the same time heartbreakingly different. Then Sadie, then Deb, and then Dorothy speak, each trading places with the person who has just finished. No one speaks in between.

Each had a child when her own childhood was still unfinished. Amina's little girl is one and a half. Amina wants to become a cook or a dressmaker to take care of her daughter, but as of now does not have a way to earn a living. Sadie's baby girl died at age one and a half. She wants to be a hairstylist, but for now sells marijuana and miraa (a local plant that produces a happy, sometimes hallucinogenic state). Deb has a daughter who is five and another who is seven. She wants to be a good mother. She does not have a job. Dorothy, whose baby girl is three years old, wants to become a secretary. Now, her only way to make a living is by trading her body. Each young woman said that she told her story today in order to get her body back. To reclaim and reenter her skin.

The next day Regina does not come to rehearsal. Frantic, I pull Kennedy outside.

"Where could she be? What do we do?"

He goes in and motions Amina to follow him out.

"Do you know where Regina is? Did she sleep at your place last night?" he asks.

"She did not come home." He nods, thanks her, and tells her that she can rejoin the group, we will be right in.

"No, no, no, no!" I cry. "Where could she be? Do you think that she went with that man? What will happen to her? Can we find her? What do we do?"

"We wait."

We go back in but I can't concentrate. I end rehearsal early. Amina, Kennedy, and I set out to look. We ask everyone we can think of if they have seen her. No. No. No. A few days ago. No.

The next day I arrive early, hopeful that she will come, that yesterday something came up, that it was just a bad day but today will be okay. Everyone trickles in slowly; Amina arrives last and just shakes her head as she comes in.

The next day is the same. And the day after. And the day after that. No one has seen her. No one knows or is telling. "But we found her a place!" I say to Kennedy. "We had the idea of the sewing group. You talked to her—you told her that SHOFCO would help. We would have found a solution. I don't understand," I say helplessly.

He places his hand on my shoulder; its weight says it all. There is such a thing as too late.

kennedy

On the first day, I watched from a hiding place as the priest stood at our agreed-upon meeting place, but I decided not to emerge. Eventually, after waiting longer than I'd expected he would, he left. The second day, when he came again, I revealed myself.

"Why didn't you come yesterday, Kennedy?" he asked.

"Father, I heard *mzungus* eat people. I didn't want to be eaten," I confessed. He released a hearty laugh and just shook his head, but upon seeing the fear on my face, he promised not to cook me.

The parish school where Father Alberto took me was an oasis of green and solid cement buildings in Lang'ata. I had no idea what was going on or what to expect. I had never before been in a real classroom with desks, blackboards, or a teacher. Father Alberto introduced me to the woman who was the head teacher and instructed her to treat me as though I were his kid. He gave me some nice clothes, some books, and a pencil. I thought I had died and gone to heaven—my dream of school was finally becoming real thanks to the benevolence of this kind man.

When I first entered the classroom, the other students were

doing math. Everyone else knew what was going on; they seemed to be copying down what the teacher put on the board into their notebooks. I tried to copy the numbers, but I sat with the panic slowly rising as the children around me raised their hands to answer questions. This isn't what I had come to school for—these scribbled symbols that made no sense. It might as well have been magic. I thought I was going to learn English! Petrified, I did the only thing I could think to do: I climbed up on a desk, jumped out of the open window, and started running.

Chaos ensued. The teacher shouted for the other children to catch me, and as I ran harder I looked back to see that a few boys were chasing me across the compound. I tried to run, but they were bigger and faster and soon had me tackled.

"We caught him, Teacher! We caught him, Teacher!" they yelled in Swahili. The teacher approached.

"You're not beating me! You're not beating me!" I shouted. "I came here to learn English and you're not teaching me English, and I'm going back to the streets, I'm going back. Let me go back!" I writhed like a wounded wild animal.

Father Alberto heard all the commotion and came rushing to find out what was taking place.

"What's going on, Kennedy? What's going on?"

I went to him and hugged him, burying my face in his robes and feeling the hot tears sliding down my cheeks. I told him I didn't trust him anymore; he had said I would go to school to learn English and they were doing something called math, some secret scribbles. I didn't understand or want to learn math. I was here to learn English, and now they wanted to beat me.

"Kennedy, listen to me. Do you want to be rich one day? Do you want to have a business?"

I said, "Yes, Father, yes. I want to."

"So here at school they're also going to teach you how to start a business and run a business, and that is called math. If you can understand math, nobody will cheat you. You will know how to give the right change. You will understand how to make a profit."

I nodded, understanding. "Father, that's a good idea. I want that."

Father Alberto knew how to explain things so they made sense to me. On the street, everything had to be practical: if you stole something, you had to be able to trade it for money. Once I understood that learning math was practical, I fought hard to learn it. I understood math very quickly. I had learned math through real life, and I already knew how to count money. Soon I was even teaching the other kids some English vocabulary I'd learned from my dictionary.

The other kids in school called me Mtoto Umuzungu, "the son of the white man."

Then one day I was called out of my class and told someone wanted to talk to me. I was immediately nervous that something bad had happened. I found Father Alberto speaking with the headmistress.

"President Kennedy is here," he shouted. "Kennedy, I'm proud of you. They say you are doing so well."

I smiled shyly, happy he was saying so in front of the headmistress. The headmistress left us alone.

"Kennedy, I have good news and bad news. The bad news is that I'm leaving the country next week to go back to Italy since I am getting transferred, but the good news is that the headmistress has agreed that you will continue with your studies here."

I felt the floor falling beneath me. "No!" I cried out, and then murmured softly, "No."

Why could my life never remain stable? In my heart I didn't trust the headmistress. I knew there was no way she would allow me to stay in school after the father's departure. But I didn't say that to him. The tears flowed from my eyes, knowing that I would not see this man again.

"Kennedy, only mountains never meet, but human beings do," he gently consoled me.

He handed me two bags full of clothes as well as other things from his house. Then he gave me a hug and disappeared.

As I'd expected, the headmistress had lied. A week after Father Alberto left, she told me that I had to find the money to pay school fees if I wanted to continue my studies. I shook my head. The street boys had been right: opportunities don't last and the feeling of losing this one—well, it felt like being eaten alive.

The church had often been a place of solace for me. I desperately needed something to believe in, and what else did I have? Every night growing up we read proverbs from the Bible. The sisters at the missionary home had given my family food. One priest had given me a dictionary; another put me in school. Through the church I found hope. From an early age, I dreamed of becoming a priest when I grew up. On Sundays different people waited on the long line to talk to the priests and disclose their secrets to them. The church could change people. At night I knew Babi would beat Ajey with our copy of the Bible, but at church on Sunday he sat angelically, his hands peaceful in prayer, reverently touching the same holy book.

After Father Alberto left and I could no longer go to school, I went back to church on Sundays. It was a way for me to see my mother and siblings, and often I would also get something to eat. One Sunday, I knocked on the door of the priest, Father John. Father John was new to Nairobi. From his regal desk he welcomed me inside. I sat on the wooden chairs and quietly ran my fingers over them, admiring their smoothness. I had never seen anything like them.

There were so many beautiful books in Father John's office that I could barely keep myself in the chair. I just wanted to get up and touch them. A brother came into the room and gave a cup of tea to me, and another to Father John. The father asked me about my family and about school. As I told him how much I had loved school before Father Alberto had left and how I was kicked out, my gaze drifted hungrily to those beautiful books. Then a miracle took place. He gave me one of the books off the shelf. My heart was overfilled with joy and gratitude. I thanked him shyly, took the book, and left. I couldn't wait for church next week.

From then on, every week after the service Father John would invite me to his office for tea and to teach me Bible lessons. I loved the stories, and my mom, who I saw every Sunday at church since I still wasn't living at home, was so proud of me—she preened like a peacock to see that the new priest had taken an interest in me. Father John was soft-spoken, and soon I began to trust him. Finally, I told him more about my problem with school fees— folding the tiny amount to rent a room into the cost of the fees, not wanting to explain my exhausting and complicated family situation. Father John didn't hesitate; he gave me the money from his own pocket so I could return to school, plus some extra—$11. It was the most money of my own I had ever held, a small fortune. My twelve-year-old self thought at that moment that if God were to take the form of a person, he would have been like Father John: generous, old, dignified, and sitting behind an oak desk and matching wooden chairs.

The next Sunday when I went to see him, Father John locked his office door as soon as I came in. Before I could even catch my breath, he threw me to the floor and began touching my body. I was too shocked to protest. I couldn't believe that a priest could do such a thing. I didn't understand what he was doing, but I cried out in pain. When he was finished, he gave me $7 and told me not to tell anyone or I would be sorry.

That night I walked around in the darkness until my hunger was more piercing than my shame. I did not know where to turn. I was in and out of my friends' shanty rooms. I knew that no one would believe me. Father John was a priest, and he was white. Even if they would have believed me, I had no words to describe what had happened to me. The next several Sundays, Father John invited me to his office after the service, just as he had before. My stomach filled with dread, and I could taste vomit in my mouth.

Every week the father touched me and threatened me should I tell. Every week after he touched me, he gave me a book, or food, or money. I wanted to just stop going to church—but because of him I was going to the school again, and I didn't want to give that up for the world. Then there were Jackie and Liz and Ajey, waiting eagerly for the food I would deliver almost every Sunday, which got them through the week. The truth was—I desperately needed what he gave me. I was scared, all the time, living on my own. I was hungry. I wanted to go to school.

I wanted to believe that there was something out there, something greater than my poverty and my suffering, but every day seemed harder than the one before. I wanted a benevolent savior, Jesus Christ, and his father, God, to *actually* watch over me. I knew that somewhere in this, there was a choice—I just didn't know what it was. I weighed the options of living on the streets, scared to completely fall asleep at night because a thief might come and finish me off, against living at home, waiting for Babi to cross the line and hurt or maybe even kill my mom or me. Or the choice between going to school—the only thing I knew could change my life—and joining the gangs of youth smoking *bange,* drinking *changaa*. There were too many possibilities, and at the same time none at all.

At church I started to feel sick when I accepted the sacrament. I dutifully handed over the food Father John gave me to my mother; I could not eat a bite of it myself. I lined the books up, neat but unopened—the only things I owned other than a bowl and my tattered clothes. I mouthed the prayers, but slowly, silently, I stopped believing in God.

Sickened by the church and denied school once I left, I searched for a job doing casual labor, only to be turned away day after day after day. Eventually, I found the Rastafarians. People in the community saw Rasta people as thieves and criminals. But the truth was they were the kindest, most peaceful and humble people, searching for wisdom. Rastafarianism enriched my brain. We would just meet and smoke *bange* and listen to reggae. The first music they played for me was from South Africa by Lucky Dube, the song "Prisoner." I knew exactly what he meant:

"They won't build no schools anymore, all they'll build will be a prison, prison . . ."

Rastafarianism exposed me to the idea of resisting oppression and being a candle for this world. I learned about Haile Selassie of Ethiopia. When I was with the Rastafarians, I forgot my poverty as they helped me understand the system that confined me:

> You know what, the rich guys who runs the businesses and the government, they don't understand we are the ones running the economy. We are the ones. The maize flour they eat, we work in the factories to package it. The cleaners in their houses, they are from our neighborhood, they are our sisters and our mothers. The security officers at their homesteads, they are our brothers and fathers. Don't forget the drivers, waitresses, and gardeners who serve the wealthy. We run this country. They can't make do without us.

Not everyone who smoked *bange* was Rasta. There were many groups of boys who spent their days loitering around, smoking *bange,* which was less expensive than food. I never had the money myself to even afford *bange*. It was curious that people would share their *bange,* but not their food. Sometimes I would just smell the scent and walk over to a group of boys who would gladly pass around whatever they had.

I began spending more time with a group of guys older and tougher than me: Boi, Bully, Dennis, and Oti. They spent their days listening to imported American gangster rap, running around looking for odd jobs, stealing something small here and there just to survive. We called ourselves hustlers, we wrote "The Cave" on the door to our shared rental shanty. After we smoked, we were so hungry and could smell the sweet scent of meat drifting up from a local restaurant. In our *bange*-induced haze, the solution seemed so simple: We were hungry—eat! Money or not!

We walked into the restaurant with confidence. When the owner came to ask what we wanted, I said with a lot of force, "Meat!" They brought steaming plates of *nyama choma* (roasted meat) to the table and we ate furiously, with glee in our eyes. After I finished, I asked with even more braveness for a second plate. I figured if they found us with no money, they might do anything, so since we'd already started, we might as well finish—no point in turning back now. We ate as if we had all the money in the world, knowing we'd either die or survive at the end of this, no fifty-fifty. I was high, my stomach was full, and life suddenly didn't seem to matter so much; even if it ended in this moment, I wouldn't mind. When the owner went back into the kitchen to bring another customer's order, we bolted. On the streets we laughed at our invincibility. Nothing could touch us.

We were not stupid. We knew we were screwing up our lives, but that only made us madder, realizing this truth. Through no doing of our own we had been screwed from the start. This was my life—all that I could expect was to be harassed by the police, to be jobless and hopeless. My only crime was drawing life's short straw. I did not know what to do, so I smoked *bange* and drank *changaa* until I no longer knew my own name.

———

What was it that lifted my spirits from this sad dark place? It was a book, *A Testament of Hope: The Essential Writings and Speeches of Martin Luther King.*

I had been volunteering, sweeping the floors, and washing

the clothes at a charity home where elderly and mentally and physically disabled people lived. These people had no families. I felt happy having something to do, as though my days were not lost, did not just fade ruthlessly into one another. I also got fed there after I did my work.

One day a white man from America named Alex showed up at the charity. We introduced ourselves, and Alex said he was attending a university in Ohio and was in Kenya for his studies. He asked about my life and my story came tumbling out.

Alex listened and then gave me his copy of *A Testament of Hope*.

"Kennedy, you have to read this book," Alex said. "You will love it. You and Martin Luther King Jr. have a lot of things in common."

I couldn't put this book down. What America had passed through reminded me of what I was living through in the slum. No matter where you came from, the struggle was the same. In America it was about race. If you were black, you were invisible just because of your color. Here it was about class. Class was the issue. Because I was poor, I was invisible. When you were poor in Kenya, nobody helped you get justice.

Darkness cannot drive out darkness: only light can do that. Hate cannot drive out hate: only love can do that.

Faith is taking the first step, even when you can't see the whole staircase.

I cried as I read about what Martin Luther King Jr. went through. Yet he never gave up. He fought for the right of his people to have a better life. He knew that success didn't spring from him, but arose when people came together as a collective. Martin Luther King Jr.'s philosophy reminded me of my mom's:

Everybody can be great . . . because anybody can serve. You don't have to have a college degree to serve. You don't have to make your subject and verb agree to serve. You only need a heart full of grace. A soul generated by love.

Reading the book, I felt like my mother and Martin were talking to me, were talking to each other—each whispering about a hope for me that I couldn't yet clearly see.

One day Alex suggested I start writing letters to a girl named Maren who lived where he did, a foreign land called Ohio. He pulled a picture of her from his wallet to show me. She was beautiful. I wanted her to be my girlfriend.

Alex told me about Maren's family—her mother, Linda; her dad, Ray; the twins, Alisa and Emily. Alex also told me that they had a lovely dog called Jette, who actually lived inside their house. I felt like I was in love.

So I wrote: "Dear Maren, I am your boyfriend from Africa. I'm introduced to you by Alex Bishara. Your picture is beautiful. You have good breasts. Your buttocks is amazing and you are white as a star and I can't wait to look at your eyes." Please remember, I was just fourteen years old.

Alex said I should write another note to Maren's mother, Linda. He said she was an amazing woman, an angel.

"Alex, you are crazy. I don't care about the mother. I care about my girlfriend!" I told him. "In our culture we don't talk to the mothers-in-law."

"Okay, but, Kennedy, it would be nice to say something. Just say hi to her."

After that, I took another piece of paper. I wrote: "Dear Linda, Alex says that you are a very, very good person and I'm now in the family, you know like part of the family because Maren and I are very close. Say hi to the dog Jette and say hi to the twins. Kennedy."

After one month, I got my reply. Maren replied that she was happy and she shared my letter with her family and it made them laugh. She said they would like to keep in touch, and they wanted to know more about my life. Upon hearing this, I started crying.

"How can this stupid white lady show the letter to her parents, to her mom. This was between us?! I wrote some secret love words that I didn't want the mother to know! Why did she do that?"

Alex tried to console me and told me to reply anyway and say more about my life and why I wasn't going to school.

"Alex, this is not about school or whatever. This is my girlfriend, man. This is my girlfriend that I want to come to Kenya."

"Yes, Kennedy, I know but listen. Just tell them more about yourself, okay? They are really nice people."

So I wrote about my life, and I asked my girlfriend to tell me more about herself. I kept on sending and receiving letters. Maren wrote me less, but her mother, Linda, wrote me a long letter and sent me pictures of the dog and the family. I read her letters each night before I went to bed. I could read her letters ten times and never tire of it—someone across the world was thinking about me.

Linda asked about my family and wanted to know their names. She asked about school in Kenya and wanted to know how much it cost. I asked around and learned about an informal boarding school outside of Nairobi that didn't care about my limited educational background, so long as I could pay.

I sent the costs to Linda and she responded "Wow! That's good. I'd like to pay for you to go."

I didn't expect that. I couldn't believe my luck. I later found out that Maren was actually Alex's girlfriend at the time; Alex had wanted Linda to help me all along.

Linda and I communicated about everything, including topics I could never discuss with my own mother. For example, in Africa we don't talk about sex and relationships with our parents, even though HIV/AIDS has become something all too common in Kibera. But Linda brought up these issues. She asked me if I ever used a condom and, honestly, she was the first person to suggest them to me. I knew people who contracted HIV/AIDS just because they had no idea using condoms would help. Nobody had talked to them about prevention.

I regarded Linda as my American mother. It made such a difference for me to know somebody somewhere in Ohio was thinking about me. Linda made me feel valuable, made me feel loved. I learned a lot about American people through Linda. She sent pictures of snow, which amazed me. She also sent me cookies, candies, and other nice things from America. I was lucky that the letters and gifts could be sent to my neighbor Baba Omondi. He had a decent job at a factory in the industrial quarter so we used the mailbox at his company as the address for Linda. He checked the mailbox, and when I received a gift, he would bring it back to me, not even opening it to look inside.

After Linda found out the cost of the boarding school, she wired the money through Western Union directly to Mr. Sidney, the principal. Suddenly I was dropped, as from the sky, into "high school." Another neighbor in Kibera, Tom, a mechanic who repaired rich people's cars, gave me one of his pairs of black shoes. This was my very first pair of real, closed-toe shoes. They were too big for me, but I took them anyway. A truly generous gift.

The boarding school was a two-hour bus ride from Kibera. It was informal, not equipped with anything typically associated with the word *school*. There were no books. The building was run-down, and urine flowed across the floor of the bathroom, even worse than in the slum.

I came from my Kibera to another Kibera, I thought to myself.

It was rough: the older kids beat the new students. I relied on the skills I had learned on the streets. I didn't want to fight, but I acted tough and dangerous. I got the nickname "The Ranking," which basically meant the king of the kings, or the crazy of the craziest.

One of the problems at the school was the food. I soon discovered they put paraffin wax in the food to make the students feel full. It made us horribly sick, causing painful stomach cramps. I decided to go and tell Mr. Sidney that this was not acceptable. He didn't take me seriously, saying that school fees were cheap and they were doing the best they could. The students would just have to understand.

There was a late-night meeting of all the students to voice our anger. We decided to pool our money—everyone except me since I didn't have any—and buy petroleum to set fire to the dormitory and the classrooms. I was insistent that all the students know about the plans so they could evacuate and no one would be hurt.

I wanted to give Mr. Sidney one last chance. I found him having bread and tea in his office, and my mouth watered just seeing him.

"Mr. Sidney," I said urgently. "Things aren't looking good. The students are planning to riot. I'm just helping you by giving you this warning, but if you could do something now, I think I could calm them down."

He dismissed me again. "Let them."

The students set fire to the dormitory and the classrooms. Quickly, everything got out of hand. The police came and began teargassing us, burning our eyes. They rounded up all the students, even those not involved, throwing us into the back of their truck. Then we were unloaded at the station like animals; the police savagely beat us with sticks and herded us into cells. The other prisoners were hard-core, the only toilet a reeking bucket.

We were imprisoned for three days, but it felt like a year. When they released us, they insisted our parents pay for the damages, though Mr. Sidney decided not to make my family pay because I had alerted him before the protest. Mr. Sidney even gave me the bus fare to get home to Kibera.

I arrived in Kibera to learn the news of the protest and arrest was all over the papers, except that the story was completely inaccurate. My mother had heard the news and was sick with worry, convinced I would die in prison. To the community, however, I was a hero. My name "The Ranking" had spread all over Kibera.

seven

jessica

My program is going to the coast for two weeks to live in a Swahili Muslim village—a true immersion experience—so I bid Kennedy a temporary good-bye.

"Good thing you've almost learned how to take a villager's shower," he jokes. "Bring me back a coconut."

In the village, my host family takes my bag and ushers me to their hut, fussing over me in the Swahili that I barely understand. Their house is made of sticks and grass and has two rooms and an outdoor cooking and eating space. I get practice with many of the tasks that overwhelmed me in Kibera. I'm expected to cook with the women in my family—the mother, two sisters, and grandmother. It is Ramadan so we don't eat during the day but prepare a big meal that is ready right as the sun sets. Coconut rice and beans. Lentils. Chapati. In the morning, my homestay mother brews me spicy chai tea and makes me eat almost a whole loaf of white bread before I can go off to "school."

Every morning, she and my host sister Fatuma dress me. The Muslim culture here is very different from what I've always imagined. My face isn't covered, but they wrap a colorful piece of cotton fabric around my head called a *lesso*. Each print has a different design with a Swahili proverb written on the edge. My regular attire is a prom dress that looks like it's from the 1980s (and I'm sure was donated to Goodwill before making its way here), and a *lesso* on my head. It feels like a Halloween costume.

During the days, we attend intensive Swahili classes. As the days go by, my ears sensitize to the music of the language. The words feel full in my mouth—like *maridadi,* which means beauty, *pilipili* (spicy), and *bahari* (ocean). I love the extended *m* and *n* sounds, the rolled *r*'s. I've never spoken a language that feels so much like it was meant to be savored.

The village is right on the beach—so every day we see the beauty of the Indian Ocean. I walk around barefoot, savoring the sand beneath my feet, the freedom of village life. People just spend the days doing their chores and wandering from house to house visiting. At night, we go swimming in the ocean and all the village kids join us—until the elders call us to a meeting. They aren't happy; they say we are exposing their children to the evil spirits that lurk in the water at night, ready and waiting to snatch people away. After that, there is no more night swimming.

At first I think this might be some kind of heaven, life in a sleepy rural village on the beach. But as the days go by, I see parts of Kibera here too. Our host families try to hide their poverty from us, but they cannot hide their glee when each day bags of beans and rice are dropped off courtesy of our program, because we are here. Sure, there is more space here than in Kibera, and it's a much more beautiful environment, but there is little economic activity. Fishing seems to be the only real livelihood, and everyone is living hand to mouth. There is only one school in the village, and many of the girls aren't enrolled.

I talk with Subiti, a young man who speaks beautiful English and has made himself into a community leader here. He tells me how few routes out there are. This little village is all he expects to know.

Subiti asks if I am married. I reply with disgust—*Absolutely not! I'm only twenty-one!* Subiti laughs. Twenty-one and unmarried? Here that is unheard of. The expectations are so different. Here in this coastal Swahili village, the expectations for a twenty-one-year-old are more aligned with what Americans consider appropriate for when one is thirty-one. It's as though you lose a decade.

Then I get jiggers in my foot. I've never even heard of a jigger before—but apparently they are sand fleas that get into the skin around your toes and then lay eggs inside. Little bumps arise, and if the eggs are not properly removed and the egg sacks break in the process, the eggs multiply and fleas spread, becoming incredibly painful. I run screaming to Director Odoch, who takes one look at me and laughs at my utter panic.

"I've seen many students before you survive," he says—and then finds a needle to get them out. "Don't worry, I got my Ph.D. in jigger removal." He laughs.

I want to call Kennedy and tell him all about this. That I feel as though I'm inhabiting another world, hidden away in this tiny Muslim village on Kenya's coast. About how I've learned to cook coconut rice and beans; about the water spirits and the village elders; the beauty of the five A.M. call to prayers that carries on the ocean breeze; my amazement at the bright night sky lit only by stars, with no interference from human lights.

But I don't. I am both amazed and frustrated by what Kennedy said to me on the hill. About how he would spend the rest of his life with me, and then never mentioned this again. We still speak easily, but our relationship since then has maintained professional boundaries. We are careful.

Somehow I know that with him, I could let my guard down. But to be with Kennedy—in that way—I'd have to give up so much. I can't picture him ever being happy in my world, and could I ever be happy in his? I look at my phone, but don't call.

———

I come back from the coast in a new dress I bought in Mombasa—covered with red and white roses—with my hair braided, and with scabies. I have to stay at my Nairobi host mother's house for a few days, because it would be easy to give Kennedy scabies in Kibera's close quarters. Plus, someone has to help me put the scabies treatment all over my body—under every fingernail and on every surface. They are incredibly painful. I have to swallow a pill to kill the mites rapidly reproducing themselves inside my body; I shudder at the thought. I ask Odoch how I might have gotten them, and he says in any number of ways but probably through some unknown contact with animals in the village.

Kennedy comes to the gate and knocks quietly. His eyes move from the house, to my host mom's run-down white jeep, to my newly braided hair. He can't mask his discomfort. It looks strange on him, a contrast to his regular easy confidence.

"They put you in nice places," he says dryly. I can feel the heat rush to my face.

"I guess so. Probably afraid of little *mzungu*s running around without gates," I joke. "Come in?"

"Why don't you come out." It's not a question. His eyes have gone hard. They don't have their usual warmth or even a glint of mischief, and my heart goes pitter-patter. I feel like I've done something wrong.

"Let me just tell Mama Rose. I'll be right there." I run inside and call out to my host mother that I'm going out. I climb the stairs to my room to grab the coconut I brought Kennedy from the coast, and on my way back through the kitchen I take several hot *chapati*s and hide them in a plastic bag. Maybe he is hungry. The thought of this sends sharp pangs to my own stomach.

I catch a glance of myself in the hallway mirror and almost don't recognize my reflection. My hair is thick and synthetic, braid after braid, wild and unexpectedly womanly. I can't help but smile as I think about my host mother and sister in the village spending the eight hours it took to make my hair this way. They wanted to henna my hands too, but the sun set too soon. I kept wiggling and crying out in pain as they pulled without pause, and they told me to stay still and be patient—words I'm not good at heeding. With my family at home, we all have what we call "ski names" that highlight our most honest, least desirable traits. Mine is Ants in Her Pants. When my host mom and sister finished, they looked at me and smiled. In my own eyes, I could only see how ridiculous I looked. How typical white-girl-goes-to-Africa. But in their eyes, the hair was a way to make me part of them, at least for a moment.

I wonder what Kennedy thinks of it. He stands outside of the gate, and when I come out, his eyes don't meet mine. I'm surprised by my disappointment, by how much I wanted him to react.

"Let's go for a walk," he says.

We amble along the road, green trees lining both sides, and then sit down on the curb, watching the traffic pass us by. I uncover the *chapati* and rip off a piece myself before offering it to Kennedy. I know he'll be offended if he senses I brought it just for him.

"You didn't call." He says this with so little emotion I can't tell if he is angry or is just stating a fact. I take another piece of *chapati*.

"It was busy, sort of overwhelming trying to figure out how to fit in there."

"Does your boyfriend like your hair?" His tone turns jovial, as if we are old friends catching up.

"He does, he likes it." I am suddenly conscious that I want to make him jealous.

Kennedy returns to his most charming self, telling stories of what the SHOFCO youth did while I was gone and accepting the coconut with glee.

Then he switches gears again.

"I'll be gone for a few days. I need to go to my family's village. My mom is living there for now, and—this is embarrassing—they don't have a toilet. I've been saving up because I need to install one. It's a big shame for my family not to have a toilet in the village."

Kennedy stands up and brushes off his pants before brusquely saying, "I have to go. Let's talk when I'm back."

Before I can say anything, Kennedy's quick steps take him away, down the road toward Kibera. He doesn't look back. Somehow, I feel as though he's just confided in me something I'm not sure he intended. I sit on the curb alone as evening settles in, before standing and walking back home the opposite way.

He doesn't call for days. Recovering from scabies at my homestay, I miss Kibera's vibrancy, my newfound sense of discovery and community there. My routine starts to resemble that of my peers in the program. I go to "school" in the morning, listen to lectures and attend Swahili classes, then come back to my host mom's house in Woodley, eat dinner and watch the news with Mama Rose, going to bed before nine.

My resident adviser from my freshman-year dorm, Gabi, calls. She is coming to Nairobi! Gabi did a similar program on the Kenyan coast, and her enthusiastic endorsement was one of the reasons I chose to come to Kenya.

I want Kennedy to meet her, so I call him. As the phone beeps, I hold my breath. He doesn't answer. I text. *Friend coming to town I want you to meet. Are you back?* Twenty minutes later, he replies. *Got back last night. Meet in Olympic 5:00?*

Kennedy waits for me outside of a small shop in Olympic where he once took me for a soda. It's only been four days, but I feel like I haven't seen him in forever. We hug shyly, careful that our bodies don't graze too closely.

"When are you coming back to Kibera?" he asks.

"Scabies medicine finishes tomorrow. So tomorrow night if that's okay with you?"

"Do I have a choice?" He winks.

We walk to Adams Arcade, where Gabi is meeting us. It's strange seeing someone from Wesleyan here, utterly surreal. Gabi arrives and we get on a bus to town—Kennedy has selected a place for dinner that is famous for its fish. The bus weaves through Nairobi's crazy traffic and eventually Kennedy says, "It's here."

As we get off, he whispers to me, "I hope you like it."

At the restaurant we sit outside, with traditional music playing in the background. Gabi looks at me and smiles. She is tan from the Mombasa sun. We each order fish and it comes whole, with *ugali* and steaming vegetables on the side. I watch how Kennedy eats it and try to copy his moves. He dips the *ugali* in the fish sauce with relish, then breaks the head off and eats the eyes and brain. We finish, and Gabi and I ask for the bill.

The waiter looks at us confused, then says, "It's already been paid."

"I took care of it," Kennedy says nonchalantly and stands up to go wash his hands.

Gabi and I stare at each other, dumbfounded. We both know it's customary in such instances to offer to pay—the reality is that Kennedy would never go to a place like this if we weren't here.

"That's a lot of money, probably a month's rent," she whispers.

I nod, overcome by this act of generosity. *African men provide.* We stay at the fish restaurant a little bit longer, but it's getting late and Gabi needs to leave to get back to where she is staying. I hug her good-bye.

On our way to catch a bus back home, Kennedy grabs my hand and pulls me inside a dimly lit bar named Tacos, although there is no Mexican food anywhere to be seen.

"Let's have a drink."

We climb into a booth at the back. The bar is filled with smoke and the smell of spilled beer. Swahili pop music blares and Kennedy shouts playfully "ehh," throwing his hands up and swaying his shoulders and hips to the music before sitting down.

He orders a round of Tuskers, and the waitress brings us each two so that she won't have to come back anytime soon.

"This was a place we used to die to come, us boys in the ghetto." Kennedy laughs nostalgically, clinking his beer bottle with mine. "Sometimes I'd sneak into reggae clubs in town with Antony, Boniface, or George. We'd pass this bar and say that's where the *watu wadozie* go—the people with money."

I look around and laugh at the mischief in his voice, taking in the friends and couples sitting at tables strewn with empty bottles, enjoying a carefree Friday night.

"When we snuck into the reggae clubs, we had to take care not to get caught or big trouble! George and Boniface always went straight to the beautiful women. Not me, I ignored them. I'd dance by myself, drowning in the messages in the music. Lyrics about righteousness, and about not giving up, and the Babylon system." With his hand on his heart for effect, Kennedy breaks into a Culture song: "*I'm a humble African, passing through Babylon. I'm a humble African, trouble no one.*'"

"My mom always said I was the worst singer, but I love it!" he chortles.

"She might be right about that!"

"Babylon, that's what reggae calls anyone who doesn't understand real hard life. In Rasta we called them 'Babi.'" He leans in conspiratorially. "Even the people here, most of them are Babis."

"What about me? Am I a 'Babi'?"

"Hard to say yet, but you're crazy and tough, more like a Rasta woman." I start to laugh so suddenly, just as I take a sip, that I start to choke, which only makes me sputter harder.

"It always used to make George and Boniface crazy. They would go up to the women, spend money treating the women to drinks, and the women would just ignore them. I'd be in my own world, dancing, moving my hips like this, and the women would just come to me. That's when I learned the secret to women."

"Oh yeah, what's that?"

He smiles mysteriously and just shakes his shoulders again to the music as if to answer. We sip our Tuskers in silence for a moment. The beers, smoke, and dim lights embolden me.

"Why did you do that earlier, Kennedy? Why did you pay for that entire dinner? You didn't need to."

He holds my gaze levelly and says, "I saved a long time for that; I know why I did it."

My insides quiver. I can't find anything to say. I'm not *that* emboldened.

It's too late for the bus, so we take a taxi back from the bar. The city looks so different cloaked in night. There are few lights, even on the main roads. Every corner looks clandestine. The driver goes fast; apartment buildings, traffic lights, people standing on corners all spin into one another.

Sitting on the torn vinyl seats in the back of the cab with Kennedy, I feel like I could measure, to the millimeter, the small gap of air between our thighs.

Suddenly his fingers are running through my hair, tracing the outline of my face, pulling me toward him. It's as if he no longer controls his hands—they've been granted a life of their own by the night and the alcohol. I feel as if all the air has been suctioned out of the car. I've wondered so many times what his hands would feel like. I can feel their strength and gentleness, their yearning. For a moment I close my eyes, wanting time to freeze.

But I can't—we can't. Without thinking about it, I pull away.

His hands instantly retreat.

"I'm sorry—"

He doesn't speak or look at me. He stares out the window, radiating heat that's either seething anger, shattered pride, or both. My typical reaction to discomfort is to let loose an inappropriate giggle, and I barely contain one from escaping. I wonder who the last girl was to say no to Kennedy Odede? My gut says he never spoke to her again. I'm so drawn to that about him: his confidence that someday, somehow, he will get whatever it is that he wants. He has an unapologetic awareness that he is special. If he somehow loved me, I would be made special too.

He says something to the driver in Luo and the car stops. He opens the door, gets out, and slams it behind him, disappearing without another word into the night.

I sit in stunned silence for a moment; and then I tell the cab-driver without flinching, "Woodley Estate, please."

The next morning I wander slowly through the market that separates my homestay from Kibera. In my head I practice conversations with Kennedy. I don't know what to say to him. My stomach fills with nerves at the thought of seeing him. When I close my eyes, a movie flashback is on repeat, complete with strobe lighting: the back of the taxi, the movement of his hands, the sharp inhalation of my breath, the slam of the door. I don't even know if he wants me to come back to Kibera.

When I arrive at Kennedy's, he's there with two men I don't recognize, huddled in intense conversation. I slip by as inconspicuously as possible and place my backpack in the corner, exiting as quietly as I came in. One of the men has an array of tools and wires, and he's showing Kennedy how he's running one of them inside the cardboard wall, gesturing to a hole he's cut on the outside. I stand outside the door frame looking in, curious.

Kennedy peers out. "Hi, welcome back."

I study his face closely, but I don't see any hint of last night. His expression is stoic and focused. I feel disappointment tempered by relief.

"Hi, what are you doing?"

"Well, you said that you need power for your computer because the battery doesn't last, so I'm putting in power."

I look at the man who is now busy connecting his improvised "power line" to a single lightbulb in the middle of the room and shake my head in amazement.

"How? Where are you connecting it to?"

"This is Kibera. These people are very clever; they can create opportunity out of anything. They tap into the city power lines and then charge people for a connection into their lines."

"So they charge you a monthly bill?"

"Yes! They make your connection, and then you pay monthly or they disconnect you. It isn't very strong power, but at least sometimes it will work. That's one way you know who is doing a little bit better in Kibera—who has power in their house."

"You never had power before?"

"I never needed it before," he says pointedly.

I wince at the slight barb in his tone, remembering the word he used last night, *Babylon*.

"Well, I can pay the bill, I'm sorry—you didn't have to put it in; I was fine charging my battery at school. I don't want to inconvenience you—"

"Stop." He cuts me short. "I could have had it before. I just never needed it. You know the problem with Americans? You always think the rest of the world is just waiting for your money." With that he goes back inside.

I sit down on the hard cement outside the door, stung by Kennedy's rebuke. I suddenly realize that I am an intruder in his normal life. He has been here, and will be after I leave. My presence has already interfered—putting in power, making it so his siblings rarely sleep at his house. He has bigger problems than reassuring me as I'm confronted by new realities that he has always known. Sometimes he pours tea into a cup that isn't there, his mind far away. The things he thinks about, that worry him, all carry weights I cannot begin to imagine. At night, he falls into bed without speaking, his body heavy with exhaustion.

I realize that what happened in the cab was connected only to the alcohol and darkness of that pub. Kennedy is back to being cordial and collegial, and so, so busy. He is so young, but so responsible. He organizes groceries for his family; he sends precious money from his job as a janitor to his mother, who recently left Kibera for her rural ancestral village. He leads meetings of hundreds of young people, and when he speaks, there is rapt silence. He talks to the women on the road and they implore him to come have tea in their houses. He helps start countless businesses. Every Sunday he leads a meeting for all the SHOFCO members in the iron-sheet office. There are so many people who come that everyone stands, and latecomers participate by looking in through the window.

Often, I'm not sure what to say to him. Kennedy's become less of a normal breathing man to me, and more of a distant hero. I get the feeling that to him I am a child, and I'm guilt-ridden because part of me feels gratitude for this, for the things I've never seen, the things from which my parents and my world protected me.

"Guilt is a luxury," Kennedy tells me.

————

Every afternoon around four, sometimes earlier, men and women—even children—gather to ask Kennedy for advice. Long into the evening Kennedy sits huddled with these visitors on the couch, listening intently. Sometimes the voices rise in heated argument, as Kennedy adjudicates family disputes or provides marriage counseling. Other times, the voices are quiet, soft and despairing—clinging to Kennedy's every word, his advice their only sliver of hope. A man standing outside the door tonight looks like he can't be beyond his midtwenties, but his shoulders already droop in defeat. Kennedy opens the door and glances back at me. This look has become our silent signal.

Caught off guard by my presence, many visitors don't pass the threshold of the door. "I'll come back later," they apologize before turning around and taking their problems back into the night.

So when Kennedy looks at me now, I slip behind the sheet dividing the room into living room and bedroom, curling up on the small bed frame. Sometimes, I listen in. Other times I put on my headphones and retreat into a world far away from these problems I am so powerless to solve or even understand. My Swahili is slowly improving, and I can understand enough to piece together the threads of the conversation. But Kennedy often switches into Luo or Kikuyu, the words flowing easier then, swaddled within the intimacy of what he calls "mother tongues." Kennedy can speak four "mother tongues," in addition to Swahili and English, and this quickly puts his visitors at ease. I love to hear him shift so seamlessly between these languages. I get lost in the different melodies and rhythms of each, transfixed by the differences in Kennedy's gestures, the distinct ways his mouth cups the words: fast and round in Luo, the words forming an oval "O" shape; in Kikuyu, the tip of his tongue presses against his front teeth, the sound forward in his mouth, light and air filled. I'm learning Kennedy also has his own language of clicks, a gentle *tsk tsk tsk* for amazement, louder for indignation, or one loud cluck when he is angry or defeated.

It's a routine, this small line forming outside the door, people waiting their turn for Kennedy's attention. By the time we cook dinner, it's often late. When he's talking to someone, he completely loses track of time. I'm exhausted by the energy it takes to simply sit still for hours, trying to make myself as inconspicuous as possible. Sometimes I excuse myself early in the afternoon to walk with Anne or Kennedy's sister Liz—doing what they call "laps" around the neighborhood. He never asks me to leave, but I sense the disturbances my presence causes in Kennedy's life, and I feel his relief when I leave him to his councils with his community members.

Kennedy is tireless. Sometimes I dread the approach of afternoon, but he seems to eagerly anticipate the time of day when everyone returns from their daily pilgrimages searching for work, fresh with worries and in need of his ear. The solutions are so often elusive, but he remains undaunted. Some nights he is openly joyful after tending to everyone who came. He'll leave the house to seek out more people in the neighborhood—to tell stories and make jokes, the sound of his laughter carrying late into the night—coming home after I've already fallen asleep. Other nights, he is shrouded by a noticeable heaviness. We eat dinner quietly, often with Shadrack, Collins, or Liz, who know how to tease out his moods, watching him carefully, eyes filled with deference. I follow their lead.

One time there's a knock on the door that, for once, isn't someone seeking counsel. Outside stands a man with a very old camera—the kind where you insert film one picture at a time. Kennedy envelops him in a hug and laughs with disbelief. It seems that they haven't seen each other for a long time.

"This man, he took the only pictures of me that I have from my childhood," Kennedy explains with reverence. "He used to come every now and then, and my mom would sacrifice anything she had, even if it meant we didn't eat that night, so that we could take a picture. I have three."

I try hard to control the muscles in my face. Kennedy has only three pictures from his entire childhood? I have an entire basement flooded with photos documenting my every milestone, and I've never given them a passing thought.

"Come outside," Kennedy says, taking my hand and gingerly drawing forty precious shillings from his pocket. "Let's take another."

Tonight, outside the door stands a man with a child in his arms; the baby's piercing cries make the house feel even smaller. The man's name is Onesmus, and he and Kennedy speak in hurried Swahili. The baby is a girl, born just two days ago. Unable to afford a clinic, her mother gave birth at home and died during delivery. Onesmus looks at the baby with sheer bewilderment. Kennedy offers to hold the child and after a long silence says quietly, "She looks like her mother." Moisture gathers in the corner of Kennedy's eyes and runs in a straight line down his face; I realize he makes no noise when he cries.

"I have no work. I can't afford milk. What kind of life will this baby have?" Onesmus asks.

Kennedy stands, holding the baby close to his chest, and says, "Let's go, I have an idea."

Once they've gone, I don't want to be alone, thinking of the baby and her mother, who was probably not much older than me. I place the padlock on the door and go to Emily's shanty. Emily is a close friend of Kennedy's sister Liz. Inside, the small TV is on as Emily and Liz watch a Nigerian movie.

I get back to Kennedy's a few hours later, surprised by the crowd of people outside. I shove my way through to the door. No one moves to let me pass, and to my dismay, the door is still locked. Taking the small key out of my bag, I turn around and see the crowd is looking at me, expectantly. I recognize a few faces, but most I don't. Many stare at me with my own look of confusion mirrored back. I raise my voice above the noise, hoping that Swahili won't fail me now. "*Ken hayuko,*" I shout apologetically. He's not here!

A few of the rowdy younger men begin to chant, "Mayor, Mayor!" I start to worry. Maybe something's wrong, maybe he's in trouble? As I deliberate about what to do next, a cheer sweeps through the crowd.

"Mayor! Mayor!" Kennedy returns just in time, but without Onesmus or the baby. He takes in the crowd, wipes the concern from his face, and begins to shake hands and fist-bump. Someone begins to sing and the scene turns jubilant. Kennedy waves his hand as if telling people to cool it, and I slip back inside the house.

It's ten o'clock, and he's still outside—I hear the rumbling voices of a meeting, people shouting in dissent, others cheering when they agree with a point. Finally, the noise starts to die down and the door opens. Kennedy looks so tired. I've made cooked bananas for dinner and bought several *chapati* from a woman on the road who makes them soft and doughy. I offer Kennedy the banana I've saved for him and he looks at me with an eyebrow raised.

"Is that what *mzungus* eat for dinner?" he says disapprovingly.

"Not usually, but it was easy. It's been a long day. What happened with the baby?"

He takes a piece of the *chapati* and scoops up a piece of the soft banana to taste.

"There is a missionary I know who runs an orphanage near Lang'ata. We took the baby there. By good luck, they took her in." He doesn't elaborate, and I don't ask more. In my head I can picture the scene. Kennedy, begging the sister to rescue this baby; Onesmus, unprepared for his request to be granted, reacting with surprise and relief. The baby will survive. She will have food and diapers, things that Onesmus cannot himself provide. A silent emptiness between them, for this is rescue, but not triumph.

"All those people outside, what did they want?" I ask.

"Elections are coming, Jess. They wanted me to run for councilor. They came to convince me."

"What did you say?"

"I said no. I don't do good work in the community because I want a role in politics, but people don't understand. What I want is just to keep SHOFCO afloat, to be able to touch one person's life at a time when lucky enough to get that chance."

"But they call you Mayor? Isn't that already politics?"

A good-natured smile breaks out on his face. "That's not an elected mayor; it's a name of affection for a man who is there for his people. A real mayor, who, not formally elected, takes responsibility for what the politicians leave behind."

I clear the dishes, finishing the remains of the banana that Kennedy didn't want. I put the plates in a plastic basin on the floor. I'll wash them in the morning. Kennedy remains alone outside, and I hear him pacing, his feet shuttling across the cement, as I drift into sleep.

eight

kennedy

One day Ajey asked me to go for a walk. We walked all along the railway tracks that lie on the perimeter of Kibera—stopping on a hilly ledge where we could look down and see it all. I pointed excitedly to our house.

"Kennedy, I want to tell you something that I've been hiding for a while," Ajey said. I was scared of what my mother was about to say. Could it be that she was infected with HIV/AIDS? Or something else? I was afraid and shaking. Was my mom going to commit suicide, like many abused women did? I held her hands tightly.

"Mom, you can tell me anything."

Tears were trickling down her face as she looked at me.

"Ken, you have passed through a lot since your childhood, and I'm sorry for all those struggles. You are honestly the strongest child I've ever had and ever known. I know many children who have had it easier than you, and they can't handle anything. Their lives are ruined by drugs, or women, or violence."

I didn't know why my mom was going on like this, without

telling me what she wanted to share with me. To be honest, the more she delayed getting to her point, the more nervous I felt about what might be coming next.

"Kennedy, your father is not who you think your father is."

I was silent. This was not what I had anticipated.

"Mom, what? What are you saying? Babi—he's not my father?"

"He is not your father."

In spite of my immense confusion, I also felt a moment of relief. Finally it made sense, even my middle name, Owiti. How Babi had always treated me: the beatings, the fury when he saw me eat . . .

She continued, "The reason I'm telling you the truth is that my life is short. I think this man will one day kill me as he has been threatening me a lot."

"Ajey, shhh," I interrupted. "I will never let anyone kill you! I'll protect you!"

We both cried together.

"Do you want to know . . . who your father is . . . ?" Ajey asked shyly. "We were so young . . ." She trailed off, lost in her memories.

"Do you know him?"

"Of course I know him, Ken."

"I mean now, do you know him now?"

"We are no longer in touch, but we know each other—"

"And he knows about me?" I cut her off.

"Of course, he knows."

"No. I don't want to know. If he is still alive and knows about me but still allows me to suffer like this—I hate him. I hate him even more than I hate Babi!" I yelled at her, before running off down the railway line.

I ran and I ran, until I was sure she wasn't following me, until I was in a part of Kibera that I had never been to before—I didn't even know if it was still Kibera. I wanted to be someplace where no one knew me, where no one recognized me as the child from that terrible, furiously fighting family, especially now that I knew at least part of why they were always fighting: me. I was an unwanted child. My life was suddenly explained. Why I ate last or not at all, why Ajey would sometimes yell that I had ruined her life, why Babi hurt me more, why he beat her so ruthlessly, why she always had to choose between protecting me or surviving with him.

In Kibera, to have a stepchild was not something normal. If it happened, it was a closely kept secret. Men did not want children who were not their own. So many children in my situation were abandoned or killed; survival was improbable.

Yet even in his deepest of rages, Babi had never told me, had never once yelled, "You are not my child! You are a burden that is not mine!" He had never said anything to give it away—no matter how drunk or mean he became. This showed how big a secret it was to have a stepchild.

There was something almost gratifying about knowing that I hadn't been making it up—and terrifying about knowing that as long as I lived at home, really as long as my mom lived with Babi, she would never be able to choose me. If she did, she could die.

On that day, I decided to take my half siblings—my mother's children with my stepfather, Babi—as more than half, as a whole part of me. I loved them so much and they loved me, sometimes even hiding food and giving it to me when he was not around.

A dream rose within me. My dream was to be the opposite of my stepfather. I never knew how a good family should be. I had no models, but I knew how bad a violent family is. I hoped one day to offer my missed childhood experience to my kids.

And what about my biological father? I didn't even dream about him. He is like someone who died a long time ago. Was he out there still? Maybe. To be honest, I didn't want to know. I was only reminded of him when occasionally someone stopped me in Kisumu to say, "You look exactly like your father." But being a parent is much more than genes, than resembling each other; it is about love and nurture and sacrifice.

With my family struggling more than ever, I had to start looking for work. I looked everywhere for a job but could not find one. I became close to another young man, named George Okewa. George came to Nairobi after finishing secondary school in the village. He was also jobless like me, but he did odd jobs in construction whenever there was an opening. I told him to think of me anytime there was an opportunity. George never said much, and so many people took him for being shy, but the rumors were that George had once beaten his teacher and gotten expelled from the school. He was tall and imposing, yet with a sweet almost babylike face. At an early age he had found work as a fisherman, struggling to survive because he was one of twenty-one children in a polygamous family. His family sent him to Nairobi to stay with a relative who would teach him to become a carpenter. However, George told me he did not like carpentry. George was about seven years older than I was, and he always looked out for me. People saw George as tough, and he commanded quiet respect. We became very close friends.

At last, I found a job in a factory. It was hard work and we earned a hundred shillings—a dollar a day—and from that we were forced to pay twenty shillings for a thin porridge at lunch. The porridge was like water; it could barely keep me standing to perform the day's hard labor. I could not afford to take the bus to work, so I had to walk two hours each way. I left Kibera very early in the morning while it was still dark. Every morning I woke at four, washed, snuck in a few moments of precious reading time, and then woke my friend Ochieng, who had helped me to get the job.

Every morning people left the slums in droves to walk to work in the industrial area. I liked the camaraderie of walking together as brothers and sisters from different backgrounds, talking to pass the time over the long distance until we reached the gate of our workplaces. Everyone around me was happy, filled with purpose—at least we were walking to work. We were the lucky few who might bring something small home at the end of the day, even though we lived hand to mouth. As we left the slums, we thought of the many who did not have any job at all.

But I was never happy. As I walked, I wondered if this would be my entire life. Was an endless series of years earning a hundred shillings a day in dangerous factory jobs the most I could hope for my life?

One day on the way to work, a passing car careening along splashed dirty water on us. The passengers had no concern for us as we walked alongside the road in the mud. When the water hit my face, soiling my clothes, tears sprang to my eyes.

"Ochieng, you know what? Poverty makes us invisible. That rich guy driving the car thinks we are nothing. You know, when I was a street boy, I would have stoned that car. I'm wearing my white shirt, and now I look dirty. I look like I slept in the mud or outside in the rain. Ochieng, why is the world so unfair? Why do some people have too much and some too little? Why can't we all just have enough?"

"Kennedy, you are crazy. You think too much!" Ochieng shouted at me. He moved away from me, walking faster.

"Ochieng, I know you think I'm crazy, but listen to me. One day I'll have a car. I'll drive it carefully and treat everybody equally," I said.

Ochieng started laughing, shaking his head, thinking I was a lunatic. "Kennedy, you will never, never have a car."

We reached the gate in the industrial area and signed in. The factory made gas cylinders. My job was to ensure the cylinders were in order by size, and then load the cylinders onto trucks and drop them at the petrol stations. The cylinders were heavy and could crush you if you weren't careful. My hands were busy all the time; they were always dry and cracked.

We had to work quickly, otherwise the overseer would complain and we would quickly find ourselves out of a job. We knew how entirely disposable we were, because every day there was a line of people outside the factory who didn't get chosen to work that day. Some lingered at the gate throughout the day, waiting for someone on the inside to fall on hard luck. We were the machines running Nairobi's economy. It wasn't our brains, but our strength that made us useful, until we had no strength left at all.

There was also a hot room in which we worked to harness the gas. I dreaded the days I would be assigned to work in this room as I knew that people had died doing this work. Once there was a deadly fire that broke out in this very room, killing many of the men inside. Yet every day I was reminded that although my factory job was brutal, I was one of the lucky ones. So many of my friends had no jobs at all.

I returned home from work tired and worn. One day George came to my house, his face serious and drawn. I saw him infrequently these days; we were both so busy hustling to survive.

"Boi is dead," he said, his voice flat.

Boi had been my childhood friend who was always happy and smiling. Life never seemed to hassle him in the same way it affected the rest of us. I felt chills up my spine. I had been with Boi only a week ago, laughing and joking together about girls.

"How?" I asked George, almost not wanting to know the answer.

"He held up a supermarket," George whispered. "But he had a toy pistol. It wasn't real. The police arrived on the scene and shot him dead. The police didn't care enough to take time to assess the situation. Boi wasn't even taking money, just some bread, milk, and flour."

I shook my head. Boi was the only one providing for his mother and his sister, and I knew how hard things could get. He was a good person, with a kind heart. Mine was broken. I had known Boi for so long, and his life was suddenly gone, in an instant. What a terrible waste.

A few weeks later I went to see my friend Calvin, whom I hadn't visited in a long time. I made my way around the street corners to his house and pushed open the beat-up iron-sheet door. I stopped still in my tracks. Calvin's thin, seventeen-year-old body hung suspended in the middle of the room, hanging from a crudely constructed noose. He had hanged himself. I felt the sobs racking my body, the sound uncontrollably coming out of my mouth. Calvin, my sweet friend, swung limp and lifeless before me. He left a note that said exactly what I felt: *I can't live this life anymore.*

I thought about suicide many times. Taking rat poison. Just ending the daily drudgery, the grinding pain. We were disposable; our lives not valued. In Kibera, people are desensitized to death. Living is understood to be the exception.

Then, a neighbor raped my sister Jackie. Late at night, he pulled her into his house as she came home alone down a winding path. It felt like my entire world shattered. Babi wanted to kill the man but was scared of going to prison. My family had no money to pay the police a bribe to have the man arrested, and we knew that if we couldn't bribe the police to keep the rapist in jail, he would easily bribe his way out. Jackie didn't laugh anymore, didn't talk. She was about to be seventeen.

A few weeks later it was confirmed: Jackie was pregnant.

My mom was devastated. Her daughter pregnant at nearly the same age she was when she gave birth to me. I knew what she was thinking. I was thinking it too: the cycle of poverty is inescapable.

Babi decided there was nothing to do but have Jackie marry the man. Jackie cried soundlessly when Babi made this declaration. I couldn't bear to see this happen, so I secretly organized a way for Jackie to go stay with relatives in the village. Jackie stayed upcountry, helped with the crops, and had her baby there: baby Kennedy. But once she became a mother, life was unforgiving upcountry—there was drought and no food; Jackie had no way to feed her baby. She came back to the city, her only thought her baby's survival—she had long given up on her own. The father of

Jackie's child worked in a petrol station, which made him better off than our family. There was no wedding, no ceremony. Jackie simply moved in with him and was considered married to the man who had raped her. The life we lived in Kibera was a life of no choices, no options. We were consumed with simply trying our best to survive.

Then one day a little girl was raped in my neighborhood. Her name was Beatrice, and she was only seven years old, raped by a man of fortysomething years, her white dress dirty and dotted with blood. The man was her neighbor, but nothing happened to him. I wanted to fight for the rights of this little girl, but, instead of the government taking any action against him, a gang in Kibera protected the man.

Another day a man beat his wife in the middle of the road— they were my neighbors. Everyone watched as she was brutalized, but we were all too frightened to intervene. From the gossip around me, I learned that the beating had started because the woman hadn't cooked dinner for her husband—even though he hadn't given her any money to buy food. Everyone I talked to said with resigned attitudes: *This is just how life is in Kibera.*

I wanted to do something. I just didn't know what or how.

Soon after these brutal events, the factory owners announced they were cutting our wages retroactively. I was the only person who refused to accept such reduced pay, and when I complained I was fired with no pay at all. Luckily for me, houses on Mombasa Road were being built and unskilled laborers were needed. The foreman picked fifteen men, including me. We each got a wheelbarrow, but when I took mine, I saw it didn't have a wheel.

The foreman kicked me and shouted at me, "Bring the wheelbarrow. You have to bring the wheelbarrow."

He wanted me to push it even without a wheel.

"This one doesn't work. It has no wheel." I pleaded with him to see my plight.

I was sorry to lose this job too, and I cried on my way home.

The next job I got was in construction, again very hard work. We did some digging; we carried bricks with our hands up to the eighth floor of a building; we mixed the heavy sand and cement. We were promised 150 shillings per day for this work, which would be paid out weekly. Yet after the first week, the Indian foreman said he would deduct 50 shillings from the pay of every employee—blatant theft as I knew he planned to pocket the money himself.

"This was not the agreement," I told him.

"Do you have a lawyer? Can you pay for a lawyer? If you mess with me, young man, I will dump you in a prison and your mama will not see you again. We will give you a hundred shillings. Take this job or go."

I took the money. Then I started organizing people.

"We cannot let this happen. Tomorrow we have to strike. This guy is cheating us. We will refuse to work until we get paid, and we are going to attract attention until the big boss finds out what is going on."

Everybody agreed. The next day we all sat down on the site and demanded our money, refusing to work until we were paid.

"*Kazi kwisha*—job finished, job finished," said the foreman. We thought he was joking, but when we turned around, we saw a line of people waiting for jobs.

"Who wants a job? Get in line!" he called out. I looked around bewildered; my guys all jumped up and left our strike to get in line. They all pointed fingers at me saying I was the troublemaker, that I had made them strike.

"You think you are smart, young boy? You are going to suffer until you die. You leave this place right now or I will call the police."

He came and grabbed me by the shirt, dragging me out of the place. He owed me pay for three days' work.

"Pay me my money and I will go. Just please give me my money," I begged him.

He refused. "I will tell these people to beat you. They will beat you."

Everyone told me to just go, and I saw that they were ready to beat me if I didn't leave.

I felt betrayed. I was fighting for my rights and the rights of the other workers. I was willing to sacrifice for the greater good, but they were not, they could not. I felt more hopeless than ever.

The foreman was just a small example of the corruption rampant in the community. Corrupt government officials stole huge sums of money and never even went to prison, but my friend Joshua stole a radio out of desperation, and a mob went to his house at night, put a tire around his body, and set him on fire. Joshua was burned to death, a punishment far more severe than his crime.

Formal law enforcement was also corrupt. The police came into Kibera, harassing people and threatening arrest unless offered bribes, searching people for marijuana and claiming people playing radios were causing public disturbances, and demanding to see permits. The police didn't curb crimes; they committed crimes. Police shot indiscriminately into Kibera, killing several people who they randomly denounced as thieves. It seemed "thief" was simply code for being poor.

George was now called Serikal, or "Government." He had become powerful. He was in charge of the unofficial government of Kibera. The group of young men did much that was good for the community, but also caused a lot of trouble, punishing rule breakers at will. At one point our landlord was selling water at a huge profit when there was a scarcity of water. Government and his people destroyed the landlord's water tanks to demonstrate that they wouldn't allow people to take advantage of others. Some people loved these young men; others hated them. Either way, there was no question that here in Kibera, *Serikal* and his group were the only government we could count on.

I was seething with anger. Anger at how every day life became harder. Anger at the senseless killing and death, the brutality all around me. I had lost so many friends. Meanwhile there were always more people coming to the slums from the villages, lured by the elusive promises of city life. Sadly, none of them could get an education or find work. There was no way out of poverty. If you protested, you would be killed. We were born poor, we would die poor.

I heard about a group of young men who, in desperation, had burned down the nearest police camp as a statement against the police's brutalization of our community. Peaceful negotiations had failed. Violence was the only statement they could make, their only way to be heard. They snuck out at night, petrol bombs ready, and they lit the police station on fire. Immediately, they were besieged by gunfire. Some ran, but others were not so lucky. Some were killed that night. I felt my fury unleashed on the world. I wanted to see the destruction I witnessed every day in my community reach those responsible for much of the damage and misery. Still, I knew in my gut that violence was not, and would never be, the answer. I just didn't know what the answer was.

I turned back to reading, grasping for answers and inspiration. I reread my book with Martin Luther King's writing and speeches and again read Nelson Mandela's *Long Walk to Freedom*. I thought about King's civil disobedience and about the sacrifice required to make a change. I went back to the story of Moses, another figure I admired. Born and then thrown away as a kid, he became a man who led the Israelis to the Promised Land, crossing over to the other side. I, too, wanted to lead my people into a new land of promise, but I didn't know how. I didn't dare dream. There was no light by which to dream.

nine

jessica

The sun, unusually orange, begins to set, and I remember Kennedy's warning.

"Makina? Are you crazy—Makina isn't even safe for me, for black people, for the people who live there. You can't spend the night there. People get killed, Jessica. There is a mosque there where a group of boys wring people's necks like chickens, in broad daylight. Makina, it's no joke."

And yet, here I am, at Alice's place in Makina, the Nubian area of Kibera. The first inhabitants of Kibera were Nubian—Sudanese soldiers—and the British colonizers "gave them" Kibera as a token of gratitude for their service in World War I. *Kibera* is the Nubian word for "jungle." Alice works for my homestay mother as her "house girl."* She smiles at me shyly, I smile back from behind a well-loved coffee mug filled with the instant coffee she's proudly prepared, having heard that Americans prefer coffee to tea. Kennedy's half-finished coffee sits on the small stool

---

* A common position in Kenyan households, akin to a housekeeper.

that serves as the room's only table. He left in a rush, anxious to leave before dark settled, and it seems he took the easy conversation with him.

Alice's eyes flicker every so often to the door, to the hook and eye that are all that keep it closed. Over her shoulder, I peer out the small window to see people scurrying to finish errands and get inside before the last bit of daylight—safety—vanishes for good.

When Alice heard that I was moving into Kibera, she pleaded with me to come spend one night with her in her house. Unaware of the nuances of the neighborhoods, I'd accepted. It gave me satisfaction to see my host mother shake her head with disapproval—she'd never go to Alice's house. Alice and I couldn't be too far apart in age. If we could sit on my host mother's couch and talk, why couldn't we do the same on Alice's?

When I'd told Kennedy my plan, he'd refused outright, explaining Makina's infamous reputation, insisting I back out. The more he'd resisted, the more adamantly I'd pushed—I had made a promise that I didn't want to break. A twinge of doubt twisted my stomach, but I didn't dare tell him, didn't dare answer the question that flashed through my mind: *What am I trying to prove?*

Seeing that he wouldn't change my mind, Kennedy had begrudgingly walked me the forty-five minutes it took to reach Alice's—his popularity made the walk longer. When we arrived, Alice came rushing out, proud to greet her visitors, eager to show me off. She wanted everyone in the neighborhood to know that a *mzungu* came to see her. All the attention made me suddenly shy, my presence converted into an uncomfortable personal trophy.

Alice served coffee and told us her story. Her husband was in jail, accused of armed robbery, and she spent most of the money she earned on food and supplies for him. She blames him for leaving her alone and without enough money to feed their children; she's had to send them upcountry to live with her mother.

"That's African men," she lamented.

"Not all," Kennedy replied. His eyes held mine for a moment.

Now I wish he'd stayed, or maybe that I'd gone back with him. Darkness falls. I realize I came here in part to prove my openness, to be able to say that I survived it, but that is not what Alice needs. She needs to get her husband out of jail, and to bring her kids home. It's not altogether unreasonable that she hopes I might be a pathway to that. I feel a faint disappointment—in us both.

Alice lights a kerosene lamp and pushes the couch against the door for extra protection.

"Has anything ever happened?" I ask, trying to conceal the concern in my voice.

Alice just laughs, and I'm too scared to repeat the question. Her frame is frail, but tough—it has already endured so much. She cooks dinner, a small portion of beef stew that I can tell has cost her dearly. Her generosity touches me; she's put a lot into this visit.

I eat the stew—it's tough and without flavor. I miss Kennedy's spicy, fragrant version of the dish, but I exclaim loudly and ask for seconds.

"I can't believe you can eat what I eat," she muses, genuinely astounded.

I smile at her, trying to be a gracious guest. In these simple expressions of shared humanity, I'm reminded of all that we do have in common.

Suddenly I'm overcome by a deep fatigue. It hits me so fast that I feel like I might fall over just sitting up.

"I think I need to lie down," I tell Alice. She pulls back a sheet to reveal her small bed and fixes the blanket for me. My body feels strange, like I no longer control my bones, and I can't help but fall into the bed.

"Jessie, are you ill?" Alice asks, startled by my quick transformation.

"No, just tired," I say, desperately hoping that this is true.

Two hours later, or maybe more—time passes strangely—my joints throb, my body is on fire.

"Water," I say, barely able to get the word out, "please."

Alice sits on the wire chair watching me nervously. She's been rocking back and forth, calling upon God and Jesus not to let the *mzungu* girl die in her house. This does little to reassure me. I sit up to drink and retch deeply. I look around and see an empty basin. There is no time to ask; I grab it and begin to vomit. The heaving racks my frame so violently that I let forth a cry for mercy—anything but this. Alice starts to pray even more fervently, and I curl up in a ball on the floor. Alice touches my forehead and recoils.

"Hot, you are so hot," she moans.

"Alice, I have to go to the bathroom—real bad."

"You can't, we can't go outside, not at night; it's very dangerous. There is no place to go." She pushes a yellow jerrican toward me. "Use this."

I take one look and shake my head.

"Alice, I have to really go, not that kind, and I have to, bad."

I'm overcome by urgency. Without another thought I frantically pull the couch away from the door, unhook the eye, and find myself outside alone in the pitch-black night. Alice follows me and grabs my hand and pulls me along a corridor of houses to a dark corner in the middle of the plot surrounded by a thin fence. I can tell she's afraid, and I start to shake uncontrollably.

"Hurry, please," she begs, looking around fearfully.

I look at her, wondering what she means. Am I just supposed to go right here? Out in the open?

"Where?" I whisper urgently.

"Here, this is the only place. I told you, nowhere else to go."

There is no time to think. Images flash in my head—Kennedy's warning—two women, outside alone. I pull up my skirt and squat, and I'm overcome by release, until the retching takes hold again. I'm too weak to stand, but somehow Alice lifts me and pushes me back the way we came, back inside the house. She latches the eye and pushes the couch back in front of the door and stands in front of it breathing heavily. It's two in the morning, but I reach for my phone and dial Kennedy's number.

He answers groggily, "Hello."

"Ken," I rasp, struck by the daring intimacy of a two A.M. phone call, the imposition. "Something's wrong. I'm sick, really sick. Please, come get me."

"I can't now—it's too dangerous. I'll come as soon as it's light. Let me talk to Alice."

I hand her the phone and there is a flurried exchange, but nothing stays in focus. My head too heavy to hold up, I lie down again on the floor, pressing myself against the cold, chipped cement. Everything hurts. I call Kennedy again, one, three, five more times—begging him to come rescue me. The morning is too far away, every minute excruciating. Night never seemed so long or so ruthless.

Finally there is a rap at the door, Kennedy stands outside. I see in his reaction how bad I look. My legs buckle when I try to stand, but the nearest place a car can reach is at least fifteen minutes away. Kennedy carries me most of the way—and the vendors setting up their small outdoor shops in the harsh morning light ask him as we pass, "Will she make it?" Others murmur, *"Pole"*—sorry. Odoch's battered blue jeep awaits us as we emerge from the market. Kennedy opens the back door for me and jumps in the front. I lie across the backseat, and I can tell by how fast we drive that it's serious.

We arrive at a clinic, and everything suddenly feels blurry. A doctor presses my stomach, and I hear him say to Odoch, *Spleen, could burst.* I don't remember anything else.

When I come to, I take it all in: the slightly faded white sheets, the mint-green tray with food untouched, and Kennedy, sitting hunched over in the one chair, hands covering his face, like he hasn't moved in some time.

I've never been hospitalized before. I lick my dry cracked lips, my head fuzzy, struggling to piece together thoughts and words. My arm has an IV in it. I don't remember that, don't remember so much.

"What day is today?"

He looks up, startled. "You're awake!"

He jumps up from the chair and rushes out of the room, returning moments later trailed by two nurses. They take my pulse, my temperature, then connect a different pack of fluid to the IV. I have so many questions, but no words leave my lips. I never noticed how much energy it takes to sit up, and I feel my weight sink back into the hard bed frame. It's bliss when my eyes close.

When I wake up again, he's still there.

"It's been like this for two days," he says gently. I shake my head, trying to process this.

"I've been asleep for two days?" I ask slowly.

"You'd wake up, toss and turn, but it was like you were still asleep—you never remembered waking up. You'd shout and talk, but they said it was the fever dreams. They've been really worried. You have malaria. Undetected, the parasite got far enough along that your spleen almost burst."

I remember now. Alice's house, the unrelenting heat, calling him, putting him in danger.

"I'm sorry."

"Your mom—you should call her. She called and I answered your phone; she's pretty upset. She made me get the doctors to list every medication they've given you. I can see where you get your determination from, she must have tried to call me almost thirty times."

"You talked to my mom?" My face flushes trying to imagine their exchanges, and I wonder what she said on those calls.

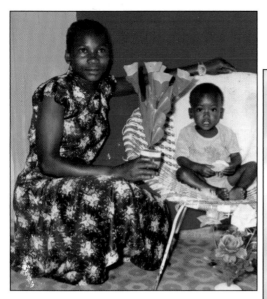

Above: Young Kennedy and his mom, Ajey, in Kibera. *Right:* Kennedy as a hopeful teenager in Kibera.

Young Jessica in Denver.

Kennedy with his siblings in their single room in Kibera. Left to right: Liz holding Collins, Jackie, Kennedy; (*front*) Jasmine and Victor.

The photograph taken on Jessica's first night in Kibera.

SHOFCO's very first office.

Kennedy in the room in Kibera that he shared with Jessica.

Jessica (with braids) and Kennedy after she returned from the Swahili Muslim village.

Jessica with Ajey (*left*) and Aunt Beatrice (*right*).

Jessica's siblings with Kennedy's siblings in the rural village outside of the "marriage house." From left to right: (*front row*) Shadrack, Collins, Victor holding Hillary, Jasmine, Raphae; (*back row*) Max, Kennedy, Jessica.

Jessica and Kennedy together in Denver. © 2015 Steve Stanton Photography

With Jessica's family at Raphae's bat mitzvah. Left to right: Kennedy, Jessica, Raphae, David, Helen, Max. © 2009 Courtney Lamb

Kennedy with Bob and Margaret Patricelli at his Wesleyan graduation.

Jessica walking in Kibera. © 2011 Benedicte Kurzen/NOOR

The first sixty girls at the Kibera School for Girls stand on the road in Kibera. © *2011 www.bellazanesco.com*

Kennedy and Nicholas Kristof on the top of SHOFCO's water tower in Kibera. © *Audrey Hall*

Kennedy and George walk on the streets of Kibera.

The wedding party at Jessica and Kennedy's wedding. From left to right: George, Liz, Jordyn, Tom, Kennedy, Jessica, Raphae, Max, Daphne, Nathan. © 2015 Steve Stanton Photography

Jessica and Kennedy dance together at their wedding. © 2015 Steve Stanton Photography

A student at the Kibera School
for Girls strikes a pose. © 2011
Benedicte Kurzen/NOOR

A student jumps rope
in front of the Kibera
School for Girls. © 2012
Paul Horton

Kennedy, Jessica, and George celebrate a soccer match with members of both
SHOFCO Kibera and Mathare. *Audrey Hall*

And equally important, what did he tell her? I'm desperate to ask more, but the door opens, and Odoch and Donna walk in, arms filled with cartons of juice.

"She's alive!" Donna exclaims. "Here, we brought you this. Absolutely horrible stuff, but it's what Kenyans always bring when someone is in the hospital!"

I'm so happy to see them.

"You gave everyone quite a scare," Odoch says in his kind, fatherly way. "Ken *bwana,* it's like you've been stuck to that chair."

"I'm leaving now," Kennedy says, tired. "I need to get back before it gets dark. Feel better. They say they might let you out tomorrow."

"Very nice young man," Donna observes as he leaves. "He's been very concerned, been here most of the days, and brought a slew of visitors with him."

I shake my head—I don't remember any of this! I wonder who else came. . . . I try to piece things together. Something comes back to me in a white flash. Kennedy's face hovering close; he wipes the sweat from my brow and whispers the words *I love you.* I shake my head, unable to distinguish between memory and fever dream.

My strength returns slowly. Walking small distances consumes tremendous effort; the smallest tasks leave me despairingly drained. The sickness brings with it newfound gratitude for health, for all the things I did before without thinking twice. On the day I'm discharged, the October sun shines brightly, and I stand in the parking lot, eyes closed, savoring the heat as it sinks into my pores, the beat of my heart more noticeable than ever before.

Odoch pleads with me to call my mom. When I do, she reads from her copious Internet research about the different strands of malaria. Exactly which one did I have, and should I come home, and is that hospital in Kenya really able to deal with it?

I insist that while it may surprise her, malaria is actually much more common here in Kenya than in Denver. I hand the phone to Odoch, who promises that the program will take very good care of me, and when I take the phone back from him, I pretend that the connection is very poor. I hang up to preempt further questioning.

Odoch begrudgingly drives me to the SHOFCO office in Olympic, muttering as his jeep sputters across the potholed road. When we get to Olympic, I take a breath before opening the door, and Odoch, sensing my momentary hesitation, asks again, "Sure you won't rest, just for a few days?"

"Not a chance." I open the door and spring out before he can stop me.

Malaria has taught me to take nothing for granted: not time, not health, and not Kennedy.

The SHOFCO office is busy, and as I walk in Anne runs up to me and envelops me in a hug. I ask her where Kennedy is, and she points to the small room upstairs. I stand for a few minutes outside the door, nervous to knock. I finally rap twice, and he opens the door, surprised to see me.

"Shouldn't you be resting?" he asks, glancing back at the several young men sitting in his office. I've interrupted a meeting.

"I'm fine."

He asks me to wait for a few minutes while they finish. When he emerges, he seems distracted, his brow furrowed.

"Are you sure you're strong enough for a walk?"

"I'm fine, only annoyed by everyone treating me like I'm made of *mzungu* glass."

We leave the office and walk in silence along the road that snakes around Kibera. I keep searching his face, wondering what did and didn't happen in the hospital.

Kennedy interrupts my thoughts: "I got a job offer yesterday, a good one."

It dawns on me that while all I can think of is my delirium in the hospital, he's consumed by something else.

"They want me to help with the elections."

The picture that pops instantly into my head is of my dad canvassing our Denver neighborhood, but I'm pretty sure this isn't what Kennedy means. The foreboding in his voice gives me the chills.

"Will you be helping people vote?" I ask.

The way he looks at me after this question, I feel I must be the stupidest person in the world.

"More like helping them not vote," he mutters.

"What does that mean?"

"In the morning I got a call. The *mzee* [big man] wants to see me. 'Me?' I thought. But they are insistent. They say they will send a car, but I refuse. I tell them I can take the *matutu*. I don't know what they want—I don't want to owe them anything. When I get there, I see a huge office—big rooms with glass windows and stacks of paper, lots of people furiously typing. I'm ushered into a private room, and then two important-looking men arrive. They ask me who I support in the election. I'm scared and take a minute before answering. I realize there was only one answer: the president, of course. That was what they were looking for. They smile; they say they need my help, my influence to win votes here in Kibera. They ask if I heard the story last week about an official caught stealing voting cards."

I nod. I've heard about this voter fraud; it was all over the national news. Machetes, commonly used to cut the grass, started to sell out in supermarkets as soon as rumblings about the election began. People are afraid, preparing for the worst. Apparently, in opposition strongholds such as Kibera, the ruling party has been paying people to surrender their voting cards, which allow people to cast their ballots.

Kennedy continues, "These men explain that they can't just buy the vote cards anymore, because it's bringing trouble. So they have a new idea. Then they ask me again if I am really with them. I say yes, since I know there is no other answer that gets me out of this room. They tell me that they want me to find opposition party supporters in Kibera and pay them in exchange for their names and identification numbers. These opposition supporters keep their cards. I am then expected to bring back the names and ID numbers of each individual. Next, someone goes on the computer, and changes the places where these people are allowed to vote. On Election Day, the opposition supporters will arrive to find they can't vote because they have been registered for a different location. These men already had stacks of paper in the office containing people's names and ID numbers. I was told that in this election, even the dead will vote."

I'm dumbfounded, entirely out of my element.

They've given Kennedy twenty-four hours to make a decision and offered to pay him in a day more than he's ever made in an entire month. These men can't even imagine that Kennedy could say no. If he says yes, Kennedy compromises everything he believes in—but perhaps he lives. And if he says no?

Overtaken by the seriousness of this, a nervous giggle escapes—my reflexive response to fear or discomfort. I try to stop. I know this is one of my terrible habits, but soon I'm laughing uncontrollably.

I blurt out, "I'm so sorry—this is just very different from what I thought was on your mind!"

The bewilderment on Kennedy's face is clear. "What did you think?" he asks, intrigued.

"I thought you were upset about the hospital—about what you said. I thought you were avoiding me—that you didn't want to talk about it—"

Kennedy starts to laugh too. The sound of his distinctive, mirthful high-pitched giggle sets me off again, and soon we're laughing so hard we can barely stand, doubled over in the middle of the road.

Suddenly, Kennedy takes my hand and pulls me off the main road, into a narrow alleyway between houses, a private corner. He takes my face between his hands, and I gasp, caught off guard by both the tenderness and determination of his grasp.

I see it in his eyes, but I want to hear him say it.

"Did you mean it?"

"Yes."

My heart has never beaten so fast, my breath has never come in shorter gasps.

"Say it then, tell me."

He doesn't flinch. "I love you, Jessica."

His lips are soft and cool, his features so close and so precious. Our first kiss leaves me nearly as dizzy as the malaria.

"They could kill you—" I break away, my hands press against his chest, pushing him gently away, unable to contain that thought as it arises.

"Shhh—" He kisses me again, this time with more force. "Now you say it—"

"I . . ." The words feel stuck in my throat, but he looks at me with that knowing look and I finish softly, "I love you too."

Wordlessly, he takes my hand and we walk down the road, past the railway, along the main path. He doesn't stop to talk to anyone along the road, a first. I feel my heart pounding. I know exactly where we are going—to the bed we've been sharing so chastely. I'm scared of what the world might look like on the other side of this moment, of the way everything might change. The way Kennedy looks at me, it's as if he sees things in me that I haven't yet discovered.

Kennedy takes the key from his pocket and opens the padlock, holding the door open for me. Standing together in his house, I blush, unsure of our new intimacy. I'd be lying if I said I hadn't imagined this moment a million times. I've imagined what his mouth might feel like. I've imagined what his skin might taste like. But I'm not sure I ever thought this would really happen.

Slowly, reverently, Kennedy begins to unbutton my shirt. His hands shake, and he makes no attempt to hide his nerves.

He kisses my bare shoulder and asks me gently, "Are you sure?"

"No—are you?"

"No—I'm worried. I might expect too much from you, more than you can give."

"Later," I say, kissing him back harder. "Let's worry about that later."

His hands trace the outline of my frame, finding the small of my back, resting on my hips. I pull his T-shirt up over his head, my fingertips skimming along his back, tracing his midline, his skin so soft. He pulls me close to him, and I feel his weight pressing against me, tethering me to this earth. Finally, there is only him and this moment, and our small single bed.

Afterward, I draw the threadbare sheet close to my chest, and we lie on our sides, just looking at each other.

He says exactly what I'm feeling.

"You bring me peace."

For one of the first times in my life, my mind stands mercifully still. I feel the fibers of the fabric as they touch my bare skin, savor the space I take up in the bed, and feel like life has unexpectedly chosen me.

"Do you think this—what we have—that anyone out there will ever understand it?" I ask quietly.

"Honestly, I don't think so," he says matter-of-factly. "In reggae, we say 'overstand,' instead of 'understand.' Between us, we have what I call *jessken* culture. We just overstand."

I move closer, cuddling into his chest, both elated by this new secret world we share and devastated to think the outside world might never "overstand" it at all.

Normally before bed, Kennedy talks to his street dog, Cheetah, scratching his ears and giving him a scrap of meat. Tonight, I talk to Cheetah myself. I give him some choice pieces of meat saved from my own dinner and bend down to whisper in his ear. I don't want Kennedy to hear the worry in my voice.

"Take care of us tonight, Cheetah. Protect us," I say softly.

Several times through the night I'm awakened by sounds I thought I'd grown used to. The sound of rats scuttling on the tin roof, a dog barking far away.

Finally, the weight of Kennedy's arms around me, holding me, lulls me back to sleep.

The next morning I wake up early, but Kennedy is already awake; he's probably been lying that way for hours.

"What are you going to do? About the elections, I mean?"

"Just don't worry about it," he says, combing his fingers through my hair. "It will be fine."

"Stop saying that!"

"I'm sorry. It's just when I was growing up, a lot of things would go wrong, but I'd always pretend to my mom and my sisters that they would be fine. Can't we pretend?"

"No"—even though a part of me wishes we could.

He looks at me, gently, but with resignation clear in his eyes, his breath heavy.

"If I say no, I'm a liability, they've told me too much. But if I say yes, then I betray my values, my dignity," he says slowly. "But maybe if we come up with a good enough reason why I can't, maybe they will leave me alone."

We lie together in silence.

"Are you ever scared? You always seem so sure . . ."

"Sometimes. Mandela has a favorite poem. I read it when I'm afraid. Do you want to hear it?"

"Of course," I say intrigued.

He leans over to grab a tattered book and opens right to the page he seeks.

"'Invictus,' by William Ernest Henley," he begins, formal as a schoolboy, becoming impassioned as he goes.

Out of the night that covers me,
Black as the pit from pole to pole,
I thank whatever gods may be
For my unconquerable soul.

In the fell clutch of circumstance
I have not winced nor cried aloud.
Under the bludgeonings of chance
My head is bloody, but unbowed.

Beyond this place of wrath and tears
Looms but the Horror of the shade,
And yet the menace of the years
Finds and shall find me unafraid.

It matters not how strait the gate,
How charged with punishments the scroll,
I am the master of my fate,
I am the captain of my soul.

He puts the book neatly back from where he got it.

"Unafraid." He smiles. "The menace shall find us unafraid, just as we found each other."

Kennedy spends most of the day seeking out his closest friends and asking for their advice about how to handle his "job offer" helping to rig the elections. One friend suggests telling them that Kennedy was accepted and given a scholarship to a trade school abroad and will be leaving in the next month. Kennedy feels he has no choice but to try this approach so he calls his contact. They seem to accept the story.

Nothing in me is as it was before. When I came to Kenya, I had certainty. I viewed this program as playing a clear role in my larger plan to make me a more cultured person with broadened perspectives: a better actress, dramaturge, director. Coming to Kenya wasn't supposed to make my life plans seem insignificant. Can so much change in so short a time? Only weeks ago I regarded love as a distraction that would prevent me from achieving my goals. Now I'm questioning the very substance of those goals, my master plan itself.

When I share my thoughts, Kennedy just says, "You have to find your place in the world."

As though finding my place in this quickly enlarging and complex world were simple and obvious. I wish Kennedy would tell me how. His place in the world is so certain, so linked to a cause larger than himself.

I can see in his eyes that he loves me, but I also know that love isn't new to Kennedy. I've never really been in love before, not if this is what it feels like. But Kennedy—he is in love with this place, with Kibera, with SHOFCO.

They say love is supposed to set you free, but I think love binds you. It's only once you're so full of joy that you can imagine the devastation of loss.

ten

kennedy

One night I was coming home, bone tired, from work at a maize factory where I carried huge sacks all day. I met a little boy selling a secondhand soccer ball and I knew I had to have it. I used my last twenty cents to buy it, taking it from him as though it was my lifeline. I was tired of being angry. I was tired of violence. I thought, if we could just come together as a community, even if this just meant playing soccer together, that could be the beginning of something good. Coming together as a community, as a people, creates more power than what exists when individuals are fighting each other for scraps. Soccer has always brought people together. Soccer was where I would begin.

I went to find George. My face was flushed with excitement, energy pulsing even through my fingertips.

"George," I said, "I'm tired of what's happening here. We must stand up and do something positive. We need to come together to try to find a solution. Enough is enough."

George was sitting in his room, tired. He looked at me like I was crazy.

"What do you mean?" he asked.

"Let's start organizing to come together around the issues we face. Let's start to address our problems and find our own ways to make changes." I held out the soccer ball, as if it should illuminate everything, but George's expression didn't change.

"Let me know what you want me to do." He sighed, with no display of hope.

First I decided to start a men's group in Kibera, beginning with my soccer ball. I thought if I could bring men together, maybe we could stop the violence. My initial plan soon changed as I realized how it was essential to bring the men together with the women.

I wanted to see the women and girls in my community have the chance for happier lives. I could no longer sit by while men shamelessly raped six-year-old girls. I had seen my mom abused by her husband—threatened within an inch of her life—too many times. The very worst part was how my mom always forgave him. I had seen my sister endure abuse also—pregnant, against her will—before having a chance to make her own choices in life. I wanted to raise my voice for the women in my community who had to turn to selling their bodies just to feed themselves.

Seeing that we needed both men and women to boost the economy, I started gathering friends to play soccer with my new ball—men and women and young people playing together. After playing, we got to talking and decided to start a group similar to my mother's lending circle that focused on saving money and starting businesses. The lending group went well, attracting many members and raising a good amount of money. I altered the strategy a bit by using money I saved from my factory job to give personal loans to people. Upon receiving a loan from me, a person agreed to simply pay the loan forward, to help someone else start a small business, rather than pay me back. People started barbershops, vegetable businesses, and more. The "pay-it-forward" approach paid off faster than I could have ever anticipated.

I started another youth group that met on Sundays after church. Because of my childhood experiences, I didn't believe in the church, but the neighborhood church gave us space and a little money. I named the group St. Dominic's. Dominic was a friend of Saint Don Bosco; both were known as the patron saints of street boys.

The St. Dominic's group would come together and read Bible verses aloud, searching for guidance and inspiration. I tried to choose the most powerful, inspiring verses in the Bible, including ones about King Solomon, King David, and Moses, explaining the significance these passages had for our lives in Kibera. Unfortunately, I stammered when I was nervous, probably due to all the abuse at the hands of Babi, and was ashamed of public speaking. So I handed over leadership of the group to my friend Charles. He was organized and eager to lead and didn't stammer.

This youth group became quite popular, and it attracted some young people who would become very close friends of mine, like Kevin and James. We earned awards from the church for being so active, winning Bible quizzes, choir prizes, and theater awards—and of course we won soccer tournaments. Before each meeting, Charles and I would meet so I could guide him. At first I liked making things work from behind the scenes. But eventually I realized the group had no significant agenda for social change, focusing more on how to get free meals from the church. We were also required to lead mass in the church and to discuss church issues in exchange for support. Being tied to Catholic doctrines meant contradicting goals for our group. The church was adamantly against family planning and the use of condoms. This made no sense. I had watched too many teenage girls become mothers and lost too many dear friends to HIV/AIDS. Using protection seemed the only option.

One day, I decided to raise my concerns about safe sex with the youth group. I spoke about the need to use condoms and to spread this message about the importance of protection. I was tired of seeing my friends die. Days after my speech, I was kicked out of the church, told never to come there again. The church leaders were furious. I felt so much of what I worked to build slip away—both the youth group I'd started and my friends.

I went to find Kevin, one of the members of the church youth group, and shared my dream with him.

"Kevin, you and I have worked hard to change our community. We tried using the church, but we couldn't achieve what we wanted. Now I have an idea. I am starting something, a movement, and I think I have the numbers and we have the people who will believe in us. What we did at St. Dominic brought people together. Now we need to set an agenda for what comes next."

"Kennedy, I believe in you. I will support you," Kevin told me. "That's the way forward, man. We have to work hard to fight this poverty."

So I invited George and Kevin and a few other friends to my house for a meeting. I prepared tea and served it with milk and bread I sacrificed to buy. There were exactly seven people: Fred, Steve, Mary, Anne, Kevin, Max, and George. After everybody had sat and enjoyed some tea, I began to talk. I had been going over what I would had been saying in my head for days.

"Ladies and gentlemen, we are coming here today because I believe together we can achieve but divided we will fall. Each of us can do something important. All of you are called to this meeting because I believe in you and I trust you can do something positive for this community."

Mary interrupted. "Kennedy, you have to pray before you start."

So Mary led us in a prayer, asking God to bless us.

I continued my "speech," sharing the stories of people we had lost through violence and mob justice. Many of us knew people who had committed suicide. We had seen our sisters, or ourselves, being raped by the age of ten. We were gathered because life couldn't continue like this. I mentioned the books of Martin Luther King Jr. and Nelson Mandela. Finally, I expressed my hope and resolve. "Today, let's decide that one day, we will look back on this moment and laugh and cry for happiness."

Fred, a very religious man, asked why these ideas could not be achieved through our church group.

"This doesn't mean that we have to stop going to church," I responded. "But the agenda there is to read the Bible. While we can benefit from the inspiration we get reading the Bible and verse, we are creating this group for action."

Next, Steven stopped me. "Kennedy? It seems like you want to start a nonprofit, an NGO, and we are ready to support you, but where is the money coming from? Do you have a *mzungu,* any donor?"

I felt the blood rise in me. For too long my community had been told that we could not do anything by ourselves without money from the outside, without the financial support and wisdom from the Western world. But since we were the ones who understood all the challenges we faced, we also had the best shot at finding the solutions.

Marcus Garvey said, "Africa for Africans," and that is what I wanted. African problems would never be solved as long as advantaged people from the Western world thought that they could save our communities by starting organizations, or volunteering in Africa, without the actual and deep engagement of the communities they sought to improve. Without mutual understanding and real community leadership, foreign-led interventions ultimately do not succeed, creating false hopes and taking advantage of the community's vulnerability. The community also takes advantage of volunteers, seeking a quick fix, a tiny drop of money. But money alone does nothing; I knew grassroots empowerment was the only sustainable solution. As my mother always said, *Only he who wears the shoe knows how it pinches.*

My wariness about foreign NGOs came from seeing several organizations working in Kibera. Rather than building free clinics that were actually accessible to people, these outsiders built inefficient ones devoid of community leadership and dignity. The majority of "local" staff who were hired did not actually live in Kibera, and they looked down on and disparaged community members. I also saw how "free" schools built by Western organizations secretly charged fees, and local staff members secretly raised the prices and pocketed the money when donors got back on their planes.

NGOs came in and paid such inflated salaries that the local government and communities couldn't compete. People stopped believing it was possible to do things for themselves. Some organizations used strategies they said came from the people of Kibera. Pretending that the locals ran the Western NGOs was a way to entice donors, grassroots was no longer a true goal but a buzzword. Sadly, the goal was not to empower true local leadership, but to find token locals to be token champions with no real decision-making power.

These organizations never helped the indigenous health or school projects that we ourselves tried to start. Outside groups seemed to feel threatened by the indigenous organizations, we who were trying to move mountains without piles of money behind us. But I always knew true, long-term change cannot happen without involving the community. I realized that my friends thought we could not do anything on our own because they had been influenced by the messages of these Western organizations.

Outsiders didn't have answers for the problems in Kibera. We had to solve our own problems. The only way help from the outside could be effective was through real partnerships with local groups—but we had to follow the examples of King and Mandela and create the local movements ourselves first.

I looked left and right and saw everyone had this question on their minds: *Where would we get the money for our movement if not from outsiders?*

I answered them then, and I found a rhythm in the words, as though I were channeling Ajey's preaching or King's from his "I Have a Dream" speech:

"My friends, Marcus Garvey taught me that circumstance should not make us inferior. He says that we must remove the cobwebs of our minds, and it is this mentality that we will never make it out of poverty ourselves, on our own, that is the first cobweb."

I paused, then continued. "We don't need money to come together and clean our streets. We don't need money to remove the garbage. We don't need money to protect our mothers, our sisters, or any little girls from being abused. We don't need money to play soccer and to just be there for each other."

As I spoke, tears came from my eyes. I tried to hide them, but down they came. The group saw them and understood how serious this was, how much this mattered.

"We cannot wait for money," I continued. "This is urgent. We are coming here today for action. We are not coming here today to start an NGO. NGOs need proposals and donors. We are here today to start a movement. A movement starts with urgency, when you have been pushed to the wall and all you can do is bounce back. That's what we are doing here. We are bouncing back."

They all looked at me and I thought of my mom's saying, *When a snake bites you, don't spend time looking for a spear. Use whatever stick you have.*

Then Mary spoke. "Kennedy, I am with you."

"Kennedy, I'm there," said George. "I may not believe your

big ideas are possible, but as a brother, I support you. Let me know what I can do."

"We will work together," affirmed Kevin.

Together we developed a list of the challenges we faced. We only had one pen, and Kevin used it to write down everything.

I started. "Crime, violence, domestic abuse, and rape."

"Hopelessness," someone said.

"Sanitation."

Everybody in the room contributed issues. Kevin wrote them all down until we had a long list.

"Now, Kevin, we will write another list that contains the ways to counterattack the problems we've written down. I believe where there is darkness there is light, and where there is light sometimes there is darkness. This is the way forward."

They laughed at me, but we kept writing down our ideas:

We could all come together to clean the streets to address the poor sanitation.

We could all come together to do street theater and performances about domestic abuse and rape and to create awareness that our women should be respected.

We could grow and continue our soccer team to give the youth something to do and to instill pride in teamwork. We wanted girls to join too.

From this list we made our programs: sanitation, theater, soccer, media and journalism, girls' and women's empowerment.

I was appointed by the group to be the head coordinator, and I gave everyone a role. I wanted to make these seven founders feel ownership of the ideas, so they would feel pride in everything we had all come up with that day.

"Now, before we leave this place," I told them, "we must come up with a name."

I knew what I wanted to call this movement. I had already

told Kevin: Shining Hope for Communities. I proposed it now to the group. At first the group liked it, but then they said it didn't work. It was too long; how would people remember it? They asked some women who sold goods on the streets and they agreed. "Too much English," one said. So we can up with the idea to call it SHOFCO for short.

George suggested that it should be something about Kibera, maybe Shine Kibera, or Kibera Stars.

I said no—it had to be about the entire world of poor people living in slums everywhere. "Shining Hope for Communities is a powerful name because it's not only in Kibera where we will provide hope. We are going to shine in other slums too. Let's start with Kibera, but I believe in the future we're going to go beyond Kibera to shine hope everywhere. Eventually the world will see the light that was lit in a ghetto house tonight."

Everyone laughed at my big ideas, but Shining Hope for Communities was born as we lit a single candle and sat watching it burn.

The seven-person SHOFCO team mobilized forty members within the first month. Most of the people from the church youth group joined us. It was really amazing and touching to see how people were coming together, though they had nothing. Soon, there wasn't enough space in my small room for everybody to meet. My house overflowed and people were sitting outside, just to participate. We had to look around for a larger space. George got us a meeting with a pastor of a church. We presented what we were doing, and when we were finished, the pastor turned us down. He said that a house of the Lord would not consider a non-religious group.

"We are not religious or nonreligious," I told him. "We are a movement."

Once again, I felt the church did not meet my needs.

So we began meeting outside on the soccer pitch, the only space large enough to hold us.

Hundreds joined in for our first cleanup activity. We had no food, nothing to offer people who helped, just singing and cleaning together. We tried to borrow some cleaning materials from a nearby organization but were denied. Despite our lack of supplies, our cleanup was so successful that I had the feeling SHOFCO was destined for big things.

We'd been working this way for nearly two years when an American organization that recognized the value of local partnership decided they wanted to support our work. At first we were hesitant, but the group, American Friends of Kenya (AFK), said that they wanted to champion local leaders and give us a small amount of money to help build our first office. We built it on a garbage heap that we cleaned up. George, "Government," let us live there rent-free. From then on we had an office.

The word had begun to spread about what we were doing in Kibera. In 2007, SHOFCO was invited to perform at the World Social Forum. We didn't know what the forum was, but we heard it was a place to meet other people and share ideas. We also heard you could sell stuff, so we made T-shirts and ornaments to sell to help fund our movement—anything helped. We had written a play about our struggle in Kibera, called *Another World Is Possible*. I played the drunken father, and Anne played a hardworking woman trying to help her family survive, a role based on my mother. The room was packed with people from all over the world; I had never seen so many white faces in one place before.

I felt adrenaline coursing through my body; I knew what a big opportunity this was to show the larger world both the problems and resilience of Kibera. As soon as the play ended, I could see how people were moved by the struggle of Kibera's women.

I was surrounded by foreigners who all wanted me to answer a burning question: What was this SHOFCO?

I was invited to give another speech at the World Social Forum about the challenges in Kibera. For the first time I spoke in front of a huge crowd without a stammer. People were really impressed by what we had been able to accomplish at SHOFCO with so few resources. We sold a lot of T-shirts and were able to raise some money. I also met several Americans who were part of a theater group. They wanted to stay in touch with me and follow SHOFCO; they even came to see our work in Kibera.

The movement was almost four years old. We had thousands of members, mostly young people and women of all ages. Many small businesses were getting started. The women's empowerment group was up and running, making jewelry and ornaments to support themselves. I had made a name for myself in the community: the people of Kibera started calling me Mayor.

And then one day, I received an e-mail from a young American woman named Jessica. She'd heard about me from some people in the theater group I'd met at the World Social Forum, and she told me she wanted to volunteer.

We weren't open to just any white person who wanted to come and volunteer. We were only interested in qualified people who had something substantial to offer the movement. I asked Jessica to send me her résumé. I was impressed when she sent it: I could tell she was smart and she had even won awards for her work in theater. I brought the résumé to a meeting of the SHOFCO leaders.

"She seems talented," Mary said.

"We can't just allow any white people to come here," said our treasurer. "Maybe we should have her pay an entry fee?"

"Let's not make it be about money," I said. "We fund ourselves. When you take people's money, you sometimes have to abide by their law. Let's see what else people have to offer besides money. This woman Jessica, we could have her work with the theater group but not anything else. No management."

Everyone agreed that if she had no decision-making power beyond the theater program, that would be okay.

I wrote Jessica an e-mail to tell her that her résumé was good, that we had accepted her application, and that she should tell us the date of her arrival so we could prepare the theater department to receive her.

I had landed a new job as a janitor at a computer company called New Horizons where my benefactor and American mom Linda had paid for me to take a few classes in computer literacy. I was to clean the company's kitchen and the floors, but mostly the toilets. Many people were rude to me when they saw me cleaning the toilets. I had to remember the words of my mom: *Whatever you do, do it well. Do it 100 percent.*

One night I had a dream about a white lady standing on a corner in Kibera wearing a dress with red roses on it. In the dream, I heard a voice telling me, "Kennedy, this is your partner."

I responded, "God Almighty, no. She's a white woman, I'm a black man. I'm a Garveyist. I believe in black power. I want a black queen."

The voice told me, "No. Hold her hand and cross the river with her. Cross the bridge with her."

The next day I shared the dream with Antony.

He shook his head and said to me, "Your dreams always come true."

"Antony, don't say that. It's just a dream. No way I'm going to be with a white woman."

eleven

jessica and kennedy

jessica

"Hi." I slam the SHOFCO office door and lock it behind me. Kennedy looks up from his writing, surprised. "No one is downstairs, the office is empty . . ."

I'm giddy at the thought of how sincere he looks, so clearly focused on the task at hand. "Everyone in theater is by the railway eating lunch; we have at least twenty minutes."

I climb into his lap, and he leans back in the plastic chair to absorb my weight.

"Twenty minutes?" He kisses me. "That's a lot of time . . . are you sure no one is here?"

We've decided to keep whatever is happening between us to ourselves for a little while, until we figure out what it means. I have to watch myself, to resist the temptation to take his hand or touch his face or laugh too hard at his jokes when we're around other people. It's harder than I thought, and yet there is something delicious about sharing this secret with him.

He stands up, carrying me with him and I squeal with glee. He sets me down gently on top of the desk and stands just looking at me. He brings his face closer to mine and touches the tip of my nose with his.

Last night he told me how afraid he is of what he feels for me—and of the future—as we near the end of my semester here.

Suddenly I remember something. "Hey, who were those people you were talking to so late last night?"

"It was nothing, not important." But the way he says it—I'm not convinced.

"It looked important, you looked so serious—" He turns and walks away, bracing his hands on either side of the small window. "I'm sorry—I didn't mean to push—"

"Do you always have to know everything?"

"I want to. I can't help it when I'm around you."

He turns around to face me, his eyes harder.

"I didn't want you to know, and I don't want to upset you. It's just that since you have been living in my house, a lot of people are asking me for money. They think because of you I must have too much of it."

It's as if someone just threw a bucket of cold water on me.

"I'm sorry, I didn't want to tell you. I knew it would hurt you." He moves close again, wraps his arm around me, pushes his face into my hair, kissing my ear and cheek.

I should have known. It's strange how when we are alone together, between us, we talk about money in this very open way; I've never talked about it so openly with anyone. Yet the world has seen too much to take a relationship like ours at face value.

I kiss him back, gently, on the cheek before leaving the office. This is my fault. He is so good and genuine, and I have put him in this difficult position.

I don't blame those people, much as I'd like to in hopes that being angry might make it easier. I'd like to blame them for assuming that I have money; for using me, or wanting to; for making Kennedy feel caught between them and me. But if I were them, I might make the same assumptions. And I can't help but think how unfair and utterly random it is that I was born into a place that gave me so much; to be so blessed that I was concerned mainly with finding happiness, not consumed by the daily drudgery of survival. No matter what I feel for Kennedy and he for me, we are from two different worlds: mine of plenty and his of want.

Yesterday, I asked when I might meet his mom. He told me that he thinks not for a long time; she will worry—he wants to protect her and me. He doesn't want to tell Liz either, not yet.

"She has seen a lot of relationships where both people used each other," he explained. "The *mzungu,* they come and then they leave; the Africans take advantage too and want money and opportunity in exchange. It's a trade on both sides."

"I don't want anything from you," he'd added, although he didn't have to.

The truth is, I can't imagine what I'd tell my parents either; my hackles rise just anticipating the inevitable questions.

I'm overcome with a sorrow for both of us. When we are alone in a room together, I want to lock the door and never leave. I could lie next to him all day and feel a more complete, vibrant version of myself. And yet, when we step outside together, the world will expect and infer certain things. There is a whole mythology, a set of rules and issues surrounding a relationship like ours, that sneaks in uninvited.

I walk to a cybercafé to e-mail my last paper for the program. Suddenly, a green indicator appears next to my brother's name on

Google. It's Max! Online! My brother and I haven't spoken since I moved in with Kennedy, since everything happened. I don't even know where to start.

> Me: Max!
> Max: Hey J, long time!

We catch up about life at home in Denver and at his university.

> Max: How is Kenya?

I don't know what to say, and I'm suddenly grateful for the forum of "chat." Max can't see me blush and scramble for a response.

> Me: Can you keep a secret?
> Max: Yah.
> Me: I moved into Kibera, with Kennedy. We're in love.

He doesn't reply for a few minutes.

> Max: Whoa, are you going to tell Mom and Dad? They
>   are going to freak.
> Me: No, and I'll kill you if you do. I g2g.

I submit my paper and leave. I can't stop thinking about Max's words, *They are going to freak.* And I know he's right, and part of me can understand that it's not for simple reasons but out of a desire to protect me. It's hard to see my relationship with Kennedy happening anywhere but here. I vow to enjoy this moment.

One day I knock on the door to the small room where Kennedy's mother used to live—it's just a few minutes' walk from Kennedy's, and it's where Liz studies after school.

Liz opens the door, and I take a handful of the spicy candies she likes out of my pocket and place them on the table, next to the splayed-open books. I sit down on the torn sofa covered carefully by handmade crochet—I wonder if Kennedy's mom crocheted it?

"What are you doing?" I ask, and Liz sighs, pushing away the book she's hunkering over.

"I'm studying; it's hard. I have my national exams coming up soon. Form four is almost over, and I need to perform well." In Kenya there is a nationally administered exam after eighth grade that determines high school options for each student, and another exam at the end of high school to decide college prospects. There simply aren't enough schools, so scores on these exams determine both whether a student progresses to the next level of schooling and what the quality of the high school or college they attend will be .

"Can I ask you something?" she says, quietly, "and will you promise not to tell my brother?" I find myself nodding my assent. We spend the afternoon talking in hushed whispers about birth control. Liz has so many questions, and I am deeply touched by her openness.

Finally I ask, "Do you have a boyfriend? Someone you're wondering about this for?" She shakes her head fervently.

"No—it's not for me! I'm just curious." I find myself saying that if she ever needs help to find a birth control method, she can tell me, but she just nods her head before burying herself again in the book on the table.

The door opens, and an older man walks in. He mutters hello but doesn't say anything else, just puts a plastic bag down on the floor and walks out as abruptly as he'd entered. His face is drawn, devoid of emotion, and there is a heaviness, almost a mechanical quality to his walk.

"Who's that?" I ask as soon as he's left.

"My uncle," Liz mutters. "He lives here."

"Kennedy never told me his uncle lived so nearby!" She doesn't respond, just turns back to her books, and eventually I slip out.

As I walk back to Kennedy's, I cross paths with Emily, another neighborhood friend also on her way to see Liz. I tell Emily that Liz seemed pretty absorbed in her studies. I also mention that I just met their uncle.

"Uncle?" Emily asks. "You mean their father?"

"No, I'm quite sure Liz said he was her uncle."

"She doesn't live with her uncle; she lives with their father. I don't know why she would say otherwise. I grew up right next door to them, and that man has a mean temper." I nod and continue on my way, thinking Emily must be confusing which person I meant. Why would Liz lie to me? It doesn't make sense.

Later that evening, while making dinner with Kennedy, I mention, "I went to see Liz today, and she was studying hard. Who is that man who lives there?" He continues slicing onions without blinking.

"Did you meet him?"

"Yes—"

"He's my uncle," Kennedy continues. I nod, convinced that Emily must have it wrong. But the next time I see Emily and tell her she was wrong about the man being their father, she insists that he is. I can't help but feel duped, excluded. Kennedy and I share so much, why doesn't he want to tell me the truth?

When I confront Kennedy, he pauses.

"Liz and I call him that to distance ourselves. We don't have a good relationship. He was cruel to me when I was a child. Liz takes my side. I raised her. I don't like to talk about him; we don't speak to each other."

"You did a good job raising Liz," I say, suddenly cautious around him, off kilter. I want to ask more about this father, but Kennedy changes the subject before I get the chance.

"Now I worry about Liz. A few years ago I found her a sponsor who took her to a good high school, a boarding school—a place where she would be safe away from this ghetto. She ran away. I've never understood why. She had it easier than I did; she had me doing all I could for her. I wonder if she understood how rare that was. She thinks chances come twice. I know they won't."

As he turns off the lights, I feel the crushing weight of the responsibility he carries. I think of what it means to be a teenager in America, necessarily pushing boundaries, making expected mistakes. Here there is no margin for error: a mistake, no matter how insignificant, dashes any small hopes to break the cycle of poverty. Here in Kibera the world is relentless and unforgiving. I sense Kennedy's ambivalence toward Liz, as he tries to forgive her for leaving the boarding school despite being deeply disappointed about this decision. At the same time, I am struggling to understand and forgive Kennedy rather than feel angry with him—for hiding parts of the vast and complex landscape of his heart.

A few nights later, Kennedy takes me dancing in a bar, deep inside Kibera. I'd never noticed this place in passing—a small, battered shack with faded blue paint and a barely legible sign that reads THE PENTAGON. Inside, it is like a secret world. Live musicians play vibrant local music called *lingala* on a guitar and an old Yamaha keyboard. The entire club is enveloped in the bright songs, the compelling rhythm. So many people are crowded in the small space, drinking Tuskers, shouting with joy when the musicians begin a familiar song. The musicians improvise as they go, "singing people," or mentioning their names in songs as an honor. I don't understand the Luo, but I hear Kennedy's name in the music and a cheer sweeps through the bar. Kennedy laughs and whispers in my ear, translating.

"He said that tonight I came with the most beautiful woman in the world."

"I don't believe you," I shout back over the noise.

"But it's true," he says in a tender whisper, as he grabs my hand and leads me to the dance floor. It is crowded, mostly full of men, although a few women also weave their way through the throng. As we walk, the large group of people make way for us, and many exclaim "Mayor!" Out of nowhere some young men appear, ushering us like royalty to a table just at the edge of the dance floor. Everyone clamors for a chance to buy us each a beer.

"Celebrity treatment," I comment, raising an eyebrow.

Kennedy just winks.

We dance, letting the music carry us away. Dancing with him, I feel graceful and even daring; the world is alive and vibrant. We dance for hours, learning each other's rhythms, trying new things, laughing as I dip so far back my head almost touches the floor, perfecting the move and doing it again and again to applause from the crowd. It's like the musicians are just playing for us, and us alone, although I know everyone is watching.

Periodically, men I don't recognize come up to Kennedy, pat him on the back, and declare, "Mayor, security is tight!," before disappearing again into the dimly lit room. Recurrent check-ins become a routine. Kennedy pulls me close to his chest, suddenly switching from playful to sensual as he rocks me gently, slowly. I've never felt both so close to home and so far from it.

When we weren't dancing, he talked, lecturing me about Marcus Garvey, about Nelson Mandela and Martin Luther King.

"I was crazy about Garvey, but I know you Americans don't like him."

"I'm not sure that's accurate . . ."

"But he was too radical for you? You guys like Martin Luther King because he behaved better?"

When Kennedy gets going like this, he doesn't wait for a response

"I saw myself as Marcus Garvey, a man who fought for the

rights of black people and resisted the system oppressing them. Garvey fought for justice, so that people would be treated equally despite their color. He preached unity, and social and economic power for the less privileged. He was a fearless person who was never intimidated by anyone. He knew the need for freedom and economic justice and preached against the powerful people who were working against the prosperity of the black community."

Kennedy hardly stops for a breath.

"I think you need both kinds of leaders. You need the peace of Martin and the radicals like Marcus and Nelson and Malcolm X. But you know, Martin knew what he was doing! He was a strategist. And Nelson—did you know Nelson was also a badass? They made him look nice when they needed him later, but he was also radical—that guy. No joke."

"Do you always call them by their first names? It seems a little disrespectful."

"They don't mind," he says with assurance. "I grew up talking to them like that. At different times in my life, I would talk to one more than the others. Martin when I needed inspiration. Marcus when I needed courage, when everyone told me it wasn't possible to escape my poverty. Nelson when I needed compassion, or lessons about leadership. My conversations with them, they saved my life."

"I sometimes just can't imagine how you didn't give up. I don't know if I would have been that strong."

"You're tougher than you know," he says—with such conviction I can't help but want to make it true. "I'll tell you something, Jess. This is the hardest university. I call it the 'University of Kibera.' Everyone must go to school, but the day of my graduation day is coming."

———

The next evening I spin the *chapati* dough into small circles like minibuns, the way Liz taught me. Kennedy makes his meat stew in uncharacteristic silence, dropping the long wooden spoon on the floor twice—unable to hide his nerves. I try to catch his eye, to give him a reassuring glance, but he doesn't look up.

For the first time in years, Kennedy spoke to Babi. He came home clearly shaken. It amazes me how Kennedy and Babi have lived minutes apart ever since Kennedy got his own house four years ago. His siblings go back and forth between the two places, but Kennedy and Babi have avoided speaking to or even seeing each other for years.

"He's not my real father, but in many ways, I guess, he is the only father I've ever known," Kennedy said last night. "He was mean to all of us, but he was the worst to me because I wasn't his biological child. Even some of my little siblings, they don't know that Babi's not my real dad. Liz and Jackie, they know but don't talk about it. Babi didn't like to mention that I was not his son. Once Jackie and Liz learned the truth, Jackie would tell me secretly that I wasn't really part of the family. Liz would try to protect me."

This man, whom Kennedy calls "Babi," had reached out to speak with Kennedy.

"It's because of you," Kennedy said. "He's been hearing so much about the *mzungu* with his son. Babi said that as a parent it's customary he come to eat a meal to see if the woman is suitable." Kennedy is shaking his head at the antiquity of these customs.

In Kennedy's voice I hear the mix of emotions, his uncertainly about talking to this man, about ending the estrangement. At the same time, he can't hide his desire to finally be welcomed by Babi.

We clean the house carefully. Kennedy intermittently offers disconnected bits of information and instruction.

"I've never been seen as a son of that house, even though I built the only toilet at the compound in my dad's ancestral village. In Luo culture, when a woman marries, she leaves her family's village and moves to the man's home. Traditionally, each son is given a piece of land in the family *boma* to build his marriage house. I may never be given such land. It will be difficult for me to be a respected leader in the community without such recognition."

I don't really understand, but I give a supportive nod. I'm nervous too, about the role I'm supposed to play tonight.

I ask Kennedy, "So I'm supposed to cook a meal—?"

He takes one look at me and laughs, shaking his head. I can tell by looking at his face that there is no way Kennedy can begin explaining everything to me. There are so many little details to execute to meet the expectations of traditional Luo culture. I realize Kennedy worries that half of the expected duties would offend me to the core, maybe even send me straight back to America. "You make the *chapati* and I will make the meat. But we pretend you cooked it all," he says hurriedly. Kennedy's face betrays concern that this gathering could be a disaster.

"Are there other things I'm supposed to do?"

Kennedy takes a long look at me, and I watch him whittle down the list in his head to just a few manageable directions.

"You offer to wash our hands, you prepare the water. Serve the meal . . . that's it."

I nod, noticing how Kennedy is nervous about my reaction, about how I'll respond to these prescribed roles. It's strange how I don't seem to mind the expectations as much as I think I perhaps should. There is something about embracing these roles for a night, about making one part of the evening easier for him, that speaks to a nurturing part of me I never before recognized.

I told Kennedy I would follow Anne's instructions exactly: Don't finish all the *chapati*s until Babi comes over, so he sees that I can cook. Prepare a pitcher filled with warm water and offer him a basin with the pitcher for washing hands. Make sure Babi takes seconds.

"Thank you," Kennedy says—his voice stopped with emo-

tion. I see how Kennedy has never stopped yearning for the childhood he did not have.

Babi enters the house, a place where he has never been, with
unexpected authority. He slowly eats the meat, trying a bit too
hard to hide how much he is savoring this food. Babi does not
want us to know it has been a long time since he last ate meat,
attempting to mask any lingering vulnerability. Neither Babi nor
Kennedy say much, both remaining noticeably guarded. Eventually, Babi turns his gaze to me. His voice has a harsh quality to it,
as if to say that since the world has not spared him, why should
he do any differently for anyone else.

"And you, what do you want with my son?" he asks. I am
caught off guard by the directness of his question, unprefaced by
any niceties or any attempts to get to know me. I look at Kennedy
for the answer, but he isn't returning my gaze. Many emotions
flash across his face, and I know he is thinking of only that one
word: *son.*

"I'm not sure I understand what you mean by that, sir," I reply.

Babi eats another few bites of stew, as if telling me he can take
as much time as he wants before answering.

"A lot of people like you, they come here, use our people, and
then they go."

I feel myself stiffen at the blatant accusation, and suddenly I
understand why Babi has come to this dinner. I meet his eyes and
offer a gentle but measured reply. I want him to know what I'm
made of.

"I don't plan on using anyone, sir."

I continue to eat in silence, trying to steel myself, to show him
that he doesn't scare me. I now feel Kennedy's eyes on me, reflect-
ing gratitude and awe. My face flushes red.

"Or you people come and disappear them from their culture.
As a Luo man, he will never have peace unless he respects our
culture," says Babi with unconcealed self-righteousness. But his
next question surprises both Kennedy and me.

"Do you love my son?"

Kennedy looks at him, disarmed confusion on his face, and I wonder to myself, *Do you?*

Kennedy looks conflicted. *Does he want to be loved by Babi?*

The reality is that Babi is here, tonight, having perhaps finally heard that unique call of parenthood, the call to protect your child. Tonight is many years too late, but he's heard it nonetheless. He is afraid of me, afraid for Kennedy. The last thing I'd expected was to share anything with this man. I'd felt my heart instantly harden toward him and yet here we are, bewildered by a shared desire to protect Kennedy.

A peculiar kind of compassion stirs inside me. Before me sits a man defeated by his own life, belittled and angry. Babi's response to the raw deal he received has been to inflict his pain on everyone else. This father and son sitting side by side are like a study in the spectrum of humanity. Both were dealt life's short straws, yet it astounds me how humans are capable of responding so differently. I see on Babi's face the pangs of regret, and it strikes me that perhaps this is some strand of unconsidered love. Nothing is as straightforward, as untinged with fear as I'd once thought. Not love, not parenthood—no act as daring as claiming another as your own.

"I do love your son," I say quietly.

Babi abruptly asks, "And how will we get your family the cows?" Officious, yet with utter sincerity. "How will we deliver your bride-price?"

My mouth falls open, and I look at Kennedy, searching for the words to explain so many things.

Babi's brow furrows. "Do the airplanes deliver cows?"

It takes everything in me to restrain my laughter as I imagine a delivery of cows to my house in Denver. To me this is utterly absurd—to Babi the idea is entirely reasonable.

"There won't be any cows," Kennedy says firmly, so many meanings in that one phrase: one for me and one for Babi. This statement distresses Babi greatly, and he doesn't say any more. He sits with his hands folded on his knees, and we all three stare in silence at the table, the chasm between our worlds laid bare.

After Babi leaves, Kennedy and I stand side by side, washing the dishes together, each absorbed in our own thoughts.

"Thank you," he says, catching my gaze.

"Welcome," I nod. I wrap the remaining *chapati* in a plastic bag, keeping it for tomorrow—it was good.

"How do you do it?" The words escape from my lips. "How can you forgive him?"

Kennedy looks at me with sadness in his eyes.

"Forgiveness is not about him; it's about me. I learned a long time ago, life is about choosing what you hold. That is what makes or destroys you."

Only two years between our ages, yet tonight I feel there might as well be twenty.

kennedy

Jessica brings home a bottle of wine to surprise me after she hears I have never drunk real wine before. CARLO ROSSI, it says on the elegant bottle, which probably cost as much as three months of my little sibling's school fees. I can't say that it seems worth that, but I know she meant well. For this special occasion I unpacked two precious glasses, made of actual glass, that I haven't even used yet. I kept them wrapped in paper and tucked carefully in their box, until tonight.

"Pour me another glass," I say to her.

She pours herself more too, and sitting on the floor, we clink our glasses and toast. "Cheers."

"You can't look away—then it doesn't count!" I say. We Africans hold on to superstitions.

The lightbulb flickers and goes out.

Jessica leaps up to get my flashlight and knocks over my book-

shelf. As she makes a grab for the falling books—not that they'd
be damaged by the fall—she knocks over her glass of wine. That
is damaged by the fall. I listen to it shatter and softly sigh. My
tornado. Jessica says that's what her dad has always called her.
Where she comes from, she can usually buy new things to replace what she breaks, and she constantly seems to be breaking
things.

"No!" she exclaims. "I am so sorry."

"I know," I tell her as I fold her in my arms and kiss her.
Glasses can in fact be replaced, but soon this woman will leave
me and return to her faraway country.

"I'm trying," she says.

"I know," I say again. "Part of what I love about you is the
way things fall when you enter a room." It's true.

I hand her my glass. It is more fun to share anyway. I sweep
up the broken glass and turn on my radio and settle down next to
her again. Bob Marley serenades us:

> *I wanna love you, and treat you right;*
> *I wanna love you every day and every night.*

I gently lay her down on the bed and cover her beautiful body
in kisses.

> *We'll be together with a roof right over our heads;*
> *We'll share the shelter of my single bed.*

As I hold her in my arms, she tells me she has always been uncomfortable in her own skin, afraid of this beautiful body with its
appetites. She has always viewed it as something to be controlled,
almost like a foreign entity.

"American men are so funny," I tell her. "I don't understand
why they like women who are so thin they have to search the bed
to find them."

I pretend to feel around blindly, as if looking for something lost on the floor, to make her laugh. I love to make her laugh, to make her eyes light up. We laugh together.

We spend our last night together at the SHOFCO office, falling asleep embracing each other.

I'm an early bird. By six A.M., I'm awake. Jessica makes fun of how I like to wake up early in the morning. She loves sleeping and to wake up late. She can even be in bed until ten, sometimes eleven. Sleeping so late amazes me.

It's time for Jessica to depart. Walking, we wipe away tears. I carry her luggage. People along the path in Kibera ask us where she is going. I tell them Kisumu, near my rural village. I call her my *Nyaloka,* which in Luo means "from across the lake."

Before she leaves, I'm taking her to Uhuru Park. We hold hands on the bus ride there, fingers interlaced.

I have brought a piece of cloth that I put down on the grass, local fabric with bright purple and yellow flowers. We sit on this cloth holding each other and looking into each other's eyes. We are crying because Jessica will be leaving.

We talk about life, dreams, aspirations.

"Kennedy, how can you be so hopeful?"

I look her in the eye. "Jessica, I've seen trouble. I've seen everything horrible that can happen to a human being. The sweetest thing is to build your own life from scratch. I was born into struggle. I know that even when the road ahead looks dark, if I pass through that darkness, I can see a little bit of light ahead. That little light that tries to shine from afar is what I call hope."

"Kennedy, you're crazy. I love you."

She is laughing, she is so life filled.

We keep holding each other.

I tell her I will be right back. At this moment I have a little money in my pocket. I walk by a tired man selling soda from a small freezer. Jessica loves a type of ginger soda called Stoney that apparently is not sold in America. I buy her a soda and a loaf of bread, a special treat.

Between us we share the one bottle of soda with a half loaf of bread. I never knew life could feel so good.

jessica

I don't want to go to that final group dinner for our program, but he insists. Somehow Kennedy is the first person I've known who's able to make me change my mind once it's made up. Afterward, everyone else is going out to a club but I've made arrangements with the bus driver to drop me off at the SHOFCO office, where we planned to spend our last night together. When I open the door, I find Kennedy sitting at the desk concentrating on the paper in front of him. I'm immobilized for a few minutes, just staring at him: trying to impress his image into my heart, trying to memorize the way he sits in a chair, the space his frame takes up in a room.

Slowly, I put my arms around his neck, kissing his hairline. He reaches his hand up and touches my hair with such tenderness I think that I might burst. I crawl onto his lap, as though I'm once again a small child, returned to some original state. He rocks me in silence. I press my face hard into his chest. Neither of us wants to move, to admit that time was moving forward.

This morning, our last morning, I wake up even earlier than he does, just to savor what it feels like to lie next to Kennedy. Looking at him, breathing peacefully, I can't imagine how I will be able to bear leaving this place. Moving slowly, so as not to wake him, I reach for my journal again. My dad always used to play me Mary Chapin Carpenter songs when I was upset, and a lyric comes to me now. *Accidents and inspiration—that's what gets you to your destination.* I rip the words out of my journal, fold it in half, and tuck it into the pocket of his jeans that lie discarded near his head.

I kiss him gently on his brow, his nose, his chin. He scrunches his face together, in what we call his "morning face," making me laugh.

"Don't move for five more minutes," he pleads, drawing me down to him.

"Five, only five," I murmur.

There is one more place Kennedy has insisted on showing me today. As we make our way through Olympic, people stop us.

"Where is she going?" one of the boys by the shoe stand asks.

"Kisumu," he answers, as he gives me a wink. He whispers in my ear, "my *Nyaloka*," the Luo word for someone who comes from across the lake—and in this case it's a very, very big lake.

We take the bus to town and get off at Uhuru Park in the city center. He takes a purple *lesso* with yellow flowers out of my backpack and spreads it on the grass. I run my fingers along the Swahili proverb printed on the side.

"This was my favorite escape when I was growing up," he says. "The place I used to walk to when I just couldn't take Kibera anymore. I wanted to share it with you." I know exactly what he means, and I can feel the tears start again, streaming down my face. I bring my hand to his cheek, wiping the moisture away, reminded how he cries silently.

"What happens now?" I ask.

"I'll take you to the bus, and then I will walk back home," he says with a sad smile.

"That's not what I mean—after that."

"Life will return to what it was—only somehow different. I have big plans for SHOFCO." He touches my face and says gently, "I have my life to live, and you have yours. But as I live it, I will often think of you."

"And us, what about us?"

He smiles at me sadly, shaking his head slowly.

And I now see it was always coming to this—to this moment where I'd have to leave, where I could leave, where that fact captures all the differences between us.

It strikes me now, how brave he is and what a coward I am. In my world, everything always just generally worked out. So I barreled along, entirely unprepared and ill-equipped to estimate the impact of loss. But he has known all along, and yet somehow he loved me anyway.

kennedy

My mom always said that if you find a butterfly and you try to hold it clasped between your hands, it will beat its wings until it dies. But if you open your hands and let it go, one day it might come back. And even if it doesn't, at least you will have held a butterfly.

part
two

twelve

jessica and kennedy

jessica

It's the end of December, and Kennedy's cell-phone number flashes on my caller ID. I'd saved his contact as "Kennedy Kenya" and that last word makes me, here at home in Denver, feel infinite worlds away from him.

I answer with giddy joy—it's been impossible to get through the phone lines since the elections and the ensuing chaos. There is a terrible buzz, and all I can hear is shouting and chaos in the background. I can make out only a few words: *Guns. Violence. Escape.* Then he is gone, and I am helpless with dread, frantic with worry.

I stayed up all night during the elections. A government website monitored vote progress. I continuously pressed *refresh* on my Internet browser. Information was added at unpredictable intervals: sometimes every hour, sometimes more often, sometimes nothing for three or four hours. Updated news was hard to get: the international coverage is a summary, delayed by hours, devoid of the detail I craved. The Kenyan news websites felt thin. I searched the web for a few hours and figured out how to stream KTN, the local channel.

Then suddenly everything changed: Raila Odinga, the opposition leader, went from leading significantly, to being only marginally ahead, to then trailing far behind. A hasty announcement declared victory for the incumbent President Kibaki, and he was sworn in at night in a rushed, closed ceremony. The EU doesn't accept the results, but the U.S. government, just as Kennedy said it would, congratulates President Kibaki. As soon as the announcement is made, mayhem erupts in Kenya: looting and burning, brutal killing targeted at ethnic groups. The entire country is consumed by chaos, and nowhere is more affected than Kibera. KTN blacked out as the government cut off all news service. Days later, when the news finally came back, I saw streaming footage of Kibera: roads barricaded, young men carrying machetes, cars burning, police shooting everywhere.

I feel as though I am losing my mind, stuck here in Denver, sitting with my family at a table at a Brazilian Steak House. I am trying to join in celebrating New Year's Eve, but watching the waiters slice steak and lamb onto our plates, my only thoughts concern whether Kennedy will even make it out of this turmoil alive. I keep looking at my cell phone, my wished-for magic thread connecting me to him, a world away.

kennedy

I hope she heard me say it: *I love you, Jessica.*

My phone is almost dead, showing just one last bar. I turn it off. I have to try to reach the SHOFCO office at night. It isn't safe to return to Kibera, not yet. I have to keep going, holding it together. Throughout the slum I see signs of death and destruction. Smoke curls up into the sky from the fires, which burn across the city.

All over Nairobi's streets, and throughout the country, violence has erupted over the disputed presidential election. Divisions are taking place along ethnic lines. What appears to be tribal warfare is not only about tribes, but also about anger over inequality and better access to resources and opportunities. Since Kenya declared independence from the British in 1963, only a few ethnic groups have dominated politics, and they have had access to better resources as a result. This election has brought to the surface all the anger about injustice and inequality that has been quietly building for forty-four years. The pandemonium in Kibera seems worse than anywhere. As news of the election results spread, people went out to the streets and began burning, looting, and killing neighbors they'd lived next to for years. As if a monster has been unleashed in Kibera's streets, angry mobs of young people ran around burning tires, their machetes already drawn.

I feel deeply sad, not only for the victims but also for these young men who have been so badly oppressed that now they have turned wild. Many residents of Kibera simply cannot imagine they have anything more to lose. I always heard about terrible things like this happening in other countries nearby—Rwanda, Congo—and I thought it would take so much to get to that point. Now I see that it doesn't take much at all, simply a spark; if there is enough poverty and hopelessness to serve as kindling, the flame burns and burns.

It's dead silent in Olympic Estate. Some houses are empty. I wake up my friend Antony, who lives in Olympic.

I knock on his door. "Antony . . . Antony . . . it's me, Kennedy . . . please open the door."

"Are you alone?"

Thugs frequently kidnap people and then force the kidnapped person to lead them to the house of a friend. The friend then opens the door, believing it is a friend who is knocking. I suspect Antony thinks I'm one of these things.

"Antony, I swear I am alone."

After watching me from the window, he opens up.

"Antony, man, so happy to see you!" I shout.

"Shhh . . . shhh . . . shhh. Don't be loud speaking in Luo!"

I know Antony to be a brave man. To see him afraid intensifies my fear.

He walks me to the SHOFCO office, giving me an update.

"A lot of sad news and I don't know where to start." Antony clears his throat. "Ken, you have to be strong."

"Antony, what will we do?" But I know I am not asking a question.

I can see the moonlight reflected in his eyes, but his face is dark. "Angel is dead."

Angel was just a baby, not yet six years old. Her mother, Helen, is part of the women's empowerment project, SWEP. We had nicknamed Angel "the SHOFCO baby." She was conceived out of wedlock with a drunkard in the community. Her mother, Helen, unsuccessfully tried to abort her. Then Angel was born so little the doctors said she would not live to see her first birthday. She was given the name Angel, an angel from God, because this baby had survived so much.

"How could someone kill a little innocent soul?"

"It was a stray bullet from the police," Antony tells me.

Tears are now falling down my cheeks. I feel my stammer and cannot talk. Neither of us can speak for a long time.

We reach the SHOFCO office. Antony opens the gate and looks around to ensure that no one is hiding. It is late, and I'm dog-tired and haven't eaten anything since the tiny sip of porridge my neighbor in Kibera gave me. We have mattresses in the SHOFCO office, where members who are working late can sleep. I say good night to Antony and we fall asleep fully clothed.

Thirty minutes later I wake to the sound of a lorry stopping just outside the wall that surrounds our office. My heart pounds as I hear the voices approaching closer and closer.

"Antony . . . Antony . . . Antony, do you hear that?" I whisper.

"Shhh. Don't talk. I hear them too."

"Oh my God . . . today we are dead."

Antony and I squeeze together on our single mattress, waiting to die together as friends.

The people outside are speaking in Kikuyu, but their voices are muffled and I can hear only pieces of what they are saying.

"They want revenge for some Kikuyus who were killed in Laini Saba village. Mungiki promised to retaliate," I translate. Mungiki is an infamous gang often associated with the Kikuyu tribe. As Luos, we are in grave danger. We would be considered worthy revenge killings.

Antony crawls toward the window. "Oh God, it's a gang. I can see the flashlights."

"Please, Antony, don't do that . . . they might see."

A light from a flashlight is directed at our window. Antony lies so flat and still next to me that I can't feel his breath.

We are on the second floor. They have not yet entered the building.

I reach into my pocket for my phone. It's almost dead, but not yet. I dial George's number, lying on top of the phone and covering myself with the blanket to suppress the sounds.

"Government . . . Government . . . this is the Mayor. George, I'm in trouble and I don't know what to do."

"What do you mean?"

"Antony and I are at the SHOFCO office. What looks like Mungiki just arrived in a lorry. We are in danger."

Before I finish the sentence, my phone goes dead.

Antony is still as a corpse.

I hear the sounds of people moving. I know if they can't break in, they might just torch the whole place—this has been happening all over.

"Hurry up, they are coming!" someone is yelling.

The lorry's engine starts and we hear it speed away, tires squealing.

"Antony . . . Antony. They are gone." I touch Antony.

"Are you sure?"

"Did you hear the lorry?"

"Yes, but . . ."

Antony moves toward the window to confirm. "Yes, they are gone."

We breathe in relief.

There is another noise outside.

"Is someone opening the gate?" I ask.

It sounds as if people are jumping into our compound.

Antony flattens himself on the floor again.

Someone is knocking.

"We have been tricked—they pretended that they were gone and now they are in our compound," I whisper to Antony.

"Mayor, open the door!" someone says from outside.

"These people might burn us alive if we don't open the door."

"I'm not opening the door. Still, we will die no matter what"

"Antony, do you think we should make noise, so that neighbors would come help?"

"No . . . No. No one is left."

The voices outside get louder.

"Someone please help us!" I can't help but shout in desperation, and Antony joins me.

"Stop making noise! This is George and his group," someone shouts.

I run to open the door. George is there, waiting for me. He is with a group of more than fifteen people, and I am overwhelmed with joy and relief at the sight of them.

George and his men had divided themselves into three groups surrounding the gang and had planted flashlights in the ground on the other side to make it look like there were many more of them than in actuality. George is a brilliant strategist.

"Kennedy and Antony, you guys were dying today. They knew whoever was living in Olympic must be Luos, as Kikuyus have already left the area. Kennedy, remember, while I'm still alive, you never fear. I will always be there for you, my little brother," George says. "What you have done for this community is so huge." He speaks slowly and gently.

Everyone is quiet as George speaks.

I am crying for the love that George has for me.

Although George is a Luo like me, I had asked him to help protect the Kikuyus in Kibera from being attacked. The previous night he hid several of our Kikuyu SHOFCO youth in his house, even as people were baying for their blood.

"At first I thought I did it for you, but later I realize I did it for myself and for humanity," he says.

George touches my heart. He risked his life by hiding others from a different tribe.

Afraid to leave us alone, George vows to stay with us until the next day. We share a little food and I am able to charge my phone. I am dead tired.

"You and Antony go to sleep, Kennedy. It's only a few hours to dawn."

After spending just one night away from Kibera, I can't take it anymore. I want to go comfort Helen and be there for Angel's funeral. In the early morning light I make my way back to Kibera. I call my friend John and make a plan to stay with him in Lanisaba, the part of Kibera farthest away from my house.

As I'm cautiously crossing the railway line, my phone rings: Jessica. I answer, bracing myself for her barrage of questions.

"Hi," she whispers. She sounds very far away.

"Hi," I say, trying to muffle the phone to mask the sounds of Kibera behind me.

"Where are you?"

I am so tired that I take the easy way out and tell her what I know she wants to hear.

"I'm with Antony. We stayed in town."

198 – kennedy odede and jessica posner

There is silence on the line, and I know she's trying to listen to the noises around me—she's smart. It is one of the many reasons I fell in love with her.

"Are you sure?" Her voice wavers, like she's on the edge of believing me, but knows me all too well.

Please make this easy, I beg in my head. I've been through too much in these last hours for an argument. I need to feel connected again, to her, to anything.

"I'm sure."

"I don't believe you. Please, Ken, be careful. We haven't had a chance to do any—to do so many things. Please take care of yourself."

Her voice is soft, and all I want is to put my arms around her, to bury my nose in her sweet-smelling hair. Then the line cuts out, and I am left with a choice. Her voice and the thought of holding her again both compel me to stay alive, to keep out of the fray, even if this means distancing myself from my community. Then I am overcome with anger. She isn't here. She doesn't understand the devastation right before my eyes. Even if I make it out alive—how do I live past all that I have seen?

But I can't shake the feeling inside me telling me to listen to her. So I call John and say I won't be coming. I start making my way back to Olympic. Several hours later I am finally back at Antony's house.

I wake up in the middle of the night covered with cold sweat. I reach for my phone and call John. He doesn't answer. I call Chris, my friend who saved my life by warning me the police were looking for me. I know Chris is spending the night with John—but no answer from Chris, either. Now I am completely filled with dread. I can't fall back asleep. Hours later, Dennis calls me. As he speaks, the tears flow down my face. It is what I had feared, only worse.

In the middle of the night, members of a gang broke into

John's house and killed the four young men who were fast asleep. The gang members killed my friends using forced circumcision, cutting them and then letting them bleed to death. My four friends were Luo like me, and we are among the few tribes in Kenya who traditionally do not circumcise—something often denigrated. My friends were killed in the cold blood of hatred. If I had been there, it would have been me, too.

Somehow, Jessica saved my life—her warning kept me from being with them—but I could not, in turn, save my friends.

As I dial her number, I am overcome by choking sobs. She answers on the first ring and when I hear her voice, I only cry more.

"They killed them, Jess—they killed them—"

"Who?"

"Yesterday, you told me not to do anything that I'd regret. I lied. When you called, I wasn't with Antony in the city. I was in Kibera. Somehow you knew. I wanted to join my friends John and Chris. I don't want to be special. I want to be there. My community needs me; I don't know where I am supposed to be. We were going to sleep in John's house, but I couldn't ignore your warning. Now they are dead. Dead and how they killed them . . ." I trail off.

"I'm so sorry, Ken . . . we will get through this."

I hear her words, but I don't know. I don't know how we will make it through.

Through the phone I can tell she is crying too. For a moment I feel sorry for all that she's been put through because of me. I grew up with violence, and still I will never become used to it. But she's never known anything like this, except in the abstract, except on the news.

There is nothing more that we can say, so we sit on the phone in silence. I know my life is still in danger—it will only be hours, or days if I'm lucky, before I'm found. If I am going to stay alive through this tumultuous time, I have to get out of this country.

"Tanzania," I tell her, my voice quiet and resigned. "Please, I need help. Help me get out, to Tanzania."

She promises to do everything in her power, and Jessica has a lot of power. She is like a lioness. Still, in this case I'm not sure it will be enough.

Vigilantes have established checkpoints and are asking people at random for their IDs. If a person happens to be from the "wrong" tribe, the individual is killed on the spot. Luckily I don't have my ID on me, and I speak both Kikuyu and Luo perfectly, the languages of the main two opposing groups. I pray that no matter who stops me, I can use whichever language will allow me to leave with my life. The police have built a barrier at the end of the road to keep people from leaving Kibera. At the barrier, the fighting is brutal—tear gas and bullets fired indiscriminately into the crowd. No medical aid, no food, nothing comes in or goes out. When I think about how many people have already died, and how many more to come, I am sick. What a waste. And what are we fighting for anyway? Neither government party cares if we, the people, live or die.

————

Jessica e-mailed everyone we know, everyone she knows—Odoch and Donna, our friends from the World Social Forum who introduced us, her family members—and collected money to buy me a plane ticket. She sent me the money using Western Union and, worried that the airport might close if we delayed longer, booked me a flight to Tanzania leaving tomorrow.

I call my taxi driver friend Mbugua to come and take me to Olympic, as I kept my passport in the SHOFCO office. I am kicking myself for leaving it there. Mbugua suggests that we should go there at around ten P.M., and so we are stuck, waiting at the edge of Kibera.

As we near the barricade, the police stop the car, check if we have any weapons, and ask for our identity cards. After reviewing our documents, they tell us to go on without even asking for a bribe. We are elated.

"This is the first time the police never asked me for a cup of tea," Mbugua says.

"Mbugua, we are lucky."

I thank Mbugua for always taking risks for me.

"Kennedy, you are a good man."

We arrive at the Olympic gate. I rush into the SHOFCO office and grab my passport, my phone charger, some books, and a few clothes.

Olympic Estate is so silent. I try to call Antony to let him know that I'll be leaving the country, but I can't reach him by phone.

As we drive back to the city, we see a line of four cars stopped by the roadside. It is almost midnight. Men walk toward us with flashlights. I look through the window. Someone is plucked from the first car. The men are asking for everyone's national identity cards. Reading someone's last name is an easy way to determine the person's tribal affiliation.

"Please don't kill me!" someone is screaming.

They chop off his head. I'm speechless, stunned. Such an atrocity is more than I can process. My breath comes quickly in short panicked bursts.

Mbugua is closing his eyes as he can't believe what has just happened. I'm trembling with fear.

Death is really following me. Twice now I'd missed it, and yet today it finds me again.

Mbugua cannot move the car forward or backward, as we are surrounded. I know the second car in front of us is occupied by Kikuyus, because I hear them speaking Kikuyu. After their IDs, they are allowed to move on.

Now the men are on to the next car, a white Subaru. The passengers are not responding in Kikuyu. I hear them being asked to produce their identity cards.

"You guys think we cannot find you. You are killing our people, now we are dealing with you," says one of the young men in charge of stopping the traffic. He is wearing black sunglasses, even though it's dark.

"One by one outside," he orders.

People are now wailing in the car in front of us. They are being slashed with a machete. Each falls on the ground, lifeless; their screams and pleas for mercy reverberate throughout the night. We can't believe our eyes.

It's our turn now. I'm trembling and crying like a baby, but Mbugua is still.

Mbugua knows he will be considered a traitor. As a Kikuyu, he too could die for trying to shield me, a Luo. We are no longer friends, no longer individual people, reduced to symbols of our tribes, of a struggle that is not even ours.

Something possesses me, and I start speaking Kikuyu to the man in the sunglasses.

"The Luos have killed my family, they burned our house, and now we are escaping! They have burned everything, even our IDs!" Tears run down my face.

Mbugua jumps in and says terrible things about the Luo.

The men look at us and feel sorry for us. The man with the sunglasses tells us to go, to be careful on the road.

I can't believe it. I have tricked death once again.

Mbugua says that he will start going to church. God has saved his life and that is a story that he will share with his family. He could have been dead. He was going to be killed for collaborating with the enemies.

We arrive safely at the cheap hotel where I will spend my last night before leaving for Tanzania. Mbugua explains that in spite of his great love for me, he will no longer drive me to Kibera. He has escaped death twice.

"We can't be lucky again the third time. That was death's last warning."

Still, Mgubua does promise to take me to the airport, as that will be during the daylight tomorrow.

That night I also pray to God to thank him for saving my life. I don't even want to ever tell Jessica what happened tonight. Some experiences are too much to bear.

A few weeks later I am staying at a run-down hotel in Dar es Salaam, the capital of Tanzania. Jessica galvanized friends and family, raised enough money to help me escape from Kenya, and I slipped out. Here in Dar, I don't know what to do with my free time. When I stop for tea in a local shop, an old Tanzanian man recognizes my accent as Kenyan. He tells me how sorry he was to hear of our troubles and buys me my first cup of chai as a welcome. His kindness only reminds me of how out of place I feel, seeking asylum away from everything I know. As the violence rages at home, I am by myself in a foreign country, the future entirely unknown. I don't know when or if I will be able to go back to Kenya. There is no way to tell how long the fighting might last. My days here consist of wandering throughout the town, checking my e-mail if there is power (Dar has frequent rationing and outages), trying to reach friends and family still at home despite the intermittent cell service, and talking to Jessica. I read the books I have brought with me—Martin Luther King, Malcolm X, Marcus Garvey. I devour them. Sometimes I can't forgive myself for leaving. Other times, I know I had no other choice.

Today, I eat rice for breakfast—a Tanzanian custom that I must admit I love. The rice is soft and melts in my mouth. I take a sip of tea, and the rice and sweet liquid go down perfectly together. I walk to a local cybercafé, hoping the power is working today. Luckily, the cybercafé is open and I eagerly log in, hoping that Jessica has sent me a note, something I can read and reread throughout the day.

But there is no love note waiting in my inbox. There is only one short e-mail from Jessica. I open it to find links to several long applications to American universities. The subject line is only one word, all in caps: APPLY.

Jessica sends me all the forms, and I fill them out. I only comply because I'm in love with Jessica and I want to make her happy. I have nothing else to do, so I figure I might as well use up time filling out forms. I cannot believe anything will result from these efforts. Jessica seems to be crazy, a crazy American lady. In America, kids are raised to believe that they can do anything. I try to be hopeful and motivated, but the difference between American kids and me is that I am realistic. I know filling out these forms and writing these essays is a waste of time. I can't get into a university in Kenya, let alone an expensive American university. But Jessica is so persistent, I fill them out all the same.

There's a form asking about my parents' property and income. Questions ask if my parents own a house, and what assets we generally hold. So many times I write zero. How much is your family income in a year? So now I decide to write $900. I fill in everything. I scan it and I send it back to Jessica.

Immediately I get a phone call.

"Kennedy, how much do your parents really earn?"

"Jessica, we earn nothing." I say. "We have no regular, consistent money. You know I'm the one supporting my family. But as an African man, I must have some pride. I was tired of writing zero, zero, zero."

Jessica sends the form back to me.

thirteen

jessica

Neither of my parents meet my gaze; they look straight ahead at the crack in between the closed elevator doors, willing the doors to open, to let them out. I look straight ahead too, signaling my determination that no matter what they say, I won't change my mind.

"This is ridiculous," my dad mutters under his breath. He's prone to mumbling, especially when he finds himself torn between his children's demands for independence, in which he is a great believer, and the consequences of that independence.

"You were the one who encouraged her to go so far away to begin with," my mom mutters back, as if by speaking to each other sotto voce, they can pretend I'm not here.

"Guys, please calm down!" I interject.

"I think we are pretty calm," my dad sputters. "What kind of parents take their twenty-one-year-old daughter to an immigration lawyer to learn more about options, even including marriage, to help her African boyfriend obtain a visa?"

I feel a moment of sympathy and deep appreciation for my

parents. My dad, enthusiastically, and my mom, reluctantly, sent away their wide-eyed daughter to Africa, and I came back feeling so much older, with everything so much more complicated.

A week ago I'd woken up my dad at one A.M. to make a Western Union transfer to Kennedy from the money I'd painstakingly raised. Western Union wouldn't authorize me to make the transfer over the phone, and Kennedy had a short window to get to town, get the money, and leave before violence erupted again. I worried if Kennedy didn't get the money right away, we would lose what could be our only chance for him to escape. Groggily, my dad had made the call, giving his credit card number, answering endless inane questions. I'd felt overwhelmed with gratitude. Still, I needed more. After the transaction finally processed, I'd collapsed on the floor and begged my dad to help make an appointment with an immigration lawyer.

The elevator doors open, mercifully. On the car ride home, the meeting with the lawyer hangs between us.

The lawyer did not mince words: she quickly appraised the situation and said that for Kennedy to have a chance at a student visa he'd need acceptance with a full scholarship to a U.S. university, and even then a visa would not be guaranteed—not even close. Laws governing student visas required concrete proof of "intent to return home," only provable in the form of bank accounts, title deeds—money. His organization, family—none of those qualified.

"Whose interests am I representing?" the lawyer had gently asked.

My parents both shifted uncomfortably in their seats.

"Your interests and your daughter's—they may not be the same."

The way I see it, there are two options: Plan A, Kennedy goes to college in the United States and comes by a student visa; or Plan B, we get married so he can get a visa and then go to college later.

Plan A seems so unlikely. I don't want Kennedy to get his hopes up, unsure if he can sustain another loss. I research which colleges even offer financial aid to foreign students, and the list is very small, containing names of highly selective universities: Wesleyan, Yale, Amherst, Hampshire, Bard to name a few. There is another problem. Today is January tenth, and the application deadlines have passed. I decide to write to the dean of admissions at each of these schools. What do we have to lose? I spend the afternoon crafting the e-mail and sending it out to over fifteen schools in total.

> Subject: Special Case
> Dear Admission Deans,
> My name is Jessica Posner and I am currently a junior at Wesleyan, and a double major in Theater and African American Studies. I am also incredibly involved in the Wesleyan and Middletown communities. I returned from studying abroad for the semester in Kenya. I am writing you about a very special circumstance that I hope you will seriously consider.
> While I was in Kenya I worked with an incredible young man, named Kennedy Odede, in Nairobi's Kibera slum. Odede is currently 23 years old, and three years ago he began the only indigenous community organization in the Kibera slum called SHOFCO (Shining Hope for Communities). Kibera is thought to be one of Africa's largest urban slums. Kennedy began by recognizing a community need for a safe space for young people to go and do something productive amidst the debilitating poverty and had the idea of beginning a soccer team—as he could afford to purchase a ball. He then had the idea of forming a theater group to act out problems in the slum—and then act out alternative solutions. Then, he formed a girls' empowerment program, computer education group, journalism group, sanitation

and environment department—as well as a microfinance organization for women in the slum who suffer from HIV/ AIDS. SHOFCO has touched thousands in the Kibera slum, and Kennedy is so loved that the community refers to him as the mayor of Kibera.

Kennedy grew up in Kibera himself. He was not able to find the funds to further his education.

Now I am writing you about Kennedy's incredible story because of very tragic circumstances. I am sure you are aware of the dire situation in Kenya. Kennedy himself is in a particularly dangerous situation. He is a member of the Luo tribe (the tribe of the opposition) and because of his incredible community work he is a very prominent leader. He has been advised to flee the country, as his life is in grave danger.

As he prepares to leave the life that he has worked so hard to build, he and I have spent time talking about any ways to find opportunities out of tragedy, which is why I am writing you this letter.

I am wondering if there is any way you might consider Kennedy for admissions to your institution under these very special circumstances. Any paperwork that would be necessary he will be able to complete by Feb. 1st. I understand that this request is very unorthodox—but thought that this consideration would be worth your while.

As a Wesleyan student, I can say with all my heart that there is no one who would add more to a community of higher learning than Kennedy. Part of why we come to schools like yours, or Wesleyan, is to meet outstanding young people from different walks of life, from different parts of the world. Kennedy's experiences have more than prepared him to excel in such a climate—and to profoundly impact the lives of the students that he encounters.

So please, let me know if there is anything I can do, or anyone I can get to speak on his behalf, as there is no one who would benefit more from, or contribute more to, a school like yours.

Sincerely,

Jessica Posner

Wesleyan Class of 2009

I compulsively check my e-mail. No colleges reply. Even if they do express some interest, the difficulties are far from solved. Kennedy has no SAT scores and his "transcript" is handwritten on a piece of lined paper after intermittent stays in informal schools that hardly amount to more than a few years in total. Kennedy's file does not contain the background required for U.S. college admittance. Thinking of him, sitting in Tanzania, unsure if and when he will go back to Kenya, I just want him to instantly appear here, next to me.

In Kenya, the violence continues. Without a power-sharing agreement in place between the leaders, it seems uncertain when it will end. I know Kennedy worries. Information is difficult to come by, and so many people are unaccounted for, so many questions. When will it end? When the violence does subside, will it even be safe for Kennedy to return?

The power is so bad in Dar es Salaam that Kennedy's phone is rarely charged. When I did manage to reach Kennedy a day ago, I suggested that the only other way for him to get a visa besides enrolling in a community college, and then eventually transferring, might be for us to get married. He didn't say much. He's much quieter these days. None of these life events are unfolding as we'd imagined. When I left Kenya, I was sure that our romance was over. Now we've resuscitated "us"—in response to extreme circumstances. A life-changing love has been reduced overnight to a practicality, boxes checked off on a marriage application.

"I wouldn't hold you to it, to the marriage, afterward," he'd said, his voice edged in defeat.

Less than a month after leaving Kenya, a month I feel contains several lifetimes, I am back—at least physically back—in America, in college, at "home." I walk down beautiful college row, lined with trees and regal buildings, in a place I once loved. I'm not supposed to feel like an outsider here, in the country where I've spent my entire life, doing the same things I've always done. But I can't stop thinking about Kibera and Kennedy.

I'm lucky to get a two-person apartment with Daphne— usually students returning to campus from abroad second semester get placed in haphazard housing. Still, nothing feels the same. The once-important rituals of classes and parties and papers feel insignificant. For the first time in my life, I can't pay attention in class. I turn in a paper late—shrugging at the thought of what once seemed like such dire consequences. Some days I sleep the entire day, skipping class, unable to get out of bed. I go to the campus health center and the psychologist says I have "posttraumatic stress disorder." I think about just taking this semester off, just going home and trying to deal with what has happened.

Many nights I wake up screaming, drenched in sweat, sequences of violence flashing through my head, and Daphne brings me back to where I am, reminds me that I am here, safe, on campus, in America—which only highlights that Kennedy is not. She brings the futon from her room into the hallway and sleeps there.

Kennedy often calls in the middle of the night. Sometimes he relays the news he is hearing. Sometimes we just listen to each other's breath for an hour or more, with nothing to say, at two in the morning, just savoring the fact that we can hear the other inhale and exhale. Kennedy often finds no words for the horrors still playing out in Kibera, or for what it means for him to live in this limbo.

Then, I get responses from Yale University, Hampshire College, and Wesleyan University, all agreeing to accept Kennedy's late application. We have two weeks to assemble recommendations, write the essays, and gather whatever remnants of his basically nonexistent educational history we can piece together. I forget about my classes almost entirely and throw myself into his application process. I send Kennedy endless forms, essay prompts, and requests for information and recommendations. I lobby friends to write letters in support of his application to Wesleyan and call upon some of the prominent people he met through his work to write letters of recommendation. Daphne helps to pull it all together.

I take charge of coordinating and compiling everything, given how poor the Internet is in Dar es Salaam. Each school tells me not to get Kennedy's hopes up as he is a *very* nontraditional applicant. Still, I can't help but hope all the same.

Then Kennedy stops replying to my e-mails, stops answering his phone. The deadline is approaching fast, and he hasn't sent his essays back. I can feel his fear as if it were my own. Caught up in the concrete tasks that make this goal feel within reach, I've forgotten what a long shot this is. Kennedy has already lost so much. Losing the dream of college and a U.S. student visa might be a devastation beyond what even he can endure.

Just when I'm sure that we won't get it together in time, Kennedy's e-mail arrives. "ESSAYS" in bold letters is the subject heading. He's attached them, asking Daphne and me to edit before submitting them. As I read, Kennedy's infectious hope comes through in every sentence. Daphne's hand squeezes my shoulder as we read the last sentence together: "I believe that another world is possible." We tell him to send them in.

In early March, Hampshire College responds with an offer of a full scholarship. We are all stunned. Kennedy is amazed, monumentally excited. He can't contain himself.

"Kennedy, this is amazing," I tell him. "But let's wait and see what happens with the other schools. I'm still hoping for Wesleyan. I want to be together." He gets very quiet.

Wesleyan says that they will have to delay their decision until Kennedy can take the SAT or ACT—in early June, and I know he's intimidated by the thought of having to take the SAT, which Hampshire did not require.

He is bored in Tanzania and, finally, decides to go back to Kibera despite the risk. The violence in Kenya is technically over, but it still flares up and there is no way of knowing if Kennedy will be safe.

Kennedy registers for the SAT, but on the day he is supposed to take the test, the paramilitary police block the road from Kibera and a fight breaks out once again between the police and the protesters. The violence prevents Kennedy from being able to take the test. If excuses are allowed, this seems as good an excuse as one could have. Kennedy tells me he's, unsurprisingly, never learned most of the content on the SAT anyway. How could we even expect he would do well?

I decide to go talk to Alice Hadler, Wesleyan's dean of international students, who has been a tremendous support and champion of Kennedy's application during this process; maybe now with Hampshire's acceptance, we can negotiate. Alice and I hope to use Hampshire's acceptance to let Wesleyan know that since Hampshire wants an answer before his SAT scores will be out, Wesleyan might lose him.

I get an e-mail from Kennedy: "The mayor has now got a ride to Hampshire, but my heart is into Wesleyan. Let me know if I'm going to join you guys or not."

Without telling me, Kennedy hunts down an e-mail address for the head of Wesleyan, President Roth, and sends an e-mail:

Dear President Roth,

 I'm writing on e-mail to the president of Wesleyan University. I am the Mayor of Kibera, hungry for books. I have reached all this with little education. I'm asking for your support that I may be allowed to attend your university. I am giving your university opportunity because I see a great future, and I want this future to be part of Wesleyan. I have met students from Wesleyan who were here and study abroad, Jessica and Matt. The way they behave, they seem amazing, critical students. I just want to know if I have the chance or no, but I would love to be at Wesleyan.

Finally an e-mail arrives from the admissions office at Wesleyan. I don't even get to the end of the acceptance letter before I call him.

"You've been accepted to Wesleyan!"

Wesleyan has agreed to pay for a full scholarship and even Kennedy's plane ticket. They are giving him a job on campus so that he can earn money to pay for other expenses.

We scream and cry on the phone together, unable to believe it.

"Life can have a turning point," Kennedy says, and I can tell he is crying. "Mine has arrived, Jessica."

I can't believe it worked. I just can't believe it.

And I can't wait to see him again. So I don't. I apply for funds from Wesleyan to spend my summer researching the postelection violence in Kenya for my senior thesis.

"Welcome back to Kenya."

My heart pounds as the customs officer stamps my visa. The administrators at Wesleyan were so nervous about my going back given the country's instability that they almost refused to fund my trip, but I was determined. To process everything that has happened this past year, I need to see it for myself.

I rush down the stairs to the baggage claim, hoping that my bag isn't the last to come out. He's waiting for me. I know he must be. I feel a surge of gratitude as my bags surface, and I make a mad dash through customs. I see him. After all that's happened these past six months, it feels surreal to see him standing in front of me—as if nothing, and everything, has changed. He hugs me, pushing my head into his chest as if he can't hold me tightly enough.

"Hi," he says.

"Hi." It seems all other words have fled from my head.

We've been away from each other for six months. *Will he feel the same? Will I?*

Breathe, I silently whisper to myself. I reach for Kennedy's head and pull his face close to mine, kissing him with every fiber of my being. Our bodies remember each other, at least.

June in Nairobi is surprisingly cold. Kennedy rented us a house in Olympic. He says he is afraid to live inside Kibera with me now, afraid that we won't get "lucky" the way we did last time. I could be raped, or robbed, or something could happen to me. When he first says this, I push back.

"I don't see why we have to live here. This place isn't very friendly. No one talks to me; it feels cold and lonely. I just don't understand why we can't live in your old house."

"It's different now."

"How? Explain it to me," I plead.

"You won't understand. You're American."

"What's that supposed to mean? I'm American? So what?"

"I thought you'd like the bed. I had it made especially for you."

"The bed is fine. I wasn't talking about the bed."

"I bought all these things for you. To make you happy. I don't want to talk about this anymore. It's different. That's all. You won't understand. I'm sorry you don't like the bed."

"Well, you could give me a chance to understand. I won't understand if you don't let me try. And I like the bed. The bed is nice. Big."

"Anything could happen. Any minute. They could close the road again and then we'd be stuck. We'd never get out; we'd never get past the barricades. Everything was on fire. Nothing was safe. Even here. Now I need to protect you, and this is the best that I can do. At least here there are real walls; there is a gate that locks."

"I'm sorry," I say softly. "I'm trying to understand. You came back, I'm back, so part of me thinks that means things are okay now."

I reach out to touch his arm, but he pulls away and my hand catches empty air.

"I'm going out," he mutters as he stands and moves quickly toward the door.

The violence is over, but something has shifted, even Kennedy, especially Kennedy. Sometimes he still laughs when I cook stewed bananas for dinner, and he sings me made-up songs in the morning. But then suddenly he disappears, going to someplace where I can't reach him. I feel terribly alone.

Kennedy shows me the pictures from the funeral of six-year-old Angel, Helen's child. I used to play with Angel at the SHOFCO office.

Since the election violence began, Kibera has become much more segregated by tribe, but everyone still lives side by side. In the fragile peace, neighbors must contend with their recent betrayals: living next to someone who killed a family member or destroyed their business or to whom they've done some wrong. I'm creating a new play with SHOFCO, trying to help them deal with this, if that is even possible. To perform the play, Kennedy chose ten SHOFCO members who had been involved with or witnessed violence against each other, in their own families or in the community, during the postelection violence.

Kennedy has been helping me with my research, conducting interviews with many people about their experiences during the violence. I listen to the tapes he brings me every night as I transcribe their contents, story upon story of loss and terror. In the taped interviews, Kennedy connects to the people as they tell

216 – kennedy odede *and* jessica posner

their stories, his questions and voice gentle. One woman, a former shopkeeper, tells the story of how people came and burned down her shop with her daughter inside. Through Kennedy's sensitive comments on the tapes I get glimpses of his own experiences, but he won't talk about them directly with me.

I wake up in the middle of the night covered in sweat, unsure of where I am. My eyes take a few moments to adjust to the dark, to the strange sounds outside. For a minute I'm not sure if I am awake or asleep, terrified that my nightmare was real. I dreamed that my mother was dead, that there was an unexpected complication at the end of a back surgery she'd actually had a few months before, and in a matter of moments she was gone. The dream felt real because it seemed to span a whole year. She died, and then I saw myself going through the horrible aftermath of losing her: the initial shock and disbelief, which merged into deep, piercing grief before becoming an ever-present pang. In my dream I continued through my life, but I was always missing something: my clothes, a paper that was due, important meetings, and most painfully, my mother at my college graduation. I was looking out into the crowd, searching for her frantically. When I finally remembered that she was dead, I got up and left the ceremony. The part of me that knew I was asleep tried to convince myself that this was only a dream, that I would wake up—but I didn't, the dream just refused to end.

I sit up in bed wrapped in a blue mosquito net. Groggily I reach for the phone and dial home.

"Mom?" I ask anxious, my voice still coated with sleep. "Is that you? Are you okay? I dreamed that you were dead."

"Sweetheart, I'm so sorry. I'm fine. What time is it there?" Her voice feels far away.

"My dream was so real. It's either really late or early here, I don't know the time."

"Honey, I'm okay. Everything is okay."

I feel sleep taking over again. "I love you, Mom."

"I love you so much, Jess. I'm thinking of you every minute."

"Me too," I say as I hang up. Still half asleep, I cuddle closer into Kennedy's chest. He pulls me to him, and I realize that my phone call must have woken him up.

"I'm sorry," I say, wiping the wetness from my face. "I'm sorry to wake you up."

"It's okay," he reassures me, rhythmically stroking my hair. "You know, in my culture, when you have a dream about someone dying, we believe it's because something good has actually happened to that person, like maybe they just ate something they like. When someone has really died, we dream that they are eating meat, because in our culture when a person dies, we kill a cow."

"So I shouldn't worry unless I have a dream where someone is eating meat?" I ask, a smile beginning.

"That's right."

I wake up a few hours later thinking about how lucky I am that I can call my mom when so many can't. All around me here in Kibera are stories of loss—loss of life, of property and of trust. People lost so much during the violence. Here I am reminded every day that life is precious, and incredibly fragile. I talk to people whose homes were destroyed, who lost everything that they have saved since they were children, who lost their means to make a living, lost their communities, their families, sometimes their eyes, legs, or arms.

Some of these people once had what I have, before it was snatched away and stolen by violence. Some were in love. Some were married. Some had children. Some probably also felt filled to the brim with the simple pleasures of daily life, overflowing with quiet joy. And then in a matter of days, or hours, or moments, all that was gone. Children were shot dead by the stray bullets fired by police. Houses were reduced to ashes. Prized possessions were looted by neighbors and friends. A man lying dead in the street never came home again to kiss his wife, who sat waiting expectantly for hours.

Yet Kennedy survived. We survived. I begin to see that in situations where there is a choice between living in fear or living fully and freely, love allows us to choose life, happiness—fulfillment. At night, I watch him sleep with quiet reverence. The way his chest goes in and out is magic; the soft curve of his eyelashes against his cheek, art.

I choose this: savoring what we have but almost lost.

I tell Kennedy we are leaving in three weeks for Wesleyan, for America. We need to begin preparing and packing.

"I'm not ready," he says, his voice harsh. "I'm not ready to leave my community."

"You'll be back," I assure him faintly, even though I am not sure this is true.

"We need to go to my village and speak to the elders. I have to build a house there before I can leave."

"A house? What are you talking about?"

"I knew you wouldn't understand." He sighs in frustration.

"We need to save money for books! And winter clothes! Not build a house in some village!"

Soon afterward, Antony takes me out for a soda and explains that Kennedy's family won't let him go to the United States until he builds a traditional house in his village. In Luo culture, this is a symbol of manhood.

"If he doesn't build this house, Kennedy will be seen as a lost son of the land; they will never accept him back again. It will be as if he has no roots," Antony tells me.

I come home and make ham and cheese sandwiches, grilling them over our small camping stove, as my peace offering.

"What's going on?" Kennedy asks when he gets home. He knows that when I cook, something's up.

"If you want to build this house, I will come with you to the village to build it."

He comes over, takes my face in his hands, and runs his thumb along my cheek.

"Thank you," he says quietly.

Liz comes over the night before we are going to leave for the village. When she looks through my suitcase, she is horrified by the clothes that I've chosen. She goes through my closet and selects my nicest dresses and my most stylish black top, saying this is what I must wear at the village. As travel wear I'd decided on sweatpants and a T-shirt, knowing we would be spending eight hours on a bus, but Liz is adamant that I wear my white capris and stylish black shirt.

Kennedy buys two chickens for us to take to the country, so Liz, Kennedy, me, two chickens, and enough luggage for a month—even though we'll only be in the village for four days—embark on the bus. It takes us eight hours to get from Nairobi to Kisumu, and then another two to get from Kisumu to this tiny village in Kenya's interior. Interior: I suddenly know why they call it that; you can feel its meaning just sitting here—a hidden pocket of the world.

I meet Kennedy's mother for the first time. She mirrors him so closely: her effusive gestures, facial expressions, and charm, and the way she is always at the center of what's happening. She embraces me with such warmth when we first meet, hugging me close and expressing dismay that we will never speak to each other in our native languages—what is called mother tongue. Swahili is just a mediated middle ground, somehow strange to us both.

I bring her a book from Wesleyan that has photos of the campus so she can picture Kennedy there, but when I show her, she just nods, closes it, and tucks the book away under a table.

"Is she not happy?" I ask him.

"My mom, she just likes me to be around," he explains with a shrug. "How much does Wesleyan cost?" he asks.

"A lot, like $50,000 a year if you had to pay."

Kennedy tells his mom something in Luo, and she immediately reaches for the book again, exclaiming loudly.

"What did you say to her?" I ask.

Laughing, he replies, "I translated that into the number of cows it would buy."

Kennedy's youngest brother, Hillary, screams upon seeing me, sending everyone into hysterics—apparently, at two, he's never before seen a white person.

Everyone spoke Swahili for my benefit when we arrived but soon gave up and switched back to Luo, so I'm relegated to being an observer for most of the visit. I sit on the narrow stoop outside Kennedy's parents' house and watch a girl younger than I am, probably eighteen, gracefully carry a heavy container of water on her head. This girl has never left this little village. She has no concept of what the world beyond this place looks or smells like, and I try to imagine what it might feel like, to be so bound to one place.

Hillary and I are playing in the grass when George, who just arrived to help build the house, comes rushing to find me. Hillary is slowly warming to me, more curious than convinced, but we spend the afternoons reading together. I read *Dreams of My Father,* marveling at how it feels to read that book only minutes away from the very same village where Barack Obama's father came from. Hillary takes the book I bought him and, of course, unable to read it, spends the afternoon pretending he can—the book flipped upside down. I can't help but notice his concentration, how at only two he can spend so many hours entirely absorbed in words he can't understand. In him I see what a little Kennedy must have looked like, with this intense determination.

"The building is starting, they need you," George pants urgently.

Hillary shrugs and runs off to chase a village dog. I wipe the dirt and grass from my skirt and follow George, skeptical of how I'll be able to help. It's early in the morning and the day feels so new and fresh, before the heat of the sun takes hold. Last night there was a feast for the entire village in celebration of Kennedy's house that went very late. At five this morning I heard people still singing outside, drunk on the local brew.

Kennedy's mother, Babi, and aunt Beatrice stand in the empty space where, by the end of today, Kennedy's house will be—in the designated place for the first son in every Luo *boma* (homestead), to the right of his parents' house. You can walk into any Luo *boma* and discern the order of the children and the number of sons simply by the placement of their houses. A few other village elders stand in a circle, and George pushes me forward to stand opposite Kennedy. I look around and smile. His aunt Beatrice steps forward and begins to pray, in Luo. Midprayer she takes my hand and places it in Kennedy's. I have a pang of suspicion. Kennedy and I, standing hand in hand in the place designated for his house, everyone else encircling us, Beatrice praying . . .

"Kennedy," I whisper urgently, stepping closer to him so that no one will hear, thankful that Beatrice's prayers have become louder, more fervent. "What is going on? This all looks strange . . . almost like a wedding."

He leans into my ear and says pleadingly, "Please, can we talk about it later?"

The look on his face—oh my God—this is a wedding. I'd recognize it in any language. We are standing here, in the middle of his village in front of the elders, and his mother and family and they are marrying us.

"Kennedy," I hiss, feeling a combination of panic and anger

rise. "Is this some kind of joke? You can't just throw someone into a wedding—you're supposed to *ask* first."

"You wouldn't have understood," he whispers. "Please, just smile?"

Beatrice has arrived at the part where now she pronounces the ceremony complete, the couple united as husband and wife. A cheer erupts and George, who is doing a very good job of pretending not to register my shock, explains that Kennedy has to complete the ceremony by cutting the first tree, and I have to mix the first mud that will be used to build the house. With everyone watching, I have no choice; I pour water into the sand and mix it with a stick Hillary brings me.

"In Luo culture, the house is actually *your* house," Kennedy whispers sheepishly.

"What am I supposed to do with a house in your village?" I snap back. "We need to talk."

"Say you're going for a walk; I'll follow you in ten minutes."

I walk brusquely along the village's perimeter. Many of the *boma*s are out in the open without a fence, cows and children running around—both seem to stop when they catch sight of me. Kennedy finds me, and for several minutes we walk in silence, unsure how to start.

"I'm sorry," he begins. "But you wouldn't have understood."

I feel the heat rushing to my face. "Well, you should have given me a chance to!"

"Let me try now."

"Don't you think now is a little late? Your whole family thinks we're married."

"In Luo culture, a man builds his house with his wife. It belongs to the wife, really. They won't let me leave without building my house, and if I do they will declare me lost. If you didn't come with me and we didn't build it together, I'd have to build it with a woman from the village."

"Like an arranged marriage?"

"Something like that. I am twenty-three—I should have been married a long time ago," he says apologetically. "The ritual is that we build the house and then tonight we have to sleep in it together—to make it official. The entire village will come and watch to make sure we go to bed together, inside."

"Kennedy . . . this is just . . . too much."

"They won't actually watch—" He jumps in, as if that might be the only thing bothering me. "They just make sure we go inside. My plan if you wouldn't come was to build the house with a village woman, but I wouldn't have slept with her."

"Oh, well, that's just great. I'm so glad to know you're so loyal . . ."

"But the thing is, I would have to send money back for her, she'd become my responsibility and I could never bring you here. You'd never meet my mom . . . so I thought about it, and I know it's too much, and we can just pretend it didn't happen. But I wanted to do it with you, so that someday we might have that chance. So someday I might bring you here for real."

"So you're saying that between us—we leave it here? Like what happens in the village stays in the village?"

A slow smile starts to spread across his face. "Something like that," he replies, his tone adorably hopeful.

After a pause, I say with a sigh, "What else do I need to know about this marriage hut ritual?"

"You have to go cook a meal in the house, to show everyone that if there wasn't anyone else in the *boma,* you would still be at home. And also whatever we do, my brothers will have to repeat it exactly with their wives."

"What if we were to cook the meal together? Would everyone else also have to cook with their wives?"

Kennedy joins me in my mischievous smile. "That will make headlines in the village. Let's do it."

When it comes time for dinner, Liz walks up holding one of the chickens we've brought. I've never killed a chicken before, but Liz holds its neck over a metal bowl and hands me the knife. I take a deep breath, look the other way, and slit its neck. The blood flows into the bowl and Kennedy looks at me admiringly.

"You never stop surprising me."

We cook together, shocking everyone and setting a precedent for his siblings.

That night, alone in the half-finished marriage hut, Kennedy holds me tightly. The sounds of the village are so different from the busy city. In the distance I hear a howl. Kennedy said there were hyenas here, and I'd been unsure if he was serious.

"What do you Americans say? You're a good sport?" he says tenderly, ruffling my hair and pulling me close.

"If you ever want this to be real—you will have to ask, and I'm still not sure what the answer would be," I say quietly.

"I know," he says. There is a pause, then, "Maybe we should complete the ritual?"

fourteen

kennedy and jessica

kennedy

The flight attendants call me "sir." They bring me food and ask if I want wine, even bringing me seconds when I ask. It is unbelievable. They are treating me like a human being. They are treating me like a king.

I almost didn't make it onto the plane. It was nearly impossible for me to pack and leave Kibera, my friends, SHOFCO—the only world I've ever known.

When I went to make my good-byes, everyone kept telling me that I would stay in America.

"Now you have a white woman. You're going to have a job in America."

"Listen, guys, I am not going to America to work in a grocery shop," I rebutted. "Here in Kibera, I'm the mayor. I'm so proud. I have my dignity. My heart will stay here with you, and I will come back after my education."

The night before we were supposed to leave, I still hadn't started to pack. When she found this out, Jessica was mad, madder than I've ever seen her, after all her work, that I could come so far and then decide not to accept the scholarship, not to go with her, not to grab onto this huge opportunity.

"It's not about the opportunity," she yelled before she slammed the door on me. "It's about me and you. I'm getting on that plane tomorrow, and if you want us to have any chance, you will be on it too."

So I made it onto the plane. And it is amazing. When you click the chair, you can lean back. Jessica says there are better places to sit in the plane, something called business class and first class, but I don't pay attention. It is all amazing. I can look down at America from the window. I can see that America is planned very well.

Jessica's friend Daphne is waiting for us at John F. Kennedy airport. She is shouting when she catches sight of us: "The chief is here! The chief is here!"

"Your airport has a good name," I tell her jokingly.

We ride in a taxi. The roads are clean. Everything looks in order. I have to be a new person. The Kennedy of Kibera is not here. This is a new Kennedy.

Daphne lives on Central Park. The building is beautiful. There is a doorman. But the greatest miracle of all is the shower. Like magic, hot water comes out from a spout above. I jump with surprise. I turn the tap from hot to cold, hot to cold—the temperature shifts instantly. I shout with delight. Jessica comes in to see if I am okay and finds me dancing and singing in the shower, shrugging my shoulders and shaking my hips.

"We're jammin', I wanna jam it with you," I sing, pointing at Jessica, and she laughs.

I just want to jump and splash, enjoying this magic. I used to have to go fetch water in jerricans, cook it to make it hot, using precious fuel, and cup it in my hands to wash. I stay in the shower for one hour, until Jess comes back and tells me I'm wasting water, and that I have to get out. I smile at this—I've never wasted water in my life.

Jessica and Daphne take me to a place called Times Square. It is crazy. I can watch TV on the walls of the buildings. Someone gives me tickets for free drinks, so we go to a bar.

"Let's get the most expensive drinks!" I say. "How about Champanzee?"

"Champanzee?" Jessica laughs. "You mean champagne?"

We stay out until five in the morning drinking and dancing.

I fly in another airplane to Ohio to meet my American mom, Linda, for the first time. She has written me and supported me for over ten years, but we have never met. In the picture I have of her she has a big smile, and at the airport when I see her it is even bigger. It is amazing to see this woman I call my mom.

They teach me to love Ohio. They buy me an Ohio team T-shirt and cap.

One time while we are driving Linda asks me if I am hungry. I tell her yes, I would like to eat some chicken. She drives us somewhere, reaches through the window, and pulls money out of a wall.

I'm like: "What's going on?"

Then we drive to another wall, and she speaks into it. She tells the wall she wants chicken.

"Kennedy, what do you want to drink?"

I say Coke.

The food and the drinks just fall into the car window and she pays with a card. What is going on in America? You don't even have to get out of the car and things just fall automatically into your lap like this? I am shocked. I can't explain to Linda and Jessica the feelings I have. Oh America!

Linda gives me advice just like a mother. She tells me about being black in America. She says that if the police stop me, I should just lift my hands up and not argue.

"There have been instances here in America where innocent black men have been shot for nothing," she tells me.

She is serious. I didn't expect that America is also scary.

Now it is time to meet Jessica's parents. We go to Ithaca, New York, to see a play her brother, Max, has written, and we will meet them there. I'm worried they might not like black people as I've read and heard so much now about black people having challenges in America. I try to pretend that I don't care if they like me or not, as long as Jessica and I are together, but I secretly will them to like me, to accept me.

The first person I see is Jessica's dad. The tears come from his eyes when he gives me a hug. Jessica has told me that he always cries at the family's most important moments. I meet Jessica's mom, who is smiling, and her brother, whose warmth is like an embrace.

They have a car and we drive together to go see Jessica's brother's play. I've never been to this kind of theater. The play is about Jessica, me, and a dog. Honestly I don't really know what's going on, but I know I'm part of the story. I hear them talking about slums, and I can see the African aspects. There is no popcorn. I thought they would give us popcorn to watch this. I'm a little bored, and I want to sleep, but everyone is looking at me to see if I like it so I sit at attention.

We go out to eat something and I try very carefully not to eat like a Kibera person in front of them. Jessica's mom teaches me how to use a fork, with the fork on the right side and the knife on the other. She tells me that Americans care about these things. It seems important to her, so I try to learn.

When we fly to Denver, I am amazed by Jessica's house, but a little overwhelmed and disappointed by how many clothes and shoes she has. Somehow, because I understand her so well, I'd thought her life would be simpler.

As I walk around Denver I am really worried that someone will shoot me, kill me. I heard that in America lots of people have guns. I don't really understand the American culture. Max, with whom I have become very close, teases me that I am "culturally illiterate," because I don't understand any of the references to music or TV shows, even popular ones.

He makes me mad when he calls me that, but I forgive him because I appreciate his honest joking style.

Jessica's grandfather, a mathematician, is also an honest man. The first time I meet him he is obviously uncertain about my relationship with Jessica. He thinks it's not realistic. He says that if we get married in the future, it will be hard for our kids. I learn that no one in Jessica's immediate family has married a non-Jew.

I love people who are honest with me, and, in this way, I love Jessica's grandpa.

Finally it is time for us to go to Wesleyan to start school. Wesleyan is a beautiful place, so green. While Jessica goes to pick up the key to her house, I kneel down to kiss the soil, this hallowed ground that took so much struggle to reach.

"May this place be my home for the next four years."

jessica

Kennedy is walking down the campus paths, carrying his books, and wearing a backpack and a Wesleyan T-shirt, looking like an entirely ordinary addition to Wesleyan's freshman class. Only I know how truly extraordinary each detail of college life is, how every mundane freshman ritual is suddenly turned magical. I relish sharing this new world with Kennedy, who makes me see everything with new eyes. We walk to the campus bookstore, and I delight in helping him pick out folders with Wesleyan's seal on the front for his classes. I notice how his fingers linger over the symbol, as if they too are trying to absorb it all.

We go to the campus coffee shop, Pi Café, and Kennedy discovers that he loves cappuccinos. We sit on the steps of the campus library drinking our cappuccinos, no words needed. I think of all the endless nights I've spent in this library and wonder about the papers Kennedy will write, the books he will discover, his own college journey unfolding before us. A foam mustache catches on his upper lip, and as I wipe it away, he takes me in his arms, burying his nose in my hair, his breath filled with possibility. He teases, "How will people know I drank a cappuccino if you wipe off the milk?" I laugh at his imitation of an American accent—or his "Denver accent," as he calls it. I notice that his Wesleyan T-shirt still has the tag on it, and I rip it off with a swift jerk.

"Hey! Now no one will know that it is new!" he exclaims.

"Believe me," I say with a smile, "they will know."

kennedy

I enjoy life at Wesleyan. The people are friendly and curious about me. There is food whenever I want it. One day Jessica sees me with a friend, who is from rural Kenya, running across the campus. She calls out to us, asking us why we are running.

I look hurriedly at my watch, it's twelve o'clock. "It's lunchtime; look how many people there are here. There is no way there will be enough food for everyone. At weddings in Kenya, you have to be first in line; otherwise you are out of luck. Let's go!"

I don't know why she is laughing instead of running. Then, Jessica tells me something incredible: I never have to run to get food here. A new friend, named Peter, explains further. He patiently tells me that here at Wesleyan the dining hall simply has times when it's "open," and when it is, they never run out of food. Nothing has ever seemed more unbelievable. Peter always looks at me when we go to eat together, enjoying my amazement at the variety—I want to try everything. Except for the salad: that is rabbit food. Peter also helps me navigate much of this new world.

When I write my first paper, I don't know how to use the printers. I am going to be late to my class, and I feel the panic rising—the feeling that I am out of place is overwhelming.

I frantically ask another student, "How do you print?"

I guess this is something that all *mzungus* just know how to do? He looks at me confused, but he presses several buttons in quick succession and my paper magically spurts out of the machine. I am so overjoyed I give him a huge hug. As I run to turn in my paper I see him shaking his head and know he must be thinking, *Why did that crazy African hug me for something so simple?* I'm realizing that the things that are simple for Americans here are not so for me. It turns out that he is the editor of the campus paper and soon he writes a story about my unexpected journey to Wesleyan.

I spread *The Argus,* the campus newspaper, out on a desk for Jessica to see. This is the second week in a row that they've run a full-page spread on my story.

"See this, Jess?"

She snatches it up. "They sure are running with it!"

"You're the one who told me that Americans will like my story." I had been reluctant to tell people where I was from at first, because I assumed I'd get the same reaction here that I always got in Kenya whenever I said I was from Kibera—fear and disdain. "I guess you were right. So many people have asked me to have lunch, or coffee, or dinner. Or to buy one of the SWEP bracelets from Kibera. I feel bad, I don't want to ask people their names if they know mine, so my phone has Lunch, Dinner, Coffee, and Bracelet in it." I shrug apologetically.

"Kennedy! You better just ask them, what are you going to do next? Lunch #1, Lunch #2?"

"*Sawa, sawa.*" I kiss her to send her on her way. "Don't be late to class!"

Soon everyone says hi to me everywhere I go. Jessica jokes that I've become the mayor here too.

I start taking her and Daphne on what I call "Meet the People Tours." We walk from house to house, and I just knock on the door and say "Hello!" whether I know the people or not. They always invite us in. We go in and have a few drinks, and suddenly we have new friends. More people on campus start wearing the colorful SWEP bracelets, and the SHOFCO movement spreads.

One night Jessica and I walk back from the library across the beautifully landscaped campus in the moonlight. We're under the same moon that hangs over Kibera, only there I never really noticed it.

"So I'm confused about something," I tell Jessica. "Can I ask you?"

"Of course!"

"So let me just get this straight. All I have to do here is read, go to class, discuss what we've read, and write some papers about it."

"I guess that's pretty much it."

"And I get to eat and take a shower, and everything I need is right here and that's all I have to do?"

Jessica just starts laughing, and it does sound like I'm poking fun. But I'm serious for once. "There is one thing I just don't understand. I think sometimes that I've died and gone to heaven, but I have one question. If this is heaven, why is it that I can still call home, I can still talk to that other world?"

She is suddenly serious too, seeing the pain in my face and hearing it in my voice.

"I guess I thought your fight would suddenly be over; instead it's just changed forms. You don't have to fight for your life here, but you do have to figure out how to be from your world and live in this one."

At least Jessica understands a little bit of what it is like, my two worlds. I take her hand in gratitude and we walk home together in silence.

I get a job at the library. My boss is a lady named Diane. She is tough, and I can tell that she thinks that some Wesleyan students are spoiled. I'm scared of Diane, and I don't want to cross her. One morning after working late on a paper, I oversleep and come into work at eight instead of seven. I am sweating. I am sure Diane is going to fire me, and then how will I help my family back home? The consequences of losing my job are dire. I go to Diane and apologize and tell her I was up late studying. I beg her to give me another chance. Surprisingly, she tells me not to worry; it will be okay. A week later, I am late again. This time is it because of something called daylight savings. No one explained to me that in America they just change the clocks all the time. I have my watch, but America changed the time on it. I don't know why.

Diane and the other lady working at the desk start laughing. She allows me to keep the job. I promise myself I will never be late again.

Another thing I don't understand, like the time change, is the gym. In my life I worked in a factory; I worked in construction. I sweated and sweated until I sweat blood. There is no way I'm going to a gym just to sweat. I just want to eat and eat and enjoy. The students drive from the dorms to the gym in their cars. Driving to the gym makes no sense to me.

I follow the news about immigration and so-called illegals with great interest. Here I am, a foreigner who has every intention of going back to my country after I complete my education. There is so much fear that people like me will take jobs away from "true" Americans. It seems to me that the United States has forgotten its glory. It was once the only country in the world that opened its door to immigrants. America has enjoyed the glory of being the superpower exactly because different people from different places contributed to its success.

Then I read in the news that the economy is falling down and something called Wall Street crashed. It reminds me of when Osama bin Laden crushed the buildings in New York. I go ask my mentor, Professor Rob. He is Rob Rosenthal, a professor of sociology, but he lets me call him Professor Rob. He once studied in Holland, and because he was American it was very challenging, and he wants to help me so I don't face so many difficulties.

"Professor, I have a question for you."

"Please feel free to ask," he says.

"Have we been attacked? Who attacked us this time? I hear they crashed a wall on the street in New York and that has affected the economy. I can't see the pictures; is everybody okay? What is going on?"

Professor Rob starts laughing. Why is my professor laughing so hard that he might fall off his chair? I feel embarrassed.

He tells me it's the economy that's crashed. It has nothing to do with a wall.

This country is so complicated.

One night there is a party on campus for Halloween. For this event, everyone is supposed to dress up in a costume, but I don't have one. My friend Nathan, who is quiet but so smart and kind, suggests we go to Goodwill to get costumes. As we drive there, I sit in the car thinking how strange my life has become, how disconnected it is from the world that I used to know, from what I would term the "real world." Now, in this new life, I am going to spend precious money to buy an outfit that I will only wear once. In my life in Kibera, such an idea would have seemed ludicrous.

When we arrive at Goodwill, we walk around for several minutes, but I feel sick to my stomach and feel my anger rising. Nathan sees that I hold nothing and asks if I plan to buy anything. I try to be polite.

"Buddy, I think I have something in the house that I can use after all."

Nathan looks straight into my face as if he reads something there. He refuses to buy anything either, and we leave the store empty-handed.

In the car I start laughing and Nathan joins me.

"Why did we change our minds?" he asks.

I become serious. "You know you are my friend, and I have to be honest with you. I felt bad, as a person who grew up in poverty, going to buy a piece of clothing that I'll only use once. I worked in the factories as an unskilled laborer for many years. I don't want to forget where I came from."

Nathan listens carefully and says he had been overcome with the same feeling, about the wastefulness of it. Even though we grew up in totally different worlds, he sees where I came from. He sees me, and he is a great friend to me.

Later that night, at the party, I notice residential life coordinators, public safety officers, and police officers who are all there simply to ensure our safety. When I was growing up, no one looked out for my safety like this. Every time I saw a police officer in Kenya, he was there to harass, not to protect, me. Police officers in Kenya would threaten to imprison me if I couldn't pay them a bribe, and my only crime was poverty.

I struggle to find my place here while I watch Jessica try to figure out what she wants to do after graduation. I wonder how her choice will affect our life together. I realize I came to the United States mainly to be with her. I hadn't prepared to leave everything in Kibera behind, or to deal with the demands and responsibilities of meeting the high expectations set for me that I don't have the educational background to meet. I am haunted by the fear that Wesleyan will discover my lack of competency and that, when they do, they will send me home to Kibera. While I'm not ready to go back home, I struggle to stay connected to the people there.

I start writing at Wesleyan. Professors encourage me to write down my experiences, and they start to pour out of me. I have a writing TA called Chachi who is so patient. She spends time helping me and tells me that I have something to say, to keep putting the words down on paper. She tells me that her mom, Abby, would love my story. I shrug; it's amazing to me that anyone could be so sincerely interested.

Sometimes my tears roll down when I remember how many years I had little or nothing to eat. I didn't care about the nutrition; I just wanted anything that could fill my stomach. I see many students who don't need to struggle because their future rests in the hands of their families. They have plenty of time to decide what to do after graduation. There are so many opportunities here in America that you don't have to rush.

In Kibera we don't have any options. When I was lucky enough to have a job, there was no option other than to wake up at three A.M. to work at a construction site, where I carried heavy blocks of stones upstairs with my bare hands and back. I feel lucky and blessed to have access to the best education here in the States. But I still think of the others around the world who don't have my opportunities. I know I don't deserve all these things that I have here in America. Life shouldn't be so based on luck, opportunities as hard to stumble upon as winning the lottery.

I am still not convinced that I am living in a world in which I don't need to walk for long distances in search of water, that I no longer have to fight with my mom about the water that I want to use for my weekly bath. I no longer have to stop eating and leave the remaining food for my little brother Hillary, who might go hungry if I feed myself well. It seems impossible that I no longer have to worry about what I'll eat tomorrow, that I no longer have to worry about whether I might not survive the year, or that I no longer have to worry I'll spend the night in the police cell—not because I am a criminal but because I met a policeman who asked for a bribe and I had nothing in my pocket to offer. I still have a hard time believing that I'm living in a world where I can decide to be a doctor, or a lawyer, or do whatever I want with my life.

After a while at Wesleyan, I develop a dream to become a doctor because everyone says that doctors make a lot of money, but I'm failing math and science. Jessica tells me that math and science build upon years and years of educational foundation, and I feel angry. I'm jealous of these American kids who had the opportunity to build that foundation. I know that although I am at Wesleyan now, I can never go back and replace all the years of school I missed.

I ask someone else, "What is the best way to make money in America?"

This person tells me to be a corporate lawyer, that they make tons of money. So now I have this idea to become a lawyer. I don't tell Jessica because she'll know that I'm failing myself. I came to America to study so I could help my community. But wouldn't I be able to help my community more if I can make a lot of money?

Then, one day, I realize I don't have to be a doctor or a lawyer. Instead, I can be a bridge to Kibera. I tell Jessica that I want to start a group on campus to spread the word about SHOFCO, "SHOFCO-Wesleyan."

"Good luck with that," she tells me. "It's very hard to mobilize people here."

Nathan loves Africa. I tell him about my idea to start a group at Wesleyan and he helps me bring people together. Six people come to the first meeting.

I welcome everyone with my thick accent. "Welcome to everybody in the room and thank you for coming. For me this means amazing things, that we do care. Wesleyan is a place of privilege. If you want to be the real Wesleyan, we have to think beyond our box. Let me start by giving my story, where I come from."

I share my story with these people, how I made it here. How with twenty cents I bought a soccer ball and started a soccer team, dreaming of a better life. I say, "Here at Wesleyan, we have more than twenty cents. We have connections, we have education, we have water, we have enough food: we can have an impact. If we can make the rest of the world a better place, that improvement will also happen here at Wesleyan."

After I give that speech, everybody is amazed. I can feel the fire coming from me and going directly into them. So we start a movement. I tell these six people to bring people, and I tell them to go share the story; it's a story of hope, it's a story of the future.

The next meeting is on a Friday night. That Friday the room is full. People pour in. Nathan is just laughing.

"Do it again, Kennedy."

jessica

I thought there would be something shatteringly equal about this trade we've made. In Kenya, I was living and walking in his world and now he is here, in mine. That maybe if we shared both worlds, they would stop belonging to either of us and both just become ours.

But we've been fighting since we got to school, little things lighting explosives between us. Kennedy always tries to keep his voice low, but it's hard for him to control, and the angrier he gets, the more his stammer takes hold.

Last night I hardly slept at all. I feel disoriented and bleary eyed, my joints achy. I'd promised I'd help him register for a class he wasn't sure how to get into, and I forgot. He was quiet, the way he gets when he is truly angry. He picked up his backpack and the MacBook that a kind librarian found for him to use and just left. I wanted to run after him, but my housemates were watching hockey in the living room and I knew them witnessing us fight would only make him angrier. All night, I've been trying to figure out what made him so incensed. All our fights recently are like this—on the surface absolutely nothing, but below them everything.

Sometimes, when we're arguing, and he doesn't answer his phone I close my eyes and try to play a game we made up in

Kibera. If, in the middle of a disagreement, one of us could track the other down, the fight would be instantly over, a winner declared, and surprisingly this still works at Wesleyan.

In my small room in my senior house, I have two sets of drawers, and Kennedy has all his stuff in one of them, even though he has his own room. During Parents Weekend, my mom came into my room and looked around, seeing how crowded it had become with our stuff.

"If he's not going to use his dorm room, you could use it for storage so at least Kennedy can see all the new clothes people have given him."

I knew my mom just wanted to help us get organized.

But Kennedy misunderstood and was furious.

"I know it! I get the message! Your parents, they don't want us to be together. I don't want to be together!" He stormed out.

I felt exhausted by his sensitivity. I have put everything into making the transition smooth for him. He didn't seem to notice or care. We didn't speak for two days after that, the longest we'd ever gone without talking. Finally I sought him out and we quickly mended things, the love between us undeniable.

Maybe it was naive to think that we could just take our love and transpose it here, with all these new expectations and pressures. He changed my life, and in turn I offered him this chance to change his. In my African American theory class, my professor said something I just can't shake: that interracial marriage is more common than interclass marriage. Even though Kennedy is now here at Wesleyan, the difference between us sometimes seems even more pronounced.

kennedy

One night, after Jessica and I have been fighting, we make up, as we always do, and decide for old times' sake to make *chapati* in her kitchen. We're working in the kitchen when my phone rings.

It's my sister Liz. I am filled with eager anticipation at the sound of her voice. But I can tell, right away, that there is something wrong.

She's pregnant, at nineteen. My baby sister. I flash back to when my sister Jackie told me she was pregnant at seventeen. I feel anger, disappointment, and frustration. I feel like I have failed her.

"How long have you known?" I ask her.

"A few months," she says.

Liz says that she was raped. She was out late one night, drinking, and accosted on the way home. She says she was so ashamed that she didn't say anything about it afterward. She thought it was her fault.

I ask her to visit a clinic and have herself tested for HIV. I promise to send her money for the test.

The phone call ends. What I feel is unbearable. Tears start falling from my cheeks.

"I wish there was something I could do. I wish there was anything I could do."

I cry all night, and Jessica holds me. African men cry inside their hearts, not outside, but this night I cannot help myself. I feel the absence of my sister, my community keenly.

For days, as we wait for the results of the HIV test, I can't think of anything else. I don't understand how these two worlds— Kibera and Wesleyan—can both be happening at the same time. I am angry at these kids here, these kids who have no idea or appreciation for what life has simply handed them. The lives my mother and sisters live haunt me. Although I'm halfway across the world, my entire mind is dwelling on Kibera.

I'm scared for the future of SHOFCO, my organization that has grown from nothing to something. It has been my everything, and it is the one sign of hope for my community.

I go to Jessica. "I know what I want to do. I want to be a bridge, but that is just the beginning. I want to build a school in Kibera, a school for girls like my sisters, so that we can have women leaders, instead of women who are raped and abused. The Kibera School for Girls."

"The Kibera School for Girls," Jessica echoes, watching my face intently and seeing on my features that this is no passing fancy. Because I tell her, it begins to seem like it could be real.

Jessica and I start discussing more openly the life of girls in my community, how Babi treats my mom, how when I walked down the streets of Kibera I would see little girls playing in the sewage and know that too often they were forced to trade their bodies for food simply to survive. I remember the tiny girl Beatrice in a bloodstained dress after she was raped. In my mind's eye, I see the boys hanging out smoking *bange* and making disparaging remarks about the women who pass by, bragging about the women they have taken. I tell her about the girls who contracted HIV/AIDS and the girls who got pregnant when they were still children themselves. My sister is only one example, but these things happen constantly in the community without being reported. Maybe we can change this.

I was born to an underage woman who was denied an education and could not prosper. My stepfather mistreated my mother, and she was often beaten almost to death, but she never gave up on her kids. She taught me how to care about other people and to take action in order to change things. My mom believes in education and instilled in me the value of women, despite all the degradation they suffered around me. I recall how my mother would always make me wash dishes, which was very unusual, taking turns alongside my sisters. When I complained that I was a boy, she told me that for complaining I could now go outside and wash them in the open where everyone could see. This school will be for her.

I want to see the women in my community taking charge, both of their education and their children's. I am willing to offer my life so that women and girls have equal access to a good future. But I want to involve the whole community: men, women, and children. For the world to change we must work in solidarity.

The school I dream of will nurture and care for students, providing them with a curriculum that will inspire them to love learning and to think critically about the world, unlike the informal "schools" that Kibera children attend. There students stand stiff, aware that the immediate result of any wrong move or wrong answer might be a beating. And teachers would use the Bible to justify these punishments: "The Bible said a child must be beaten to be a better person." Of course children detest going to this kind of school. Given the conditions, they have no reason to want to keep struggling for an education when they have to struggle for everything else.

The Kibera School for Girls will encourage little girls to believe in themselves and nurture them to become future leaders.

One afternoon, Jessica comes rushing up to me.

"Come here," she implores, practically dragging my full weight. "There is something I want you to see."

She pulls me into the campus center and points to a sign: 100 PROJECTS FOR PEACE, $10,000 GRANTS. The Kathryn Wasserman Davis Foundation will fund a hundred projects that contribute to world peace. Each project will receive $10,000 to make its proposal a reality.

"What?!" I ask her, confused. She wants to work on world peace now?

"Your school for girls!" she exclaims. "We could apply to build your school for girls."

"It's for peace projects, Jessica. That means stuff in war zones."

"Educated women invest 90 percent of their earnings in family, have children later who are more likely to survive, and are significantly less likely to become HIV positive. In communities where more women are educated, child mortality drops, and economics improve; it impacts everything," Jessica lectures me. "I think we can make a strong case that a school for girls in one of Africa's largest slums does contribute to a more peaceful world."

"I don't think we'll get it," I tell her, shaking my head. I walk away, afraid to fail.

But Jessica, like a dog with a bone, refuses to drop it. A few nights later, she hands me her first draft of the grant application.

"What do you think?" she asks nervously. "Of course it's not done. I would need you to tell me how we actually do this, like fill in the details about where we would get the land to build it, how we would find teachers—I've outlined all those questions in bold . . ."

My heart is full of emotion. I look her in the eyes. "It's great." I see in her eyes that she will make me go through with this. Her belief in me makes me in turn believe in this crazy, impossible dream.

I read a line aloud, a great line:

"This is the very first primary school for girls in the slum providing a superior, creative education, daily nourishment, and a refuge from the pressures of the slum."

"My God, Jess. Do you think we could actually do this?"

She takes my hand in hers. "If you tell me how to navigate the logistics, I understand the educational piece and can make a plan for your school."

I take her hands in mine now. "I believe it. You can make anything happen. And it's *our* school." And it is, I want it to be.

"You need to make it more personal," Daphne says after reading our grant proposal. It's one in the morning and the proposal is due at noon tomorrow. "I'm thinking, if I'm the committee, how do I know that you guys can do this?" Daphne asks. "It sounds pretty far-fetched to me, that is, if I didn't know either of you."

"Daphne has a point," Jessica says. "We should add in some more specifics." She's been hounding me for what she calls specifics, but I already have a very clear vision of how I want the school to be.

It's got to be a primary school, because by the time secondary school begins, the most vulnerable girls have long since dropped out—already locked out of future opportunities. By starting with early childhood education, we can teach the brightest and the most vulnerable girls from the start, when education is so important.

I add more about the obstacles that the girls will face, which could keep them from showing up every day. Girls in Kibera are sometimes left with no options but to trade their bodies for food because there is no other way to survive. The lack of access to quality health care and resources often prevents girls from staying in school. The lack of value placed on women and girls means many of the most vulnerable girls never start school at all. This school will clear the way for these girls to reach their full potential.

I even have ideas of people who could be the teachers, the lucky few people I know from Kibera who received a church-sponsored education and went on to make something of themselves, becoming teachers. I might be able to persuade some of them to return to Kibera.

We get an e-mail saying we're finalists for the prize and must come in for an interview. The committee asks countless questions: *How will we get the land? Who will build the school? Who will run it?*

I just follow my heart and my instincts as I answer.

"Was any of that true?" Jessica asks me afterward, incredulous.

"Well, it will be. We'll make it all come true."

She shakes her head.

A few days later, I receive an e-mail, and I start screaming for Jess.

"What is it?!"

"We got the 100 Projects for Peace!"

We are jumping up and down. I call my mom to share the news. Ten thousand dollars seems like all the money in the world.

fifteen

jessica

Kennedy's dream of the Kibera School for Girls has started to become a reality, and now it's my dream too; it's powerful to share a dream together.

We're on our way back to Nairobi—my brother, Max, in tow—with just six weeks to execute our school plan. Kennedy has won a human rights fellowship in Paris for the month of June, leaving us only July and half of August in Kenya. He talks endlessly about going back home for the summer, about seeing George and Liz, about his mom.

I spend every hour after we get the Projects for Peace grant embroiled in planning. I make detailed daily schedules outlining construction progress and deadlines, hiring plans, budgets, student admissions policies. I work with a volunteer architect from Architects for Humanity, who designs beautiful plans for the school. I read every book and article I can find about early childhood development and curriculum. The curriculum and teaching style I envision are based largely on my own background attending an experientially based K-8 school in Denver. When I feel overcome by the many challenges of implementing the class-room mission, I think, *What would Lisa Davis*—the teacher I had for kindergarten and first grade—*have done?* A former head of my school in Denver, Marty Caplan, and his wife, Arna, spend a few years helping our teachers implement innovative math and literacy curricula. The Chapin School, a premiere New York City girls' school gets involved, helping develop admissions tests, curriculum, and teacher training. Organizing all of these pieces feels vaguely familiar—like producing a play, only with real-world implications.

On the plane I pull out the folder with my Excel spreadsheet. We have so little time in Kenya before we have to go back for the start of Kennedy's sophomore year and the start of my fellowship at Wesleyan. Six weeks—nowhere near enough time to build an entire school. I have every day meticulously planned out with goals and milestones. I have deadlines for hiring teachers, teacher training, student recruitment, and the purchasing of furniture and materials. If everything goes exactly according to plan, six weeks will be just enough, although I haven't really calculated time for sleep.

I keep asking Kennedy if the land is really there.

"Don't worry. I'm the mayor. I'll figure it out when we get there." I want to strangle him.

No matter what I ask, he says the same thing: "Don't worry. We'll figure it out when we get there."

"Passengers, we're approaching Nairobi."

I feel the plane start to descend, and the butterflies flutter in my stomach. I can't believe I'm going back. I felt so certain when we left to go to college last summer that I had said my last good-byes to Kenya. I can see Kennedy's excitement and also his nerves, which I share.

Kennedy's mom and Liz, who's very pregnant, and Kennedy's other sisters, Jackie and Jasmine, all stand waiting for us as we exit customs. They shout with joy. You can see the surprise and delight on their faces that Kennedy has actually returned. They hug me and I feel enveloped by the warmth of their skin, the perspiration on his mom's big cheeks. They hug my brother, Max: he looks less than comfortable.

Kennedy is so excited to get to Kibera that he can barely sleep. He wakes up early, and together with Max we take a *matatu* to the SHOFCO office in Olympic. But when Kennedy opens the door, he's horror-struck. We all are. The office has been ravaged. Some of the furnishings are gone and all five computers donated by the American Friends of Kenya are missing.

kennedy

I never should have left. The desks where our precious donated computers used to sit are empty. I want to wind back time and find them still there. I'm in a cold sweat of anger and betrayal.

I imagined being here would feel like coming home, but home is not the same because people here don't see me in the same way. Some are shocked that I am back, calling me stupid for not staying in the land of milk and honey. Others are welcoming, their joy palpable, but it's as if they no longer see the street boy who ate chips on these corners and grew up in these crannies. Now I am seen as different and because of that they want something from me. I start to feel like there is some hidden intent behind every exchange. I am suddenly the lifeline not only for my family, but for the whole community—fielding requests for money, for jobs—and sometimes this burden feels inspiring but other times it's unmanageable. Thankfully I have Jessica to share some of this weight, but the implications of leaving, the impossibility of returning—it all makes me feel like I can't breathe.

It turns out that Antony sold the computers in my absence. He is nowhere to be seen and doesn't answer my phone calls. My friend since the age of nine, Antony bought me my first pair of underwear. I kept my secrets with him. Jessica kept her passport in Antony's house for safekeeping when she first lived at my house in Kibera. He was one of SHOFCO's biggest supporters. His betrayal is unexpected and monumental. It's becoming clear just how much I gave up to come to America: not just the forward progress with SHOFCO, but the trust that I had with my people here.

I take Jessica down a garbage-lined path to see one of the houses I lived in later in my teen years with a gang of local boys. The trash is deeply layered and wet from the recent rain, and it seeps into our shoes; I notice its squelch as never before. We have to crouch when we get close; the alleyway is so narrow and the overhangs of the sharp iron-sheet roofs protrude. I reach out my hand protectively to block Jessica from cutting her head on a particularly sharp corner. We arrive at one of the crudest shacks on the alley. Made from mud and sticks, with huge holes in the walls and cardboard and patches of iron sheet on the roof, this used to be my shack. So small and exposed to the elements, it seems impossible that I once found a way to survive here.

"This is it, I lived here," I say quietly. Jessica doesn't speak, pain apparent on her face. I know it's hard for her to think of me living here. I knock gently on the door and a woman opens it.

I see instantly that she knows who I am.

"Mama," I begin respectfully, "I used to live here. Could we come in?" Her face dissolves in disbelief, and then she grabs my hand and pulls me inside, shouting with pride so that all the neighbors can hear that Kennedy Odede once lived here too.

jessica

As the next several days unfold, I learn that there is, in fact, no land on which to build the school, only potential locations, but nothing agreed or concrete. The problem is that there is just no empty land in Kibera. Without a place to build the school, well, there will be no school.

In despair, I look at the schedule and all the spreadsheets that I've created, and it feels like everything is falling apart. I feel like giving up—we didn't have time to lose even a day.

In the face of Antony's betrayal, Kennedy grows even closer to George. George was the person who helped Kennedy secure the land for SHOFCO's first small iron-sheet office near the railway line. Every afternoon George and Kennedy meet for drinks, talking for long hours, strategizing and planning—often switching from Swahili to Luo, leaving me out of the conversation entirely. Their heads are bent deep in thought. George is a man of action.

After a few days, George discovers a piece of land in the heart of Kibera. An international organization had secured the rights to build on it, even getting letters and approvals so everything was ready to go. But when they went to build, the community protested, making construction impossible.

Here in Kibera there are two governments: one is the formal government, and the second is the community with its complex hierarchy of elders and local leaders like George. You can get letters upon letters from the formal government, but if the community doesn't agree, it doesn't matter—nothing will ever be built.

To secure this land for the school, it seems there are several steps. The first is to get permission from the community. The second is to get permission from the local informal government. The third is to somehow secure formal approval.

So Kennedy works tirelessly to get everyone in the community on board with this idea of a school for girls. He wants everyone to know that this is a local project, part of SHOFCO sprouting from the inside, and that it belongs to the community.

I'm not allowed to go and see the land; in fact, I am forbidden to leave Olympic. Kennedy's convinced that as soon as people see me, they'll think that there is *mzungu* money or that Kennedy is beholden to someone in America. For this school to survive, it will have to grow entirely out of the community, not be seen as imposed from the outside. No matter how much respect Kennedy commands, if Max and I show up, the price of the land could skyrocket, the sellers eager to capitalize on *mzungu* money. That makes it easier to stay out of sight: our budget doesn't even have wiggle room for extra pencils.

I spend hours staring at my Excel file every day, wishing there was some way to reorganize the cells to increase the money or make it go further. On top of the $10,000 from 100 Projects for Peace, we managed to raise another $8,000 from the family of Kennedy's classmate Yael Chanoff, to which we added many other small donations from friends and family. But even in Kibera, where every dollar goes so far—building an entire school, hiring staff, buying furniture and school supplies—it will be a very close shave.

I repeat this to Kennedy every night as we're going to bed, but his response only makes me more nervous.

He merely repeats, "This is an idea whose time has come."

I wish I could share in his undaunted optimism, his conviction that there is always some way—that money doesn't matter.

We are too far along to change course, but only now do I fully realize what a gargantuan commitment this is. Even if we manage to build the place with the resources we have, we will still need ongoing cash flow to pay salaries. Since we are targeting the most vulnerable girls, the only meals they are sure to get will be at school. What good are lessons if they have nothing in their bellies? So we'll also need to find money to buy breakfast and lunch for years to come.

And nothing is happening. My meticulous plans have proven completely useless. Max and I spend our days in the SHOFCO office talking, napping on a mattress, waiting for word of what's happening. We are already almost a week behind. I call Kennedy at nearly hourly intervals to check on his progress. Fifty percent of the time he doesn't answer, so I call George. Eventually Kennedy tells him to stop answering too. I still call, because there is nothing else to do.

"You should stop that. You're making it worse," Max says as he reclines on the mattress, throwing a tennis ball up and down.

"Would you stop it with that tennis ball? You're making me dizzy. And if I don't call, who knows if anything will *ever* get done."

"You know your strength and weakness, Jess?" Max asks. "If there is a burning building, most people cross the street. Not you, you run right in."

Suddenly a tiny version of Kennedy comes tumbling through the door: three-year-old Hillary, whom I met in Kennedy's village. Kennedy's mom, Ajey, has been unwell, so she's come back to the city, bringing Kennedy's youngest brother. Ajey spends her days resting—overcome with fatigue, as if the past thirty-nine years have finally caught up with her—while Hillary runs the streets unsupervised.

Babysitting a three-year-old isn't what I'd envisioned doing for the summer, but it looks like this is it. He and Max hit it off. Hillary doesn't speak any English, so Max takes it upon himself to teach him. I hear them practicing and shake my head at the few phrases Max has deemed important starting places.

"Are you mad?" Max asks.

"MAYBE!" Hillary responds.

"Are you crazy?" Max asks.

"WHAT IS WRONG WITH YOU?" Hillary shouts back.

"Get out!" Max points to the door.

"I'll fight you," Hillary says, pumping his fists like a boxer. "John Cena!" he shouts, before running to the mattress and throwing himself on it sumo-wrestler-style, as if he's just won the boxing world series.

"You do realize that those lovely phrases are all the English he knows, right?" I ask.

"Isn't it great?" Max smiles.

Kennedy and George wake up early the next morning to get the final permissions they need for the land, and they come back elated. Everyone has agreed. But Kennedy warns me that it is not as big as we hoped.

"What does that mean?"

"Well, those plans you've made. They are going to need some adjustments."

I think about the beautiful plans, about all the back and forth that I engaged in with the architect. The building was designed to maximize space and natural light and ventilation—the plans consumed nearly a month of my attention.

I just nod my head. It seems at this point "adjustments" will be inevitable. I'm starting to learn that it's easier here not to have expectations.

Over the next few days, George and Kennedy frantically engage construction workers and a man named Subiti, who they say is the best local architect. I still haven't even seen the site. Subiti and I go over my plans. He takes one look and starts drawing all over them, striking through many of the ecofriendly features that I had worked so hard on.

"What are you doing?" I cry with alarm.

He smiles at me, three of his front teeth missing. "I am making it good for Kibera."

"You're ruining it!"

"He's not ruining it; he's just trying to adjust," George intervenes, trying to mediate.

On the first day that the crews start construction, George calls me at about twelve and all he says is, "Don't worry. Everything's fine, no matter what you hear."

He hangs up. I try calling back and calling back and calling back, but he doesn't answer. All I can think frantically is *What's going on? What might I hear?* I am not allowed to go to the site until construction is halfway complete. I fume and pace in the office.

Late in the day, Kennedy and George make their way to the office, the mood heavy. As the groundbreaking commenced, a few men with machetes had come barreling in, trying to sabotage the construction.

"What happened next?"

Subiti and his local crew had their own machetes, and before Kennedy could intervene, Subiti slashed the cheek of one of the attackers, yelling, "You can't stop community development!"

Kennedy jumped in the middle of it and told everyone to calm down. He immediately paid for the injured man to go to the hospital.

The community was dumbfounded, and Subiti yelled at Kennedy, "That guy came to overthrow your project and you're paying for him to go to the hospital?"

But Kennedy shrugged. "Poverty will make people do some crazy things. I just felt sorry for him."

The next day, the attackers come back to apologize to Kennedy and admit they had been paid to cause trouble. A few days after that, they show up to help with the building.

George pulls me aside. "Ken doesn't want me to tell you this, but I think you should know. Antony paid someone to hurt Ken. By good luck most people he can pay here are loyal to Ken, so the guy told Ken. But he needs to be careful."

This knocks the wind out of me.

So many people seem genuinely surprised that Kennedy's come back, most of them elated. As he walks Kibera's streets, he's even more of a celebrity than before. Everyone wants to talk to him, to congratulate him, to feel that through him their struggle is also recognized. But I'm sure that there are some people who see his success and ask *Why him and not me?*, when the answer is, it should be both.

The more time I spend here, the more intelligent and enterprising people I meet. One of the cruelest aspects of this place is simply the wasted human potential, the brilliance and creativity that exists. It shouldn't be impossible to break out of poverty—talent and hard work should matter—but here they don't. If our school can do one thing, maybe it's this: reward the talent and hard work of girls by providing a path out and then back in like the one that Kennedy has forged.

But in one moment, Antony or someone else overcome with envy could take everything away.

"Why? Why does Antony want to hurt Kennedy?"

"Jealousy is something powerful. He wants to show Ken how important he was in SHOFCO, and how Ken can't succeed without him."

"And so he wants the school to fail? And he'd go so far as to hurt Kennedy?"

George shrugs; in his world, that is just how issues so often get solved.

"Thanks for telling me," I say.

"Talk to him, he'll listen to you. Tell him not to take risks, not to be out at night, to take different routes when he leaves."

I nod, understanding. "I'll talk to him."

I confront Kennedy about the man who was bribed to hurt him. My breath catches in my throat and I ask how, how much, why.

Kennedy shakes his head sadly in confirmation and says, "Only a thousand shillings can hire a gun for a day, here. Antony wants to make sure that I don't succeed."

"Is this for real? Seriously, Antony?"

"Yes. George thinks that he could do anything. He's become crazy with jealousy."

It does feel real. I feel vulnerable, as if everything I have and love could be taken from me in an instant. I have a sudden memory of the year before when I lived with Kennedy and his family deep inside Kibera, of how carefree I felt, how naive I was and, as Kennedy said, how lucky that nothing had gone wrong. I struggle to match up the Kibera I knew with the Kibera Kennedy described during the election violence.

"Should we stop? Should we go home?"

"No. The school must be built."

George and Kennedy successfully convince the city power company to put in our own legal power pole, but it's going to add $1,500 to our budget that we just don't have. I'm trying to cut expenses everywhere, but between teacher salaries for six months, school supplies, money for the meal program, furniture, and finishing construction—by my count we're another $1,500 over our original budget, bringing the total deficit to $3,000. We've asked everyone we can think of already. I don't know how we're going to make up that difference, and if we don't, what then? No power? Or delay construction?

I write furiously on the yellow legal pad where I meticulously record every purchase before transferring it into Excel, and I reach for the accordion file where I keep all the receipts. I add and re-add, but soon I'm just punching the calculator buttons in frustration.

"NO."

"Take it easy there, cowgirl," Max says.

"Shut up," I shoot back. "Kennedy is late, as usual," I mutter.

We're supposed to meet him and George to hand over money I withdrew at the bank. It feels strange, to have a few hundred dollars in cash on me, but we can't afford to use checks because all the materials we need are cheaper on the local market from small-scale suppliers who don't accept any other type of payment. It's amazing to me, the different economies that operate simultaneously. Because SHOFCO and Kennedy are beloved locally, they can buy construction materials, even pens and pencils, from the local stores and vendors at incredibly affordable prices—prices given to no one else. It's because of Kennedy's ability to do this that our money has gone even this far. If I walk into the same shop, they'll sell me the exact same item for almost double the price.

At first I found this strange or even unjust—that people would mark up their prices to nonlocals, even when dealing with well-intentioned organizations providing education or health care—but the more Kennedy and I talked about it, the more it started to make sense. It is almost like a sliding scale. People just assess that outsiders could afford to pay more and still call it a deal, and in this way everyone does well. For Kennedy, it is as if the cheapest price was almost like a partial donation, each individual vendor's way of telling him they believed in what he was doing. And we're extremely grateful, since every single shilling needs to go as far as possible. I'm meticulous about documenting everything, keeping every receipt in order, every cent carefully accounted for.

This is especially important since Kennedy and I have been discussing another groundbreaking idea. We don't want to charge school fees. The school itself will be entirely free, and this will include everything: school supplies, uniforms, breakfast and lunch—even an after-school snack—so that our girls never struggle to learn on an empty stomach.

Our idea is that instead of collecting money, we will require families to volunteer at the school five weeks a year in exchange for their daughters' educations. While many of our students may not have parents, it can be anyone willing—a sister, brother, father, aunt, a neighbor—anyone willing to contribute a very valuable form of payment: time. Kennedy isn't sure it will work, but we've agreed to give it a try, so when we conduct the admissions interviews, we'll ask families if there is anyone willing to make this commitment.

Finally I am allowed onto the site of the school. Our school.

I close my eyes and inhale the smell of cool earth. I marvel at the structure; the frame of the building and each room consists of a lattice of strips of wood, packed with mud. Once dry, they will cover these walls with plaster. I walk down the narrow corridor—only enough space for one person to pass at a time—into my favorite room at the end: the library. I stand in the middle of the room. It is big and open—especially compared to the other classrooms, which are small by necessity. This room feels so peaceful.

We're on the hill that is the very edge of Kibera, right above the river that once flowed clear when Ken was a boy, but now is little more than sewage. Still, somehow being on this hill, looking out into the green suburbs on the other side, I feel alone with the trees.

When they dug the foundation, they found an inconvenient layer of rock in this room about three feet high. We couldn't bring a machine down here to remove it because there is no power that reaches this far, so the men and women building the school chopped at it with little axes, breaking it piece by tiny piece. Then Max had the ingenious idea to leave a strip at the back of the room as a "stage."

I sit on the "stage's" edge. It's still jagged, but I imagine it after it's been covered by concrete—smooth. I smile thinking of the performances that might take place on this stage, the poems, songs, plays. I picture this entire room with the walls covered by children's artwork, when windows fill the now gaping holes, when one day there will be tables and chairs and books. My further conversations with Subiti the architect had gone much better over beer, and he agreed to the skylights and the airways, along with the general design.

"You look happy," Kennedy says softly, standing in the empty door frame. I didn't even notice him there. He is smiling and sweaty; he's been helping with construction too since everyone started to make some good-spirited fun about how America had made him soft, no longer able to perform the hard labor that was once his entire life. Never one to let a challenge go, Kennedy grabbed a shovel and, for the past three days, hasn't put it down.

No one seems overly concerned about getting it all right. The skylights, which everyone fought me on terribly, are not evenly spaced. The ventilation gaps—between where the top of the walls and the ceiling meet—are smaller than I'd imagined. I kept writing down the daily changes in the measurements, trying to keep up, to adapt to Subiti's daily alterations, in my obsession to capture it all. It seems that to get a builder who cares about exact measurements, you might have to pay more than we have.

One day George gently explained that while I might not be able to let go of my own vision for the school, I should trust Subiti. Here in Kibera, he is seen as a man of vision too—the best local architect around. The school might not look exactly as I'd so carefully measured and planned, but it might turn out just as beautiful, even endearing in its imperfections.

"I *am* happy," I breathe quietly. I can't believe that we've made it this far.

Kennedy stands in the doorway taking it all in.

"Want to sit?" I ask. "This stage is comfortable."

"The stage was a good idea." He laughs. "I've never seen those people who were hacking away at the rock look so relieved. Max was like a small god."

"It's going to be beautiful," I say.

"I told you not to worry," he says. He gently pulls out a bit of dried mud from my hair. Today, I joined in the construction too, motivated mostly by anxiety about how long it's taking. I thought if I participated, it might spur things along. For the first thirty minutes no one took me seriously, everyone laughing and yelling things at Kennedy in Luo that he didn't translate. But I stuck with it, and it turns out I'm a faster mud layer than a lot of the men. Many of the women are still faster than I am. And today, we got much more done.

Subiti and some of the other men had been skeptical about hiring women at all, but Kennedy and George insisted. Now no one makes a big deal of their participating in construction, but because I'm white they see it differently. People make fun of Kennedy for it, as if he is somehow implicated by my unruliness.

"You're stubborn!" he had whispered as he inspected my handiwork and handed me a better shovel. Now my arms ache, but I think I made my point.

"Next time you tell me not to worry I won't believe you, seeing how you didn't really plan anything, and yet you still told me not to worry!"

"But it's working out, right?" he says with a devilish smile.

"Not yet . . ."

"You'll make it work out," he says with an unconcerned wave of his hand. "Say you'll stop worrying," he insists, kissing me abruptly. He takes my flip-flop in his hand and tosses it across the room in one swift motion.

"Kennedy!" I shriek. "Don't you dare."

He flexes his fingertips menacingly, in the way he always does when threatening to tickle me. He moves to my other foot and grabs hold of the shoe.

"Say it," he says again.

"Give my shoe back!"

He drops it just out of my reach and starts to tickle me, and I shriek helplessly. I try to squirm away, and we slide off the stage and onto the dirt floor. He's stronger than I am and ruthless. I grapple for his armpit, and he squeals and slithers away, still holding my foot.

"Stop, stop! You know what they say in my culture; if you tickle a man, he won't be able to ever give children!"

"You're such a liar. You can't always use that, just make up that something is 'against your culture' when it's convenient." I giggle.

He raises his eyebrows in feigned innocence.

"It worked in America!" He moves his hand up to my ankle. "Say that you'll stop worrying."

"Fine, you win, okay? I will *try* to stop worrying."

He kisses me, gently this time, laying me on my back on the unfinished floor. I pull him down toward me.

"I like doing this with you," he whispers.

"I know," I say.

"I didn't mean that." He grins. "I mean this, building this together with you."

sixteen

jessica

Now that the building is well under way, George and I put up signs advertising admission to the school. We make hundreds of copies of the ad and put them up on all the streets of Kibera. We also get on the radio to announce the opportunity: "We are taking girls from the ages of four to six to fill our preschool, our kindergarten, and our first-grade classes."

Before we left for Kenya, people often asked me if parents here would allow girls to go to school, even if such a school existed. Kennedy got worked up at that question, and he would respond that he believes the gender disparity that exists in Kibera's schools is not cultural, a statement of the relative value of girls, but actually primarily economic. In Kibera 43 percent of adolescent girls are enrolled in school, compared to 29 percent of boys.[*] But Kennedy explained that when families are forced to choose which child to send to school because they simply cannot afford to

---

[*] A. Erulkar and J. K. Matheka, *Adolescence in the Kibera Slums of Nairobi, Kenya* (New York: Population Council, 2007).

send both, they choose the boy because they see his education as a long-term financial investment. In Kibera, men are much more likely to get the only jobs available, working in a factory or at a construction site. There are hardly any actual jobs for women, and so it is assumed that instead of being economic contributors to their family, they will get married.

The morning we start doing the interviews for admissions, the line of parents bringing their daughters forms well before 6:30. We can only accept forty-five students: fifteen each in preschool, kindergarten, and first grade. Kennedy and I push through, and people crowd around us as he takes out the keys to open the gate. Working quickly, we put chairs out, but it's clear that we don't have nearly enough. I instruct Max to make a sign-in sheet and try to register people as they come and ask for the age of their child. Soon, he yells at me in bewilderment, besieged by clamoring parents trying to get their names written down first.

"Everyone is saying their child is the 'right age.' How will I know?"

I raise my eyebrows at Kennedy, looking for an answer.

He shakes his head. "Most people don't have birth certificates. If they have anything, it's a clinic card." This is going to be even harder than I'd thought.

Kennedy and I set up the interview room. We stack several plastic chairs atop one another facing the desk, so that the child will be at eye level. I unpack the tangram puzzles and photocopied assessments. We've thought a lot about the interviewing method and rules we'll use. Just thinking of the teeming courtyard, I can feel how hard this will be and am grateful for the clear guidelines we've set. I'm responsible for the first round of interviews, which will be an early childhood assessment that measures the student's potential through testing her verbal competency, fine motor development, problem solving skills, determination, and creativity—potential. Developed with the help of several early childhood education experts, the assessment includes a tangram puzzle, on which points are given both for perseverance and for quickness of solving. In one part the applicant is asked to draw someone important to her. As she draws, I'm to ask questions about the person. Some children will be able to draw and talk at the same time and others won't—points are given for multitasking, as well as for the number of body parts the figure drawing has.

Without the funding or infrastructure to accept all the girls who deserve this chance, we've decided we want to make the highest-impact investments possible with our limited funds. First, we want the very most vulnerable girls. Girls who, without this opportunity, will never have the chance to go to school. Even in Kibera, class exists. Some families earn enough money to pay to send their children to informal schools—inside the slums there are no official government schools. Those exist only in Kibera's surrounding lower-middle-class neighborhoods and they don't have enough spaces. While primary education is supposed to be free in Kenya, it isn't always because the schools don't get the support they need. Thus schools often invent their own creative fee systems. Sometimes these alternative fee structures become more expensive than schools were before primary education became free. While Kibera's informal schools may not provide the best quality, at least if a girl is in such a school, she is off the streets.

Second, we want the very brightest. By educating the next generation of girls who will grow up to be successful leaders—lawyers and doctors and maybe even government officials—the school can effect tremendous long-term change in Kibera and beyond. Just one of our girls might one day affect millions of lives, more people than we will ever reach directly. Indeed, the success of our girls has the potential to have a powerful multiplier effect.

After the first round of assessments is done, we'll take about the top 50 percent of the scores (a pretty generous spread), and Kennedy will proceed to conduct home visits to each and every one of these families to assess the family's need, looking for details to evaluate their economic status. How many other children are there and are they in school? Do they have power? What is the house itself made out of and how many household items are owned? Are there other factors that make this child more vulnerable? Without us, will they send their daughter to another informal school? We'll then rank using the combined "need score" and "potential score" to admit our first students.

We've also agreed on a few other things—we have a one-child-per-family rule so as to spread out the opportunity as much as possible. We will also look for ethnic and religious diversity. With the postelection violence in mind, we can't help but think that if children go to school with others from different ethnic groups and religions, tolerance will result.

These rules give me some semblance of a system to cling to, and frankly, to hide behind. All these girls deserve a chance. I can't help but feel anger at the world's disparity that denies each of them the tremendous opportunities they all deserve.

I walk downstairs and get the list from Max—already fifty girls long and it's not yet eight o'clock. I see clearly on these hopeful parents' faces that they know that education is the best pathway to a better life for their daughters and for their families.

Hillary trounces through the courtyard and confidently makes his way upstairs. He doesn't ask before sitting down in the chair we've set up for the interviewees and starting to arrange the tangram puzzle. In about a minute, he's completed it perfectly.

"Well, we don't have to worry about his determination or fine motor skills," I mutter to Kennedy. "What am I supposed to do with him here all day? Can you take him?"

"Jess, I have a meeting with the chief of the area today, and then the district commissioner and the district education officer; you'll have to figure it out."

He kisses me on the cheek before leaving, and I suddenly feel completely desperate, entirely unprepared.

"Not one peep," I tell Hillary, pressing my finger to my lips to make sure he understands. He shrugs impudently in reply, but he does get out of the chair for the applicant. He pulls another chair to the side of the desk, as if setting himself up to be an assistant judge.

"Robyn Adhiambo," I call out from the top of the stairs. A little girl comes forward with perfectly even braids in her hair, and her mother starts to follow her upstairs—she looks much younger than me. I tell her in Swahili that it's children only; we talk to parents later. We decided that applicants have to do the interview alone, because Kennedy worries that parents will want this chance so badly that they might punish their children if they see them not doing well.

Robyn continues up the stairs without looking back at her mom—clearly confidence isn't an issue. She hoists herself up in the chair and looks at me, waiting for my next move. She's incredibly together for four, adorable and entirely serious.

"Your name is Robyn?" I ask in Swahili. I've been practicing the assessment in Swahili for days to make sure I can do it flawlessly. She raises her eyebrows to say yes, making her eyes big. She completes the assessment flawlessly and then just sits back to look at me, as if now I'm under examination. Then I invite Robyn's mom in to tell me a little bit about herself. Robyn's mom looks like she can't be more than early twenties. She's skinny, with striking features, and carries another little baby with her. Is she willing to work five weeks a year in exchange for Robyn's free education?

"Absolutely." She says she never went to school but knows that Robyn is bright and has potential, and that she would do anything to make sure she gets that chance.

In the courtyard another little girl stands perfectly still, wrapped in a white sheet. When it's her turn for the interview, her mother unwraps the sheet to reveal a beautiful pink dress—she wrapped her up to keep the dress clean. Her name is Mackenzie, and she is so determined; even though it takes her a while to do the puzzle, she gets it. I am impressed by her persistence. We're taking a photo of each girl so that we remember who's who. When we tell her it's time for a photo, her smile opens her mouth so wide, it's like she's biting an apple.

A girl named Michaela comes up, with the cutest little braids and the most mischievous smile. When we ask her to draw and tell a story, she draws her father and talks about how he died. She says she loves him so much even though she doesn't remember him clearly.

There's another little girl named Belinda, who's incredibly matter-of-fact. Everything she says is so clear and measured, she seems like a tiny adult in a child's body. She tells us that her parents died from AIDS, and that she and her other siblings were all farmed off to relatives. She lives in Kibera with her uncle and her stepmother. There's no emotion in how she says any of this. She's just very factual, and so bright. She just shines.

I'm falling in love with all of them. There seems to be a brightness underneath all of the darkness of this place that I never saw before. Perhaps one girl at a time we will uncover more of the light.

After only ten interviews, I feel absolutely drained, but there are so many more families sitting patiently downstairs that I keep going. It's fascinating: the clear developmental differences and verbal and imaginative inclinations between children. Some can put together the tangram puzzle with ease and can draw a person with all the body parts and tell an elaborate story about the person they're drawing as they do it. For others the tangram puzzle takes longer, but they are incredibly creative and persistent—and we've worked out the scoring so either outcome can result in equivalent points.

Hillary doesn't make it any easier; as one little girl struggles with the puzzle, he cups his hands over his mouth and emits a sitcom-worthy "ha-ha-ha" giggle. Another struggles to jump on one foot during a test for motor skills, and he does it himself before pointing at her and saying, "DO IT!" At that, I kick him out. He gives me a menacing stare before running out, but when I next look outside I see him playing happily with the little girls who are still waiting their turn.

The interviews continue for five days, and each day more parents arrive with their little girls than I could have possibly imagined. On the final day of interviews there is so much chaos, a last-minute flurry of people just hearing about the opportunity, that I don't wrap up interviews until six P.M. Afterward, I sit in the office entering the day's scores in the master Excel spreadsheet so that I can sort it, to generate the list of who Kennedy needs to start home visits with tomorrow.

A little girl stumbles in crying, looking confused and lost. She is tiny and has puffy lips and long eyelashes now thick with tears. I look outside in the courtyard—no one else is around. Suddenly, I remember her interview. She was playful and bright, and when asked to draw a picture of a person she loved, she'd drawn her mother, narrating a story so sweet in its detail of how her mother likes to take her for walks.

I greet her in Swahili and ask, "Where is your mom?" At that word she starts to hiccup and cry more, shaking her head in bewilderment.

"Did you get lost? Where did you last see her?"

She opens her eyes wide but still shakes her head. I go to the bathroom and tear off a piece of toilet paper. "Here, blow."

She presses her face into the tissue and blows her nose, and I wipe her tearstained cheeks. Slowly, she stops looking at me with fear in her eyes and starts to play a game of peekaboo, hiding behind the desk. I play along. She holds on to the edge and hides her face by turning away and burying it in her arms, her smile now mischievous. Then she pops up suddenly and I feign both fear and shock.

Her mom bursts in the office door—overcome with joy at seeing her there.

"Priscilla!" she cries, rushing to sweep the little girl up in her arms. Priscilla presses her face into her mother's neck and peers over her shoulder to look at me with a smile.

"Thank you," she says. As she and Priscilla leave hand in hand she tells me, "Please, you're welcome at our house anytime."

After they leave, I check the score sheet: Priscilla's score places her among the very highest. All night, I can't get that image of Priscilla and her mother hugging out of my head: a universal image of motherhood.

It's early morning and a haze hangs low. I pull my sweater close against the chill and struggle to keep pace with Kennedy and George, watching carefully where I place my foot to avoid stepping into ankle-high mud. On this pathway the smell of the river is suffocating—a combination of stale urine and sewage. It takes all the willpower I have not to press my nose into my forearm. Kennedy and George are starting the home visits, and I've asked to tag along. Kennedy is insistent that I wait a little bit away until he goes first and does his initial inspection—he feels that my presence might impede his ability to make an honest assessment. George stays with me.

Priscilla's mom meets Kennedy at a corner and they disappear down a side pathway, while George and I poke our heads into several small shops along the road. One woman sells an assortment of white stones.

"What are those?" I ask George.

"They're for pregnant women." I look at him sideways and he elaborates, "They eat them, when they are pregnant."

"They *eat* them?"

"Yes—they have iron in them."

I want to ask more, but my phone beeps. *Done. Meet me at that corner.*

I show the phone to George and he nods. "Let's go."

Kennedy is trying to keep a neutral face—he's committed to

impartiality in the selection process—but his expression is pained.

"What happened?" I ask, worried something is terribly wrong.

He shakes his head, indignant. "People suffer," he whispers.

Priscilla's mother follows hesitantly behind Kennedy, but when she sees me, she smiles.

"*Karibu chai,*" she says—Welcome for tea.

I look at Kennedy to get his approval, and he nods before signaling to George that they better continue, to have any chance of finishing all their visits in the next several days.

I follow Mama Priscilla down a very narrow winding path. We make a right and walk down a small alleyway in between two rows of houses that face each other; there is less than a foot between them. There is laundry hung on haphazard lines and I have to duck, but I still run into wet clothes, the moisture sticking to my face. Priscilla's house is tucked away in the back of a long row, and I see the little girl playing outside, throwing her head back in laughter. She looks up and sees me, then runs toward me.

Mama Priscilla invites me to come inside, and I stop at the door to remove my shoes. I walk down a single crude step, and my eyes take a moment to adjust in the dark. The room is so small, hardly big enough for two grown adults to stand in. There is a small wooden table stained with blue paint—the room's only color. She gestures to the small couch made from what looks like refurbished metal. The room is sparse—no bed or "kitchen corner," only an old metal trunk for storage. I sit down gingerly, and Mama Priscilla places a plastic cup filled with hot tea in front of me, apologizing that she doesn't have any milk. I think about giving the tea to Priscilla, but I remember the last time I refused tea, thinking that I was being respectful. Kennedy was livid—explaining both the pride and generosity I was simultaneously rejecting.

Mama Priscilla doesn't say very much, and I don't ask, but I can tell she is happy that I took her up on her offer of tea. Priscilla pops in and out of the doorway, trailed by her little brother, still playing peekaboo.

"Where is Priscilla's father?" I ask quietly, unsure if I am over-stepping.

"He doesn't live here," Mama Priscilla says. "I'm a second wife."

I have so many questions I want to ask, but I don't know where to start.

"I only finished eighth grade," she continues. "We didn't have money for more. I want better for Priscilla. I want her to depend on herself."

I think to myself, *So do I.* I thank Mama Priscilla.

"Come back, anytime," she calls after me.

All afternoon, as I read prospective teachers' résumés, I think about Priscilla's smile.

In my bank account in America, I have exactly $3,000, care-fully saved from summers spent waitressing in a Japanese restau-rant, babysitting, and working at a day camp. Impulsively I pick up my phone and compose a text message to Kennedy: *I found a donor who can close our gap.*

A moment later, my phone buzzes with his reply. *You're kid-ding. How?*

I know how, but I don't know why. It's seems completely arbitrary—and completely unfair—that I am even in the posi-tion to offer this small, yet entirely meaningful sum. But it does feel like a step in the right direction.

———

It's two in the morning, and the sound of Kennedy's phone jerks me from sleep.

"Kennedy, your phone, again!" I tap him.

His phone rings at all hours, although I'm always pleading for him to turn it off, to give us a few hours' respite from the endless demands and questions.

"What's going on?" Building the school has made us both very heavy sleepers, and we fall into bed exhausted at the end of each day. He gropes around to find his phone and answers groggily. Then he sits up sharply, the tone of his voice intensifying in Luo, and I know something is wrong. Still on the phone, he switches on the lights and pulls on the first pair of pants and shirt his fingers grasp.

"What's going on?" I ask again. He holds up a finger to say one minute and motions toward the door. Finally he hangs up, but instead of walking out the door he sits down on the bed.

"Liz is in labor," he says quietly. "She's going to have the baby." I immediately fly out of bed and pull on a sweatshirt and jeans.

"Where? Should we go?"

"At St. Mary's clinic; it's a small clinic in Olympic. I know the nurse who runs it. I set it up weeks ago with a deposit so that she could go there whenever the time came."

For people without any insurance, hospitals in Kenya can be expensive, and Kennedy slowly siphoned money from his job in the Wesleyan library for the birth and to help Liz.

I sit down next to him.

"Is she okay?" I rub his back soothingly, using my nails the way he likes, but he doesn't say anything—he's lost in thought. "We should go," I say gently.

"I don't know if I can." He burrows his head into my chest, and I wrap my arms around him, pulling him to me.

"Liz was my baby," he whispers.

"I know," I say.

"I wanted so much to keep her away from all this. I tried to get her into the parish school. When I saw the boys she was keeping around, I warned her and them too. Maybe I protected her too much; she never knew how fast Kibera lets you fall, because I tried to hold her up."

"She knows you tried, baby. And she needs you now."

"You don't understand." He pulls back, catching me off guard with his vehemence. "My mom was fifteen when she had me. Jackie was seventeen. Liz is only nineteen. We're trapped."

And he's right. I don't really understand the cycle of poverty he has seen all his life, this cycle that refuses to let go. Sometimes there is nothing to do but to stand by while his heart breaks, and then keep standing there as, slowly, he pieces it back together.

Liz gives birth to a beautiful, healthy little girl. She names her Jessica, and I am deeply moved. The clinic is small—only four rooms, each shared by four people—but it is clean. I sit on Liz's bed holding baby Jessica. The baby's hands are so small, clutched in little fists—I've never before held a baby on its first day of life. Her features are beautiful, so small and precious. She begins to cry in my arms and Ajey stands up, reaching out to take her. Liz lies still, as if in shock.

I stand outside the door to the room, struggling to reconcile all our collective feelings and hopes for this baby and for Liz. When I was her age, I had just finished my freshman year of college and was home in Denver for the summer, making out with my boyfriend, staying out late, and working a few jobs to make money. That summer I felt sophisticated, independent. I'd survived a year away from home at Wesleyan, and as a result I knew everything. I was filled with politically correct opinions and absolute certainty. My parents looked at me and smiled gently, knowingly, because once they had been nineteen and insufferable too. I was a child becoming a woman, but allowed that period of transition.

I think I understand why Liz is so ambivalent toward this child, toward being a mother. She knows that she has been forced to become a woman before she is ready. She is in mourning for a childhood she never got to finish or live fully.

"Is she okay?" Kennedy asks, hovering in the doorway.

"Let's go outside," I whisper.

I drag my feet through the stones in the courtyard, making patterns.

"Is she okay?" he asks again.

"I don't think so," I say, looking him in the eye. "But I think she's going to be. That baby is so beautiful, once she recovers from the shock of what's happened to her, she's going to see that. She's going to become an amazing mom."

"I need to talk to her," he says. Half an hour later, Kennedy reemerges, looking lighter.

"She's keeping the baby," he says.

I nod, unaware that she'd been considering another option.

A week later, I drop off a bag of clothes and toys I bought for Jess—unsure of when she might be big enough or ready for any of them. Liz sits outside, holding her.

"I hope she's like you," Liz says. "In Africa we believe that when you name a child for someone, they take some of their character."

"Which parts of my character do you hope she takes?"

"Your stubbornness."

I laugh.

I hug Liz, and we sit together looking at Jess, her eyes half open, dozing and so content. I want nothing more than a world in which, when she is nineteen, she has my opportunities and Liz's strength.

Once we've admitted the girls, we need to get them uniforms. George and I troop into downtown Nairobi through streets bustling with merchants. We go to a shop called The Uniform Distributors and look at ten different uniforms. George, it turns out, has very strong opinions about what uniforms our girls should have. One uniform is a faded yellow, and he says it will get dirty too fast. Another is bright red, and he says it's too much red.

"They have to look the smartest."

Then we look at a blue dress with a white collar. This is the one we decide on, paired with a red sweater. George is so happy. As we walk out of the store he is almost skipping down the street.

"No one has ever seen brightly colored girls like this in Kibera. They'll stand out. They'll stand out the way they should."

I never thought I would be so excited about giving out a uniform, but when the time comes to hand each one out, it's so clear that for these girls it is a symbol of education, a symbol of everything that lies ahead. Big, tough George stands in the doorway, grinning as he watches each girl walk in, take her uniform, and walk out, head held high.

Just before we open the school, we get a call from Babi that Kennedy's mom has collapsed. Kennedy face goes white, and I snap into crisis mode. We're at the SHOFCO office in Olympic and Ajey's in Kibera, so we have some of Kennedy's friends carry her up to the nearest place that a car can reach. I call an ambulance.

When the ambulance comes, Ajey is shivering and unconscious. Kennedy and I ride in the ambulance with her to a small hospital. He is so scared that all I can be is strong. At the hospital Kennedy is paralyzed; he can't talk to the doctors or the nurses. It's so unlike him. I find out from the doctors that Ajey has gone into shock because she has high blood pressure that has gone untreated.

Kennedy just sits by her bedside, refusing to move. I can see that the thought of losing her overwhelms him with terror.

Ajay recovers slowly but surely. On the day she's released, we get a taxi to take her back. Kennedy and I pool our small amount of remaining savings to rent her a place in Olympic, so that she will have a more comfortable place to live. She's so happy, she decorates and invites all the members of the SHOFCO staff over for tea.

My parents have decided to fly over for the opening of the school. Kennedy is nervous for their arrival, and I, too, wonder what they will think. Seeing my parents and my eleven-year-old sister, Raphae, coming out of the airport feels like all my worlds are suddenly colliding and yet complete. I'm so happy that they're here in this place that's come to mean so much to me. My mom hugs me. My sister looks like a zombie.

"Kiddo, it's great to be here," says my dad, hugging me.

We go back to the apartment we've rented on their behalf, so they can take a nap. When they wake up, we go to Nairobi Java House. My mom is relieved.

"At least there's coffee," she says.

I roll my eyes and say, "Mom, Nairobi is a huge city. You'll find there's pretty much everything."

Kennedy and Max both shoot me a look that says *Be nice!* and I hold my tongue, willing myself to be patient as my parents go through what I went through not so long ago.

We take them to Kibera, first pausing at the overlook to take it in from a distance. I look at my mom, trying to read her reaction. She doesn't say anything.

"Are you okay?" I ask her after a few more moments.

"Where did you live exactly?" she manages.

"Well," I say, "we are going to have to walk a ways to reach it, because it's way down there. Let's go."

She shakes her head and says deliberately, "I will never trust your judgment again."

I look at my dad worriedly.

Walking through Kibera with my parents makes me notice things I stopped seeing long ago. The smells, the dried fish lying in the hot baking sun, the heat as it cascades down the iron-sheet roofs. I remember the first time I walked to Kennedy's house and what an impossible maze this all felt like. Now, two years later, it is deeply familiar.

People we pass ask me in Swahili if that's my mom. I nod and smile. I keep looking at my mom, desperately wanting her approval. Everyone on the road exclaims with happiness that my family has finally come, calling out that their "in-laws" have arrived for all to hear. I'm silently thankful that they are speaking in Swahili; all my family can grasp is their welcoming excitement.

The school emerges in front of us, a beacon of hope in the midst of this chaos. When we reach it, my family stops and is uncharacteristically quiet. I realize how deeply I want them to celebrate with me what we have created here. My mom is the first to speak—"Jess, this is amazing"—and I feel my face flush red, glowing with her praise and recognition.

I know it doesn't look like much, a small, crudely plastered building. But now, looking at her, looking at my dad, I know they see the same potential that I see. It means everything to be standing here, sharing this with them.

There's one other tiny challenge to tackle with my family, in preparation for the trip we'll take with them to visit Kennedy's family in the village before the school opens. I select an appropriate restaurant, one of Nairobi's nicest, and, once we're all sitting down, I clear my throat.

"Guys. You know the village?"

They nod, and my dad says that they're looking forward to seeing a different part of Kenya. I catch Kennedy's eye and he nods at me. His expression is the one that often comes over his face when he suspects things won't go according to plan. There's a mischievous glint in his eyes.

"Yeah, so about the village," I continue. "Okay, in Kennedy's culture, before he could leave the country to go to Wesleyan, we had to build this house. It's more like a hut. We had to build it, because otherwise he couldn't leave. They would say he has no roots without it. And, well, it turns out that in his culture, that house means, well, his family thinks that we're married."

All of a sudden, no one is chewing. The silence is thick enough to cut.

"They think you're what?!" My mom is incredulous.

I try again to explain slowly, "Mom, Kennedy *had* to build this house."

She interrupts, "I know, you've said that. Cut to the part where you said the house means you're married?"

I nod, trying to pretend this is all perfectly standard.

My dad, who's been silent to this point, says firmly, "Well, we'll just have to explain to them that in our culture, you are most definitely *not* married."

"Dad," I say very quietly, my teeth clenching, my jaw tight. "If you can't just pretend to be respectful, then I will never invite you to share someone else's culture again."

I get up and storm off to the bathroom, leaving Kennedy alone with my family. I feel trapped and confused. Which world is mine? I can understand my family's resistance to their twenty-two-year-old daughter being married in another country in a strange house-building wedding without their knowing. I also understand why having these roots matters so much to Kennedy and his family. Do I belong to Kennedy's world? I feel like I exist in a strange middle place, neither here nor there.

I walk back to the table. My dad looks contrite. Kennedy's face looks as if he's about to be sick.

Max is just laughing. "This is going to make a really great play one day."

"Dad?" I say. "Can you just agree to be respectful?"

My dad nods his head and says, "As long as you tell me that you're not really married."

Kennedy jumps in to reassure saying, "We promise. We'll tell you if that ever happens."

Raphae finally says, "Can we go home?"

The day of the opening arrives at last. We wake up early, and I have chills of anticipation all morning. The classrooms are set up with small tables and tiny plastic chairs. I imagine the girls sitting there, debating, learning about themselves and the world. The teachers have been training and preparing for weeks. Raphae and Max carry the bags of school supplies my parents have brought.

As Kennedy and I walk through Kibera, it feels entirely different, alive and washed with hope.

Hundreds of people attend the opening of the school, everyone deeply invested. Forty-five little girls in matching uniforms, the chosen ones, their faces appropriately serious, are flanked by their parents and sisters and brothers and neighbors, whose buoyant pride shows on their faces because they have been chosen, too.

"*Erokamano*," a parent sings—her beautiful clear voice so vibrant it sends a shock down my spine. Soon, everyone is clapping and echoing her words—her song translates to mean "Thank you, when we thought there was no reason to live, God has given hope, a reason to keep moving forward." The mother who started the song belts it out, truly bringing it home, bringing us all together.

More people have come than even Kennedy expected, men and women alike who have no affiliation to the school but are here to celebrate all the same. People from the community, youth leaders and village elders, shouting and praising a school for girls. Children stream in, their curiosity irked by the commotion.

Kennedy stands in the center clapping his hands in time and dancing too. When the song is over, he speaks. He begins by saying that his mother told him when he went to America not to forget: not to forget her, not to forget Kibera, and not to forget where he came from.

"Look at me. Today, one year later, I am back, and together we have built this. We have made this possible."

I love watching Kennedy in front of people, in his element. He comes alive reading the responses of the crowd and changing his tone to speak to what people really need to hear. I stand off to the side as I watch him. The audience guffaws and cackles in response. As he talks, a lightness comes over the crowd. Everyone who came in a bit unsure, nervous, not trusting what this was all about, knows, when Kennedy talks to them, that it's theirs. It's a special gift to be able to connect to people in that way, and as I watch him in front of the parents, I realize that although our love binds us in a special way, he is not mine alone, but belongs in deep and complex ways to this place and to these people, too.

Kennedy calls me up to speak in front of everyone. I shake my head, but he insists, grabbing my hand and pulling me through the throng of girls.

"What language should I use?"

"Swahili," he says. "You can do it."

I stand up, feeling the eyes of the elders and community, the eyes of the parents, the eyes of the girls, and then I speak. I thank the parents for giving us this chance to educate their daughters. I thank the community members for coming up to support this day. I thank my own parents and Max and Raphae for traveling across the world to share this moment with me. And I thank Kennedy for inviting me to be part of something that I didn't completely understand until today, until I'm standing in it, standing in the light of what is possible.

I feel the girls' keen attention and I tell them, "Girls, you can be anything you want."

I know that this will be a hard promise to keep, but I resolve to dedicate myself to ensuring that this contract holds true.

seventeen

jessica

I am not ready to say good-bye to the school, to the girls, to the teachers, to this Kibera that feels utterly different from the post-election Kibera to which I had sworn I would never return.

Back in Connecticut at Wesleyan for Kennedy's sophomore year, we run the Kibera school long distance, which has its challenges. I've gotten a job on campus working for the writing program at Wesleyan, but I spend most of my time working on the school. There's so much to do. We have about two weeks' worth of operating funds left in the bank, so raising more money is a matter of urgency.

Before we left Kenya, Kennedy came up with the idea of setting up a committee of parents to oversee the work, making sure each parent showed up for their volunteering. This committee would also meet monthly to provide the school staff with feedback; the chairperson would be elected by the parents on an annual basis. George also promised us he'd take care of things. We boarded the plane with our two suitcases neatly packed with fifty pounds of crafts made by the SWEP women. We plan to sell their bracelets and bags to help the women earn a living and help raise funds for the school.

The level of detail Kennedy is able to negotiate from this distance amazes me. Half a world away, he knows everything that transpires in a day. The phone rings in the middle of the night almost every night, when it's daytime in Kenya. Kennedy sleeps with it next to his pillow.

"Hello?" His brow furrows. "Uh-huh, uh-huh."

"What is it?" I ask. He motions his hand at me telling me to wait; he's listening.

Sometimes it's parents just calling to say how much they love the school or how happy their child is; other times it's community members congratulating him or George relaying the details of running the place. Money is so stressfully tight. We're literally counting pencils, with everyone instructed not to sharpen them more than twice a day so that they last longer. Every child has to sharpen under a teacher's supervision.

Sometimes the calls are about problems: a teacher who came late to school, a parent who didn't show up to work, the ins and outs of running something, of managing people, of trying to keep everyone motivated even when there is no financial motivation. I'm trying to keep everything together.

Then good news comes too. George reports that the girls are starting to speak and understand English after only one month.

"These girls are geniuses," he tells me on the phone.

I laugh and tell him, "George, all kids are like that. When they're little, they're like sponges; they soak it all up."

George also tells me, "I've decided I'm going to take my wife out for dinner. I've been looking at the girls in our school. I think people in Kibera now see there's a lot they didn't know about women and what women can do. I think there's a lot I didn't know about what my wife can do. I should take her for dinner."

I laugh at George's disarming honesty.

"George, take your wife out somewhere nice."

kennedy

"It's not enough. The school is not enough."

I want to expand the girls' school to serve as a center of wider community transformation.

"We need to create an incentive structure for the entire community to place value on these girls, on all the women. The only way we can accomplish this is by providing men, and the entire community, with social services. They will support the girls' school if we also offer things like a library, toilets, a health clinic, clean water, a job center, financial literacy and economic empowerment, a community center . . ."

This vision emerges nearly complete in my mind, of making a girls' school a portal of large-scale change, placing it at the center of an ecosystem of value.

Then I think of the realities of managing just the school—I wonder how on earth we would develop all these other programs and services, much less fund them.

But it's not in Jessica's nature to hesitate. "When can we start these other services?" she asks.

I laugh. "I guess we should try to get some money to keep running the school and then we'll figure it out from that."

"There's your problem," Jessica tells me.

"What do you mean my problem?" I ask.

"You're always afraid to jump in."

"I'm trying to be realistic. I was talking of an idea for five years' time," I explain.

"Don't be," Jessica says. "Nothing was ever changed by someone trying to be realistic."

The following week Jessica sees a notice for a grant competition for a fellowship called Echoing Green. To win you have to pitch an innovative model to transform the world. Even though fewer than 1 percent of applicants win the fellowship, it seems like an obvious fit for this wonderful, unrealistic idea of a girls' school connected to community services.

We stay up for three days straight, putting ideas into writing, articulating ways we can connect the girls' school to transformative social services like health care, clean water, economic empowerment, and violence prevention. Jessica's parents even help with the budget, the formatting of which was more complex than anything we'd managed before. With twenty-four hours to go before the deadline, her dad reworks all the numbers in Excel.

Not quite willing to put all our eggs in one basket, we look for other grants and awards, and I am amazed at how resourceful Jessica is, how much she finds, and I marvel at her determination.

I ask her incredulously, "What makes you think that we can win any of these?"

She replies simply, "Well, doesn't someone have to?"

We submit a grant proposal to the Dell Social Innovation Competition, which requires gathering votes. Voting goes viral on campus, and we get thousands of clicks. A small team of dedicated Wesleyan students stays up day and night helping us to finish the grants. Our idea seems to be contagious.

We also apply for the Do Something Award, for "America's Top World Changer, 25 and Under." Jessica writes an application for me, but right before the deadline, we see that you have to be American. So we quickly rework everything and put Jessica's name forward. Then Jessica wins the award live on television. I am so proud to see her receive such deserved recognition. I know in my heart that it is her drive that pushes all of this to become possible.

There's so much energy and momentum behind our vision. Jessica is wired all the time, thinking about our to-do list and our plan's potential. I am determined to go back to Kenya the next summer and build the health clinic. Jessica is helping me to leave caution behind and is unfazed by our lack of health-care experience.

"We'll just find the best people to do it with us. But we have to do it."

I nod. She's right, and she immediately begins to learn all she can about the best approaches to health care. I begin talking to the Kibera community to listen and understand what is really needed.

One day at Wesleyan, I have lunch with a kind man named Bob Patricelli. Professor Rob comes with me, since Bob and his wife, Margaret, sponsor my scholarship at Wesleyan. Bob speaks thoughtfully and wants to hear all about my experiences at Wesleyan and my hopes for the future. We talk easily, connect naturally, and I have a premonition that he will mean much in my life.

After lunch, I am skipping and laughing and run to find Jessica. I have something to tell her. She tells me to slow down. I'm speaking too fast, and she can't understand.

"God is great sometimes," I say. "The spirits said this was something whose time has come. And Bob has . . . Do you know someone named Paul Newman?"

Jessica bursts into laughter. "Paul Newman? Everyone knows Paul Newman!"

I shrug and say, "Well, I guessed he was somebody important. Me, I've never heard of him before. But Bob helps out with something that is in his memory, and he set up a meeting. They want to talk to us. They want to help us. The Patricellis want to help too."

"You mean the Newman's Own Foundation?" Jessica asks.

"Yeah, that's the one," I say. "How do you know it?"

Jessica shakes her head. "Let's go to WesShop," she says.

At the campus grocery store, Jessica takes me over to a fridge filled with orange juice and lemonade. She pick up a carton of lemonade and says, "Look, Ken, this guy is Paul Newman. They sell lemonade and pretzels and popcorn and salad dressing, and all the money, they give back to charity. We always bought Newman's Own in my house. Paul Newman was a movie star, an icon."

I see the label, recognizing the name and agree, "That's the one! We have a meeting with their organization next week."

"Next week?" Jessica exclaims. She begins to talk in a flurry about all the things we need to do before this meeting. All the more-detailed budgets we need to tie down, all the plans and visions we need to put in place.

"We have a lot to do," she declares, and I nod my head, knowing she can do anything. "Here." She thrusts the lemonade into my chest. "You buy this. I don't have any more points."

I roll my eyes. "You're going to use up all my points!"

"You wanted me to stay in Connecticut." She smiles.

It's true. I kiss her and go dutifully to pay with my Wes card. This plastic card never gets old to me. Imagine, you can just swipe it and buy food. Magic.

We work frantically for the next week, until the day of our meeting with Newman's Own Foundation. And when we get to their offices, we're both nervous. A warm, but professional woman named Pam lets us in. We follow her back into her office. We tell her about the school, about the girls, about our plans to build a health clinic and a source for clean water. I talk about my own story, and how I was driven to start this bigger movement. The conversation flows easily once she warms up to us, going on for an hour and a half.

Pam gives us each a big hug as we leave and says, "Just keep up what you're doing. You're going to make it."

In the car ride home, I feel ecstatic.

I put my head out the window and let the wind hit my face, screaming, "Aiiieeee, aiiieeee!"

"Kennedy," Jessica says, "people are looking at you like you're crazy!"

"I don't care!"

A few weeks later, we meet Bob Forrester, the CEO of Newman's Own. He is an energetic and kind man, with a hint of mischief in his eyes. He tells us that Paul Newman would have written us a check on the spot, and that Newman's Own Foundation is giving us $50,000. Bob says he believes in taking risks, and that Paul always wanted to use his own personal luck to create luck in the lives of others. This strikes me deeply, this notion of both the power and cruelty of luck, and I wish I could have met this man Paul Newman. I am touched by his selfless legacy and dedication to change the luck of my community and so many others. Bob is filled with witty and powerful advice. He tells us that one of Paul's favorite things to say was that "there are three rules to business, and luckily we don't know any of them," and the spirit of this resonates. Bob's clear belief in us and the promise of funding is a tonic, and Jessica and I truly begin to feel as though anything is possible. Later, privately, we jump up and down, and hug, each saying to the other, "You knew we could do it," even if we weren't sure.

jessica

After the summer together and the palpable growth of all our services, I can't leave. While Ken has to return to Wesleyan, I decide that I will remain to keep propelling our progress forward. We have big plans, and with the staunch support of Newman's Own Foundation we can now accomplish them—we can make the girls' school directly benefit the rest of the community, turning it into the source of vital social services. We win the Echoing Green Fellowship and Dell, and other interest and support begins to follow. We begin to dream even bigger.

But mainly I just want to see the girls. When I tell Kennedy this, he kisses me.

"You're crazy," he says.

"I know."

———

There is still traffic at the roundabout after I drop Kennedy at the Nairobi airport, after the summer we've spent together in Kibera. The taxi driver keeps asking questions that hang between us unanswered, but he isn't deterred. All I can think of is Kennedy standing in line with his first "frivolous purchase," a new red duffel bag ordered off the Internet—in America he'd discovered a love of luggage. I'd hovered, standing on the curb even though the taxi driver didn't like it. But I needed to see Kennedy for every last second possible—as if each one might be the difference between resolving to stay and following him home. He kissed me good-bye, held me so close, and then he was gone, through the metal detectors and on the other side. And it feels like a well-practiced routine done in entirely the wrong order, like brushing your teeth and then putting the toothpaste on the brush. I am alone in his country, and soon he will be alone in mine. It strikes me, as we weave our way through the traffic, still thick at ten P.M., that countries, unlike baseball cards, are not so easily traded.

Being in Kenya without Kennedy is simply strange. No matter how much time I spend here I can't escape the whiteness of my skin, the way I stand out no matter what I do. But it's more than my skin. It's my privilege.

I think about our girls and what I want them to be when they grow up, what I want them to imagine for their lives. Kennedy from the beginning felt very strongly that foreign teachers should never teach in the school. They should work in partnership with our teachers to build capacity, to build skills, but they shouldn't be the ones here teaching. He didn't want our girls to see foreigners, Americans, as their role models. He wanted them to see local Kenyans doing something to give back to their community. Sometimes when I walk these roads alone, I think about that, and what my presence here means. Will this ever be my place?

In some ways, though, this time feels precisely like an opportunity to make this project and community my own. I'm clear that I'm not just working to help make Kennedy's dream come true. This has become my dream too. It's the most independent I've ever felt in my life—and, one day, as I'm walking through Kibera to the school, I begin to feel brave. I am living in Kenya on my own. I am growing up.

But the bravery comes and goes.

One night, I sit straight up in my bed at the sound of people outside, their voices floating up through the window. I clutch the sheet close to my chest—barely daring to breathe. Without him, I wake up a lot. But tonight is different. I reach for my phone ever so slowly—as if my motion might catch their attention. It's 1:31 A.M.—people don't usually walk around Olympic this late. I close my eyes and listen, willing my ears to pick apart their sounds—to make meaning from the bits and pieces that waft in.

Mzungu anaishi hapa jua, peke yake. A white girl lives upstairs, by herself.

I inhale sharply.

I picture the gate to this small compound. There's a padlock on the inside, but they could climb over the walls or cut the lock, climb the single flight of external stairs, and then be here, at my door. It's metal and solid, also locked by one sturdy padlock. I close my eyes, my heart beating fast, trying to think of what Kennedy would do. We don't have much to steal. I don't keep money in the apartment and we have only a bed, some plastic chairs, a small wooden table, pots and pans, and my laptop. I wonder if the downstairs neighbors would come to my rescue—I don't know them. Here in Olympic, people are determined to show their propriety by being less friendly than the people in Kibera, less involved in every aspect of each other's lives.

If they want to, it would be only a matter of time before whoever is out there would get in. I can still hear them, whispering, and I shake my head—it's not good that they are still standing there. I know that sometimes when thieves don't get anything they want—like cash—things turn violent.

I lick my lips, trying hard not to think the worst. I walk to the kitchen and take our only sharp knife, clutching it to my chest. I go back into the bedroom and lock the door from the inside. *Shit.* I hear a fumbling at the gate, the sound of metal on metal, and I know that my fears weren't just the misplaced anxieties of a girl far from home. They must have found something to cut the padlock. I don't know if they are armed, and I don't want them to hear me, but I dial George's number and close my eyes, just willing this not to happen, praying that he'll answer.

"Hello?" he says groggily.

"George, it's me, I have a problem. There are some guys here—they're trying to break in, please help," I whisper urgently.

Suddenly awake, he says, "Five minutes and I'll be there."

Five minutes. I hope that's fast enough. I find I don't have complete control over my hands, and with slow, sticky fingers I fumble through my phone numbers for the local police inspector Kennedy asked to look after me. I've never spoken to him so I send him a clumsy text: *This is Jessica of Kennedy I have trouble please help.*

Outside I hear fervent whispers, movements slowed down to conceal noise, and then suddenly silence. There is a creak as the gate opens, and it sounds like now they are inside the compound, any minute walking up the stairs and at my door. I am frozen, I can't tell how many people there are, but it won't be long before they figure out a way to get through the door—the small window in the bathroom flashes in my mind.

I don't want to die—here alone and without Kennedy. I'm scared, and I feel the vulnerability that so many women in the world feel—that they feel because they are women. Before now I couldn't have imagined this paralyzing fear, this sense of powerlessness.

Not often one for prayers, I find myself repeating fervently, *Dear God—if you're listening, I promise if you protect me I will pay it back somehow.*

Someone is thrusting his weight against the door and I know that any minute they will be here inside, and that the bedroom door is easy to break.

But then, I hear a flurry of exclamations. I can't see what is happening but there is frantic activity outside the window. I hear footsteps running down and then up the stairs and then my phone is ringing—George.

"Let me in," George pants.

I take a deep breath in, overwhelmed by gratitude. I run to the door and open the lock. George stands outside, with five other men waiting respectfully at the bottom of the stairs.

George is huge. He is probably at least six feet tall and burly and strong. His forehead is high and his face is still, rarely betraying any of his emotions. I have never felt closer to him than in this moment.

"That was close," he says. "Julius tried to chase them, but they got away, there were four of them."

I shudder. "Thank you, George, thank you—"

As the months pass, people greet me more often as I pass, calling me *shemaji,* meaning "daughter of here" or "sister-in-law." Today, I feel like I've started to make my own home here. A few of the girls run past me. Their bright red-and-blue uniforms pop against the browns and grays of Kibera.

Robyn turns around and waves and says, "Hi, Jess."

"Hi, Robyn," I say, still shaking my head at her latest feat.

Last week, Robyn, only in kindergarten, organized a strike.

She got the whole class of girls to sit on the classroom floor and refuse to go home.

Our kindergarten teacher, Julia, called to me from the office down the hall.

"Jess," she said, shaking her head, "the girls are striking. They're only in kindergarten. Just wait to see what they're going to be when they grow up."

"Striking?" I ask. "For what?"

"They just don't want to go home."

"Do we have a leader? What do we do? Do we negotiate?"

"Robyn." Julia shook her head. "Robyn is, without a doubt, the leader."

Robyn, only six years old, but already an organizer.

We sat her down and explained to her that although we'd like her to stay in school too, her parents would miss her if she never went home, and the same was true for the other girls' parents. Eventually, after some complex negotiations, she agreed.

Seeing her bright red form disappear into the street, I shake my head at how empowered, how bold these girls already are.

As I walk home, I see Mama Priscilla. She rushes up to me, her face lined with worry.

"Jess, can you come?" she says to me in Swahili.

"Sure," I say, "where?"

"Home." She grabs my hand and pulls me along the streets. She walks fast, and I struggle to keep pace. She turns down a narrow alleyway and I follow her. She pushes open her battered wooden door.

Priscilla is lying on the couch, fast asleep.

"She's sick," Mama Priscilla says. "Very sick."

I put my hand to the little girl's forehead. She's burning hot.

"Please sit," Mama Priscilla says.

I sit, unsure of what to do, acutely aware of the seriousness of the situation.

"Do you know what's wrong with her?" I ask.

She nods. "She's positive." Positive for HIV.

Priscilla's lips are swollen. There's something that looks like a cold sore. She's sweating profusely.

"Have you given her any water?" I ask.

Mama Priscilla nods and says, "But she doesn't want to drink. All she's doing is vomiting and sleeping. Vomiting and sleeping. I couldn't even take her to school today."

"We need to take her to a clinic first thing in the morning," I say. I sit with Mama Priscilla in silence, afraid for Priscilla, and of how frail she looks.

At the clinic, they say Priscilla's CD4 count is very low—340— and her viral load is very, very high. They tell Mama Priscilla that Priscilla no longer has HIV, she has AIDS.

Priscilla is coughing, so they do a chest x-ray. The doctor comes back, shaking his head. Mama Priscilla clutches the sheets, bracing herself for what looks like bad news.

"TB," the doctor says. "She has TB."

Priscilla has to start taking antiretroviral medication, or ARVs. They refer us to another small clinic nearby. No one is very friendly; no one looks at us when we walk in. Mama Priscilla grips my hand, scared. A nurse comes out and says they're very busy, that we should come back in a few hours. We look at Priscilla. Her eyes are glazed over and she's perspiring, burning up.

I think back to the day when she came for her interview, our game of peekaboo.

Mama Priscilla shakes her head and says, "Please, my child is very sick."

"Come back later," the nurse says. Defeated, Mama Priscilla carries Priscilla and we go outside.

We sit in a small shop drinking a cold soda, while Mama Priscilla tells me her story.

"We're a polygamous family, but I am alone. When I first came to Nairobi, I stayed with my aunt. I was helping her to sell fruits in Gatwekera. I met Priscilla's father there. He told me that he wasn't married, that he was single.

"After three months," she says, shaking her head, "I realized that he has another wife with three children, but by then I was pregnant with our first child. I had no choice, nowhere else to go. My family had no money for school. I dropped out in class eight. My aunt was the only person who wanted to help me. When I got pregnant, that was it. She told me I was on my own now. I gave birth to Priscilla in Kibera, but then my husband sent us upcountry. He didn't want to take care of us anymore.

"Priscilla got sick, so sick. My husband, he told me that he'd bring me back, but then he refused. My only way to survive was to dig for other people, hard work. I saved the bus fare myself to bring Priscilla back to Nairobi, because she wasn't well. I didn't know what was wrong."

I nod, unsure if she wants to continue, but she just seems like she wants to talk, wants someone to listen.

"I lived with a friend for three months when we came back," Mama Priscilla says. "She introduced me to the job of selling fruits on my own. I saved a thousand shillings. It took me long. But that's when I moved to that house you came to. That's *my* house, not his," she says with emphasis.

"In December 2007, that's when I found out my status," Mama Priscilla continues. "Priscilla was two and a half years old. I also found out about her. She was always sick. I went to the hospital. They told us we were both positive. When I left that hospital, all I could think about was giving this child poison so I could go on with my life. I couldn't imagine how to live my life and also have her. A counselor advised me there was a group for children. I went to that group, Jess, and I saw so many children who were also positive. I said I think it will be okay. My child, this child, will grow.

"In 2008, I got pregnant again, and gave birth in 2009. I thought this child will be positive, too, but my boy was negative. After I gave birth in 2009, that's when I saw the posters for School for Girls. I remember that day. I took Priscilla to Olympic and she passed the exam. I went with some of my neighbors and their children failed. Priscilla got lost. She was the last one."

I nod. "I remember," I say.

"My husband is positive," Mama Priscilla says, "and the other wife, too. Imagine, he doesn't help with anything. Sometimes I see him outside on the streets, but he doesn't even give me any money for food, so I go to wash laundry for people outside. That's how I eat. Recently, he got another wife. He never has money. The wives are the ones who have to struggle for the children to eat. If he has found that you have cooked, then he will stay. There was a time he beat me up so bad my eye was swollen. He came in the house in the morning. I was washing clothes. I forgot to wash his vest. He asked me if I washed it and I said I forgot. Then he beat me. I went to the hospital and they gave me medicine to put in my eye.

"Another time, he beat me up because he came at midnight and I didn't hear him knocking. He says, 'This house is mine and I can come at the time I want.'" She shakes her head. "When he says that, all I can think is about those thousand shillings I saved to find that house for myself, for my kids. I am the breadwinner. I pay rent, school fees for my other children. I buy clothes."

We go back to the clinic, walking slowly. She tells me she is a skilled tailor but has no way to start a business.

I sit outside as Mama Priscilla and Priscilla are in with the doctor. When she comes out, Mama Priscilla looks stricken. I ask her what's wrong.

"They tell me now that I have to agree, Priscilla will be on ARVs her whole life, every day, morning and evening."

I nod, looking at Priscilla, seeing how sick she is. We don't have any choice.

Two weeks later, Priscilla is still sick, vomiting and sleeping. Every morning at school, we administer the ARVs once Priscilla's had her breakfast of porridge. The medicine is so strong it's almost toxic and it must be absorbed with food. There's no money for food at home, so she eats only at school.

I call Kennedy each evening and give him the update. He's worried too. He can't figure out why Priscilla isn't improving, even after being given the medicine. Luckily, he will be back soon. I don't know what to do and I'm afraid.

In the summer, Kennedy returns to build our health clinic. Seeing him again feels new and strange and exciting after spending so much time here on my own. Even though we've only been apart for a few months, it has felt like forever. When we first hug on Kibera's main road and he kisses me, everyone stares. He doesn't care, he kisses me again. I feel the glow of being next to him here; I feel his glow rub off on me. As we walk down to school together many people shout to Kennedy, *"Telo,"* which in Luo means "boss." With him here, this place feels complete.

Every day is frenetically busy as we work to get the clinic open. Kennedy finds a great doctor who helps put all the plans in place, figuring out what services we'll provide, working with the Ministry of Health to get us registered, finding out where to buy the lab equipment from, determining what drugs we'll need, hiring the best staff we can find.

We collect detailed information from people in the community about their previous experiences with health care. People tell stories about the lack of privacy given, and the absence of dignity; waiting for hours and hours, their illnesses never explained. Sometimes people die in hospital waiting rooms, as was the case with one SHOFCO youth affectionately called "Councilor." Councilor was one of SHOFCO's very first soccer players, only a teenager.

I remember Kennedy telling me the story of how he died.

"When they got there, to the government hospital, Councilor was struggling to breathe." Kennedy had explained, heartbroken. "His father begged the nurse to take him in quickly to see a doctor. She insisted he pay first. In Kenyan hospitals before any services are rendered, even in emergencies, you have to go to the cashier, pay, and then get a receipt. His father begged, 'Please, I have money.' He even showed her his money, and just begged her to help the boy. But she refused and he rushed to pay. He waited in the queue, and by the time he came back with the receipt, his son was dead."

Anger overwhelms me at the senselessness of this loss, its needless cruelty. I remember Kennedy's heaving as he'd told me this story, his tears of both pain and fury.

His pain makes me consider that I've never seen a person die, never imagined how with such little ceremony everything could end. It takes me a long time to gather myself. All I can think is that there is a side to life that has been well hidden from me, but that's been there all along nonetheless. Councilor died, and no one moved to save him, to fight for his life. His loss was simply accepted, almost anticipated. While I live my life expecting to live, others expect that they might die. The rules of the world are not the same for all of us.

I think about what we've gone through with Priscilla. When we went to one hospital in Kibera, the doctor disclosed her HIV status in front of a whole waiting room of patients. I saw her mother's face flush pink. The doctor didn't think twice about what this public announcement might mean for Priscilla or her mom.

We have been advertising for places for a second round of girls at the school. In the school's first year, word has spread far and wide that this place is very different—with food, uniforms, and an amazing education—from the traditional Kenyan school experience. Our girls prattle away to one another in English, and the sophistication of their vocabulary amazes me. I love to overhear their conversations or see their delight when they learn to read. The Chapin School continues to send teachers to train ours, and our curriculum flourishes. Our girls and teachers talk nonchalantly about literary strategies like metacognition. I walk into a second-grade classroom and hear our girls discussing writing "juicy sentences" and techniques like show don't tell, repetition, and imagery. When one of our very first teachers, Julia, gives her kindergarten students a third-grade science test equivalent to what might be given in the state-run schools, the lowest score is an 88 percent. When our initial group of students take their first government-issued district exam, they are first in the entire district by a fifty-point margin. We shake our heads in amazement. The girls are just little sponges soaking up everything in their eagerness to learn. On weekends, they're always in the library. Their determination, their hunger for this opportunity is palpable.

Kennedy is a force of nature. He wakes up every morning so early, rushing to school, making preparations for the clinic.

As I'm walking to school one day, I notice a huge construction project. I call Kennedy.

"Hey, Ken. Someone's building something really big, halfway to the school."

"Yeah, that's our community center."

"It's our what?" I say.

"It's our community center. They started yesterday," he says, as if this were no big deal. "You remember my housemate from Wesleyan, Yael; her family is helping us to build this. Can you believe that? I've never even met her dad, Matt, but he sent us a second donation. People are sometimes just so good," he continues.

"Kennedy," I exclaim—surprised, impressed, exasperated— "we have to plan things like this!"

"We'll plan . . . later," he assents.

While preparations for the clinic are under way, a visiting group of volunteer doctors from the American Friends of Kenya offer medical exams for all the girls in our school. When they're doing the physicals, they discover that one of our first-grade girls has been raped—Annette. They call me and Kennedy into one of the tiny offices to tell us. The expression on Kennedy's face is complete devastation. I reach for his hand, unable to imagine this happening to one of our little girls.

"I'll talk to the mother," Kennedy says.

He calls Mama Annette and she comes to school. At first, she's quiet and reluctant to talk, but eventually she says that Annette's eleven-year-old brother sleeps in the same bed as Annette. Annette doesn't understand what's happened but describes her brother hurting her.

Annette's dad died in the election violence and her mom spends her days looking for work, unable to supervise her children. The mother is upset, but resigned.

When she leaves, I tell Kennedy, "We have to do something about this. We need a place for kids like that, for kids like Annette, who are not safe in their own homes."

Kennedy doesn't speak. I can tell he's really angry.

"I'm tired," he says. "I'm really tired. You can do everything and still you can't stop, you can't protect them. You can't end it."

He takes a deep breath.

"But you're right, Jess, we need to do something. We need to involve the entire community to end this. I want everyone to know, every man, every woman, every child that this clinic"—he points right outside of the school where, sure enough, a clinic is being built in place of about twenty houses, families whom

Kennedy has convinced to move, a nearly impossible task—"all of this is because of these girls, that girls are a point of value."

It turns out that many of our girls have been raped or abused. We can no longer ignore the need to have a safe place for girls living in such terrible situations. How can we expect them to function, to benefit from their education when they're in constant peril? There is five-year-old Maureen, whose mother went crazy after her father was killed in the postelection violence. Her mother cuts her, and a neighbor rapes her every morning. She is scared and can't control her urine, and we find out she has a fistula.

Then there is Ava, whose mother threw her in the garbage when she was a baby, and who was rescued by her grandmother. Ultimately, her grandmother abandoned her too, leaving her with a sixteen-year-old aunt who beat and abused her, forcing her to sleep on the streets. And Michaela, whose mother has no way to make a living except for brewing *changaa*. At night so many men visit their house for the drink that Michaela is often victimized. Her mother cries, but she simply has no other way to survive.

The girls tell their teachers what's going on at home. They come to me and Ken asking what they should do, and we're tired of having no answer.

We decide to build a safe house for them.

Kennedy talks to Bob Patricelli, and Bob and Margaret decide to donate the money to start Margaret's Safe Place, a boarding facility for girls for whom no other living accommodations can be found. We find an empty house in Olympic, the lower-middle-class estate that is a little bit farther away, harder to find in a gated neighborhood.

The safe house will be for both long and short stays, and there's a social worker who will live in the house full-time, as the housemother.

The first girls in the safe house are most interested in the second floor of the house because many of them have never been on a second floor before. They call the house a tower, and their delight at being able to look out the second story's window and watch the street below gives me previously unimaginable joy.

At five thirty one morning, George is waylaid outside the school by the father of the youngest student at the Kibera School for Girls; the man, Otieno, is known as Baba Julie—Julie's father. Baba Julie has been up all night waiting for school to open in the morning.

He tells George that his daughter, Baby Julie as she's called in the school, has been assaulted. She's only four and a half. She has chubby cheeks with dimples and a bright smile. Baba Julie's eyes are lined with worry. He is angry and frustrated, a fierce advocate for his daughter. Our social worker and volunteers stay with the family as we figure out what's going on. Julie is admitted to Nairobi Hospital where she undergoes surgery.

I am in absolute disbelief. Four and a half years old and having surgery after an intensive assault. Baba Julie storms out after the doctor says, "Well, she wasn't technically raped." The perpetrator, an eighteen-year-old boy, used his fingers instead. Baba Julie punches his hand into his fists and yells, "That is the same thing!"

Julie is in the hospital for nine days. George organizes transportation so the entire school can visit her. The girls troop up to her bed one by one.

We go to the police, but nothing is simple or straightforward. Baba Julie, George, and I are told that there are letters we need to get from the doctors. Baba Julie goes back to get the letters, but the doctors refuse to give them to him.

"Corruption," he says, shaking his head.

George and I go to the police station every day.

We work with the family to get everything in line—Baba Julie often arrives out of breath to meet us after walking an hour and a half from his construction job—and still the case doesn't move forward. Eventually the boy is arrested. I spend days sitting with Mama Julie on the grass outside of the police station, keeping watch. She doesn't speak much, her eyes fixed on the small plain of grass opposite us, where the boy's family also sits. We are afraid that if we leave, his family will succeed in bribing the police to free him. People often look at me strangely as they go in and out of the police station, but after a few days no one seems to notice; we blend into the environment now, another fixture of this defunct system.

It's all for nothing. Weeks later, the boy is out on bond. The title to an old car was sufficient for his release.

Baba Julie asks George and me if we can meet.

"I want to start a committee so that no other parent goes through what I am going through. Without you guys"—he looks at me and George—"I would have given up. Now, I will never give up for Julie."

We organize a group of community leaders to come together and form what they decide to call the SHOFCO Gender Development Committee. There are elders and community members from all over Kibera. One of the members is named Editar. She's beautiful, tough, and says exactly what she thinks. She was assaulted as a child and teenager and is determined stop this pattern of assault, most of it unreported, in Kibera. Every day she goes door-to-door just listening to what's happening and, with the rest of the committee, spreading the word that cases like Julie's can be reported to them. They promise to serve as victims' advocates through every step of the inevitable medical and legal battles. People begin to make reports. Slowly, cases begin to go to court. Editar trains young people to also educate about family planning services. She says, "When we break the silence, we end the violence," and she makes herself right.

Priscilla still isn't getting any better. This time when Mama Priscilla and I go to hospital to get another refill of the drugs we also ask for Priscilla's medical records. Mama Priscilla isn't sure it's in her power to request a transfer, to request her own daughter's medical records.

We walk into the room, make our request, and the chilly doctor refuses to release Priscilla's records.

I say, "Excuse me, but she's the parent. It's her right to have access to her child's medical information. She'd like to request a transfer."

The doctor shakes her head and says, "We won't release records and we won't make a transfer."

She doesn't say why, but perhaps she is just lazy. Mama Priscilla is poor, and the doctor thinks she can get away with putting Mama Priscilla off.

They do give us a refill of Priscilla's drugs—nevirapine, zidovudine, lamivudine. Mama Priscilla takes these drugs to Kennedy in a small brown package. He makes several calls on his phone. About an hour later, a young man shows up and says, "I'm looking for Ken." Kennedy and George give him the little brown envelope and he disappears.

"Who is he?"

"He's a friend," Kennedy says. "He works in a lab. He's going to take them and do a test. I have a feeling one of those drugs is not real."

"Not real?"

"Many times there are rumors that we get vaccines that aren't real. I don't believe those, but I do believe that sometimes the rules are not followed."

I start to feel like we're in some sort of medical thriller. How could a doctor give a sick child a placebo drug? I think about Priscilla coughing and coughing, sleeping, and vomiting. The next day, Kennedy comes into the office, where I'm reviewing the teacher's lesson plans.

"I told you," he says, slamming his phone down on the desk. "No one has any respect here. One of those drugs that also helps to prevent the development of TB, that one was not real."

Kennedy goes with Mama Priscilla to demand a transfer from the clinic. You can't get ARVs from a new clinic without a transfer letter, and we won't give up until they give it to him. At the new clinic, they change the combination of drugs, and a few weeks later, Priscilla is stronger.

Our own clinic at SHOFCO opens tomorrow. Construction has been ongoing day and night, and as usual things are running behind. Though we'll just barely pull it all together in time, I am adamant that we must add HIV care, which requires several added steps, to our services. Kennedy is excited because yesterday he and George were finally able to get someone from the Ministry of Health to come to the site to do the inspection we need to get our license.

"No one wants to come to Kibera. They're afraid," he says, shaking his head.

It's always amazing to me how few Kenyans have actually walked through Kibera and how deep a divide this illustrates between rich and middle-class Kenyans, and those who live here. Kennedy hired a taxi, went to pick up the district health officer, and said he wasn't going to leave until she came with him. Somehow his charms worked, and our license is on the way.

We've painted the clinic a bright blue and pink and named it the Johanna Justin-Jinich Memorial Clinic after a classmate who was tragically shot on the Wesleyan campus. Johanna had dreamed of working in the field of women's public health, and it's wonderful to see her name on the clinic, as if her dreams are still alive here. We are joined by several of Johanna's friends from Wesleyan: Leah and Ari, whose dedication helped make the clinic happen along with the efforts of other volunteers; Inslee, Ilana, and Kyla; and the expert team of clinicians, nurses, lab technologists, and community health workers we have hired. We have boxes of medications, a few precious pieces of lab equipment, and a committee of community members who have helped plan every part of the clinic. We name the toilets we've built in conjunction with the clinic after Paul Newman, as Newman's Own Foundation funding made the entire clinic possible and, impressed with our results, the foundation increased their grants to support the organization as a whole. Bob Forrester laughs, saying Paul Newman would have gotten a kick out of his name being on a toilet.

"This is the thing I'm good at," Kennedy says, laughing when I share the details I've learned about health and sanitation. "I find the best people, people who really understand health and education and I bring them in together. They're the ones who will actually do it."

This is something I love about Kennedy: his willingness to share and collaborate—to find great people and bring them together around a cause. I look around at the team of professional Kenyans we have assembled to provide the very highest-quality services. SHOFCO's staff is made up of both locals from the community and talented clinical officers and nurses who commute into Kibera from the greater Nairobi area. A "reverse" commute, Kennedy jokes.

Kennedy goes back to Wesleyan after the clinic opens, leaving behind plans to build a substantial supply of clean water and to launch big economic empowerment programs. Foundations and many individuals begin to come forward with amounts large and small to help us build these desperately needed programs. I spend my days working diligently to execute every detail and find the support I need in George, in Kennedy's family, in our amazing local staff, which seems to grow by the day, and in Jordyn, an American who comes to volunteer and then, compelled by our work and the endless activity, decides to stay. Jordyn is dedicated to helping measure the impact of SHOFCO's programs and to creating structures that allow them to grow. Our collaboration soon blossoms into a friendship that without Kennedy's presence in Kenya is a constant source of grounding and inspiration—as well as a boon to the organization. In Kenya, I truly feel I have my own family and community, and beyond that, I see daily proof of our work as patients flow through the health clinic getting treatment and the girls at the school thrive.

Jordyn teaches art classes, one day making beautiful papier-mâché masks and on another painted pasta necklaces. The girls go home for the weekend and come back with only the strings, no pasta. Jordyn learns that they were hungry over the weekend, so they ate the pasta—paint and all. This hits both Jordyn and me—the reality of the need our girls face every day. Beyond working with the girls, Jordyn comes up with the idea of issuing everyone who uses our programs an ID card with a barcode that is scanned upon each use and can track the user in real time. The card contains information about each family's starting socioeconomic status so we can see how they're affected through their participation in our programs. Kennedy realizes that because so few people in the community have formal ID cards, these SHOFCO cards can become a source of real pride, as well as a way to track what is working.

I follow our second-grade class on a field assignment in the community as part of their social studies unit on "community." They set out to map all the facets that comprise a community: businesses, homes, religious institutions. Today they are interviewing a local business owner who runs a small shop, effectively a small convenience store. One girl raises her hand and asks, "Excuse me, sir, can you please tell me where you got your start-up capital?" Teacher Julia and I look at each other in shock. I am so impressed, and can't help but think that even a year ago, start-up capital was a new concept to me. Every day, as I walk to SHOFCO, I see what has already happened, and all that it is yet to be. SHOFCO has come a long way from a twenty-cent soccer ball, but without that first step, none of this would exist.

eighteen

jessica and kennedy

jessica

"I want to take you somewhere," Ken says, waking me up early one morning the week before Christmas. He's back in Kenya on Wesleyan's winter break to get our clean water project flowing. The health clinic only makes so much sense if people don't have access to clean water.

"Don't go back to America," I say, still half asleep. "Stay here with me. It's too hard. I miss you too much when you're not here."

"Pack," he says.

"For what?"

"We're going to the beach," he says.

"The beach?!"

Kennedy never takes a vacation. He doesn't stop moving, and he doesn't like to stop working. Together we've been relentlessly focused on building the infrastructure for clean water, the pinnacle of which will be a huge 100,000-liter tank, the largest supply in the area. Last week, Jordyn and I listened in stunned disbelief as Kennedy and George recounted how they rolled 10,000-liter tanks, huge black plastic barrels bigger than VW beetles, over the rooftops of Kibera.

"Yes. Let's go to the beach," he says. "We deserve a rest, some time together."

This is exactly what I need to hear. There's been so much to do that I've hardly seen him since he's been back, and before I know it he'll be gone again. Every time he comes and goes, it's as if I find my feet and then lose them again.

We take an overnight bus from downtown Nairobi to Mombasa. We find the cheapest place to stay, some tree houses on Diani Beach. Our tree house is simple but beautiful, about a ten-minute walk to the ocean. We spend our days reading and talking about everything, our plans for SHOFCO, the realities of life at Wesleyan without me, and Kenya without him.

Each day feels languid and hot. We walk along the beach feeling the sand in our toes, feeling what it's like to be together again. As I feel the weight of responsibility slide off my shoulders in the Mombasa sunlight, I realize the immense pressure to hold everything together while Kennedy's been gone, to live up to the tremendous potential of this shared vision.

Early one morning we walk along the beach holding hands; the ocean is a transparent blue. All of a sudden, Kennedy is no longer holding my hand. He is down on one knee. My heart drops. He holds out a card.

"Open it."

My chest pounds, as if it might explode.

Dear Jessica, you are the love of my life. This is one of my most important days. Will you spend your life with me? Kennedy.

There's a ring taped inside.

"Yes," I say, kissing him, clutching the card to my heart, pulling him toward me. "Yes."

He puts the ring on my finger.

kennedy

I check with Jessica before I delete the e-mail, thinking it is spam.

It's an invitation from the Clinton Global Initiative, and it's real. How could the former U.S. president share a panel with a slum boy? A junior in college?

Bill Clinton became the president of the United States of America in 1993. That same year, malnourished, I almost died from malaria. In 1993 my family hovered between death and life. My mom left me alone all day while she looked for odd jobs in the slums so that we might survive. I was always hungry and sick, and we had no money to do anything about it.

A little boy striving to survive in the slums could never dream that he would one day meet President Clinton. I barely dreamed of going to school.

Also onstage at the Clinton Global Initiative University event will be the award-winning actor Sean Penn. Sean Penn starred in *Dead Man Walking* in 1995. That was the year I started living on the streets. I joined the gang, slept cold on the streets, and stole food in order to eat.

I feel a bit of a connection to President Bill Clinton, as his father passed away before he was born and his stepfather mistreated his family. Clinton also came from a humble background and was the first one from his family to attend college. He is generous and kind, and when he speaks to me, I feel truly heard.

It is surreal sitting next to him and Sean Penn onstage, and at first it makes me nervous. I know that in Kenya, Liz and George are watching this on a live stream with Jessica even though it is four in the morning there. I don't want to let them down, and knowing they're watching from so far away gives me strength. Soon I am speaking as myself, in my own skin. I even get a little carried away, and as President Clinton winds up the panel with closing remarks without thinking, I ask, "Mr. President, would it be all right if I added something?" He looks at me for a moment with a glint in his eye, but then he smiles, hands me the microphone, and says, "All right, everyone, we'll let Kennedy have the last word." Later, Jessica called to tell me that my sister Liz was horrified that I'd dared to interrupt the former president. Apparently Liz had exclaimed, "Ay ay ay, those people will think we never taught him any manners!"

Later, at the conference, when a speaker tells the story of a fifteen-year-old girl in an African village who got pregnant, had a child, and lived a life filled with suffering and abuse, I can't help but see my mom.

"You must really know what he is talking about," says an important-looking woman in a blue suit. In that moment I feel two burning sensations simultaneously. I, Kennedy Odede, born to poverty and suffering in one of Africa's largest slums, have made something of my life. I look down at my name tag and it reads MEMBER CLINTON GLOBAL INITIATIVE. My dinner place is unmistakably marked KENNEDY ODEDE. The people sitting at this table want to talk to me. I'm on the inside now. But I also feel that, in some ways, I'll forever be sitting on the outside.

Later I will call my mom and tell her about the people I met and spoke to today—and she will not know who any of them are, as she goes to sleep in the small house I'm scraping to rent. That night I cannot fall asleep. I can't help but think that because I belong in some ways to the worlds of Kibera and of the Clinton Global Initiative, I ultimately belong to neither—or maybe in some strange way to both.

jessica

I hold my breath as Kennedy ascends the stairs to the podium, radiant in his bright red graduation cap and gown. I can tell he is nervous. Choked with emotion, I think about the song that came on this morning, "Sunny Days," by Akon. The words echo in my head: *Who'd ever thought that I would see this day.*

Hillary sits to my right, watching his big brother with rapture in his eyes. He now lives with us full-time, and this is his first trip to America.

"Ken is going to be a lawyer now?" he asks me.

"No," I say, shaking my head. "Kennedy is going to change the world."

Liz and George are here too, sharing this moment with us. George is beaming. Yesterday he gave a speech in front of the SHOFCO-Wesleyan group about how much Wesleyan's support means in Kibera. I've never seen George speak in public before, and he was great.

Kennedy begins speaking, and I see how moved everyone is as he shares the improbability of this moment.

"Today, I stand before you as one of the first from a large African slum to graduate from an elite American university. For most of my life, I never imagined that one day I would be standing here.

"For me, Wesleyan is HOPE.

"You, the class of 2012, and my time at Wesleyan have changed me forever.

"I grew up in Kibera. I was the oldest of eight children in a family that could not afford food, much less school fees. In Kibera, I dreamed of many things: food to eat, clean water to drink, safety from the violence, and relief from the oppression that surrounded me.

"Today, I want to tell you three stories about hope:

"One day when I was seven years old, my mom and I set out early in the morning with $3 that we had saved over many months. My mother wanted to enroll me into an informal school in the slum. As we walked through Kibera, I went on about learning to read, growing up to be a teacher or a doctor, and my mom told me, gently, not to get my hopes up too high. When we reached the school, I was smiling from ear to ear, so excited about the bright future ahead. The principal told us that while they did have open spaces, the school fees were $5 per month—not $3. My mom, a woman of great pride, begged and pleaded but had no luck. As we left, I saw the children playing in their bright school uniforms, and as I looked down at my torn clothes, tears began to stream down my face.

"I wanted to be them so badly—I saw opportunity in front of me but knew that I could not be part of it.

"My mom told me that she was sorry. She had tried her best. Love gives us hope, and none of us got here today on our own. Throughout our journeys many people have shown us this kind of love and dedication—which in turn fuels the hope and love that we share with the world. Today my brother, sister, and best friend came all the way from Kibera to celebrate with us, and I want to thank them for being a part of my journey.

"My second story. When I was eighteen, I had a job in a factory. My work started at 7 and ended at 5, with a 2-hour walk each way. I could not afford the 15 cents needed for transport. I performed hard labor—dangerous work—for $1 per day. One day I realized, this was going to be my whole life.

"When I arrived home to the slum one evening, I was horrified to discover that my friend Calvin had hung himself—tired of living a life confined to poverty with only one possible goal: survival.

"This was a moment that changed me. I did not want to waste my life. With twenty cents from my job I bought a soccer ball and started a movement of young people fighting for social justice in Kibera. While I was growing this movement, I met a Wesleyan student studying abroad in Nairobi.

"She thought I should apply to a school I'd never heard of, and without knowing what would happen, I said YES. I was awarded the Bob and Margaret Patricelli scholarship. My mom was so sad to see me leave—but then I translated the cost of a scholarship to Wesleyan into the number of cows that you could buy for the same amount. As you can imagine, it was a lot of cows. Then, she almost picked me up and put me on the plane herself.

"When I first arrived at Wes, I was totally confused. Luckily—I met all of you at freshman orientation.

"I did not know how to work a printer, use a shower, and couldn't understand how money could be stored on a little piece of plastic known as a "Wes Card." During the first week of classes, I would furiously sprint from class to the dining hall, determined to be the first in line. I learned that here the food doesn't get 'finished,' Usdan is open until lunch time ends.

"What struck me the most about the class of 2012 was the kindness exhibited in explanations like this.

"Never before in my life had I felt valued. I always felt that growing up poor was something to be ashamed of, and at first I was scared to talk about my past. I had arrived at an incredible place.

"I said YES, and my life changed. I believe we will only live in a better world if we are willing to take the risks to make it a reality, only if we are willing to say YES. My fellow graduates, I hope that we continue to say YES today, tomorrow, and throughout our lives.

"Finally, when we dare to hope, we create more hope in the world, which is my last story.

"In my freshman dorm room at 200 Church St., I grew my

nonprofit Shining Hope for Communities with the help of another Wes student, Jessica Posner.

"Through Shining Hope we built the Kibera School for Girls—the slum's first tuition-free school for girls. Shining Hope grew because the entire Wesleyan community embraced it.

"From my mentor Professor Rob Rosenthal, who first told me, in true Wesleyan fashion, that I should 'go for it,' to every student who has ever bought a bracelet, Wesleyan students, professors, faculty, and alumni fueled this change in my community. SHOFCO has grown to build a health clinic and provide clean water and community services that will reach thousands of people this year.

"Together we are building hope across the world. My dream is to attend a Wesleyan commencement 13 years from now, and sit where our families are today, to watch a graduate of the Kibera School for Girls accept her Wesleyan diploma, proving yet again that it does not matter where you come from—only where you want to go."

kennedy

As I finish my speech I'm crying. I look at Jessica, and she is shaking. Like me, she can't believe that all this is a reality.

George, Liz, and Hillary are here; it's unbelievable to see their shining faces. Of course at first they denied the visa application for George, and for my little brother Hillary, who is almost like my son in that Jessica and I are raising him together, but now I have connections and was able to rely on them to get the visas. The day before my graduation, I take George around. He can't believe how many people know me—he says it's like walking with me in Kibera.

"Here I'm still the mayor!" I tell George.

George is laughing. "You are truly the lord mayor."

After I give my speech, I am surrounded by so many people. One man comes up to me. I've never met him before, but he gives me a huge hug. "I'm Todd Snyder; let's have dinner in New York. I want to help you." He has tears in his eyes. I think of how special this place is. A few months ago I had lunch next to another alumnus named Tim Dibble, who after meeting me came to visit Kenya with his daughter and joined the board of SHOFCO. He danced in Kibera, and all the mothers of the girls laughed in joy, to see that people from all over the world want to be part of our little movement.

Whoever imagined that all this would be possible? Certainly not me, not me. I can hardly believe my life.

As I walk down the aisle to take my place and wait for Jessica, I see people from every point in my life. Liz, George, and Hillary, who is our ringbearer; my American mother, Linda; all of Jessica's family and friends; people who have helped to build SHOFCO. Bob and Margaret Patricelli and their daughter Alison hosted an amazing event with African food and music in Denver. Bob takes the role of my father. But mostly I have eyes only for Jessica, who is radiant as she walks toward me, waiting to begin the rest of our life together.

When I first met her, I couldn't imagine that she would call Kenya her home one day. Together we create a powerful battalion that is unshakable. A man is just a man, and without her, I could never be where I am. It's always good to have someone who understands you better, someone who does not judge, and someone who is focused on things beyond the material world. Jessica is a gift to my community in Kibera and to all the stakeholders in Shining Hope for Communities. She knew how much I loved Kibera and instead of uprooting me from my community, she rooted me more deeply there. She draws me nearer and closer to my culture, spiritual life, and joyous happiness. I can't describe how I view her, as I don't see any blackness, whiteness, greenness, or redness. But I see love in her, I see peace.

I feel like I've married her before, but this time I take it as a way to share our love with the world.

"Loving you, Kennedy, has taught me that nothing is impossible if you believe it enough," Jessica says in her vows to me.

Feeling very lucky, I read my own vows to the woman I love.

"Which wedding is this?" Jessica's dad jokes at the party afterward.

"Number four," she replies, her face bright with laughter, "if you count the wedding I didn't know about beforehand."

"It's much calmer than the Kenyan wedding," says my new father-in-law.

A few months ago when her family came to Kenya, we invited them and my family to a dinner at my favorite fish restaurant in Nairobi. It was supposed to be an engagement party. My relatives traveled into Nairobi from the village: grandmothers and aunts and cousins. Of course everyone took the occasion very seriously, and soon the dinner had morphed from an engagement party into a wedding, with my family singing and dancing and then demanding that Jessica's family give her to them. Her dad didn't like that idea.

He stopped the whole ceremony and said, "Wait. Now you guys have to give Kennedy to us."

Silence. The men in my family looked confused, angry.

"That's not how it works," said my uncle Dan.

But then my aunt Beatrice, a secret feminist, stood up and exclaimed, "Exactly."

She took me by the arms and pushed me across, giving me to Jessica's family, fair and square.

Afterward chaotic dancing and celebration erupted.

George ceremoniously gave Jessica's dad the rope that should go around a cow's neck, saying that he'd thoughtfully left the cow at home.

epilogue

jessica

Two white tents stand illuminated, in the early morning light, on an open acre of ground that is the only space of its kind in Kibera. SHOFCO is here now. The initial building for the school for girls is presently just a tiny piece of the sprawling compound of buildings and activity that have since sprouted. Several months ago, almost a hundred families voluntarily moved to give us more space to continue to expand. Behind the tents the bright blue of the expanded Kibera School for Girls emerges; the water tower stands high, and the clinic is always teeming. The toilets have now multiplied all over the community, and the tiny old first school building has been converted into a community center for our economic empowerment programs. In the rare early-morning quiet, I sit in the middle of what we've built, amazed that in six short years all this stands here, each little piece impossible yet realized.

People begin to arrive slowly. There are tables where staff members in blue SHOFCO shirts check people in—women, old men, young people. The chairs fill. The tents are now spotted with color. Today is the launch for Kennedy's SHOFCO Urban Network, called SUN, which, we hope, will help women and young people to come together and organize for their rights, talk about peace and justice, access services, learn financial literacy, and start saving money that will enable them to open businesses. Hundreds of people stream in past the borehole that we sunk only last week—the huge trailers with massive machinery miraculously making their way down the narrow main road thanks to George. It's amazing to see everyone assemble here in this place that five years ago didn't exist. All the people gathering register at hastily assembled tables, and our staff works diligently to accommodate them. SHOFCO's team has grown to over 235 employees. Jordyn and George, along with so many others who began this journey with us, are still committed to the growth of our work.

I walk through the halls of the empty school, looking at the brightly colored artwork and posters about ecosystems. Downstairs in the lower school, there is a wall dedicated to the idea of human rights. Each girl has written what she has a right to: the right to freedom of expression, the right to assembly, the right to housing, and one says the right to dream. Now our classes are much bigger, forty girls a year in each class instead of our original fifteen.

In the economic empowerment room, there's a wall we call the "magic wall." People are saving and taking loans. Currently about nine million shillings, over $100,000, is in savings and being loaned out by our trained facilitators to launch over four hundred businesses a year. This system has utterly changed the realities of families like that of Evelyn, who started a peanut butter business, or Mama Mary, who started selling tomatoes and expanded into *sukuma* and avocado. Today her vegetable stand is booming.

I look at one sign in the corridor. It's a picture of a girl with a backpack and a Kibera School for Girls uniform. It says "Chief Justice 2034 from the Kibera School for Girls." Another one says,

"Name: Martha Achieng. Age: 10 years old. Dream job: President. What you are doing to reach your goal: Being proactive, working hard, being optimistic, being fair, practicing being a leader." I shake my head in amazement.

In the gender violence office, another chart hangs on the wall. Last year, 273 cases were reported to this office. Cases are being reported that before were silenced by the fear of the sheer difficulty of successfully bringing cases to court. Today we have 55 active cases, including the one we brought for Nancy, who is four years old and an orphan, abandoned by her parents and living with an uncle and aunt who never watched her. She was raped by a fourteen-year-old neighbor. Today she lives in the safe house. Shy at first, Nancy smiles sweetly, proud to show off the new English words she learns every day. Mario, one of our caseworkers, and Baba Julie, who still works in the gender department, heard a story about a nine-year-old girl who had been locked in a house for a weekend and raped repeatedly. Without fear for their own safety, they charged into the house, breaking down the door, where they found Caroline tied to a bed, unable to walk. Mario carried her out of that house, through the slum, to us. Today, Caroline attends the same boarding school where my sister Raphae helped raise money to send Kennedy's siblings—and she is thriving.

Baba Julie still has not seen justice in his daughter's case. We've been to court over ten times and worked with countless lawyers, but somehow, something always goes wrong. The perpetrator has money, and we've never figured out which judges or magistrates or clerks are in his pocket, but that doesn't deter Baba Julie. He's determined to get justice for all of these girls. Julie is thriving. She doesn't like to be called baby anymore. She says she's big now, and she's right.

Priscilla is healthy and back at home with her mom, who started a tailoring business and is now making enough money to support herself without having to rely on her husband.

Our clinics alone will serve over sixty thousand patients this year. A nutrition program saves lives. Our early childhood program provides immunizations and deworming, allowing mothers to deliver safely and their babies to grow up healthy. The water infrastructure that Kennedy put in place is robust and growing. Not a day passes without water, and now we're planning to expand the system throughout Kibera with a one-of-a-kind aerial piping system. We've opened a community preschool and day care to give children the chances they deserve right from the start.

As I walk back outside to this open space we used to dream of—a space big enough to build an expanded school, more water, a meeting room big enough to hold huge gatherings of the community—Kennedy's urban network launch is well under way. He stands in front of the crowd, where he belongs.

"Alone there is nothing we can do, but together we are powerful," he intones, and the crowd goes wild.

In the summer of 2014, we held a peace rally. There was word that intratribal violence was brewing as it had in 2007 after the election. So Kennedy brought together fifty community leaders, the people most likely to start the violence, and, most important, their wives. He invited them for lunch in Kibera. In SHOF-CO's largest meeting room, everyone stood up and introduced themselves. These were people who had held animosity against each other for decades—from the Nubian community, from the Kikuyu community, from the Luo community—all together, peacefully, in one room. Everyone present agreed to sign a public peace declaration. One by one, the leaders stood up, their wives cheering them on.

Many women stood up and said, "I'm a leader, too. I have to sign."

We were still worried that violence was a possibility, but on the day of our peace rally we marched through the community, a thousand people strong, shutting down the main throughway of Kibera, the *matatus* surprisingly agreeable as we passed. We arrived at Kamukunji, the big open ground before the railway, and over five thousand people came to demonstrate their own commitment to peace, to living in a community together. There was no violence. When it was over, Kennedy and I looked at each other and breathed out a sigh of relief, and that's when he'd said, "We have to start our own urban movement; together we are strong." Hundreds of people came to the launch of the urban network, and a subsequent event is planned for thousands.

In September 2014 we opened a School for Girls in Mathare, Nairobi's second-largest slum, to which we are working to add a health clinic and clean water—all started and led by local young people from the Mathare community. Mathare's gender violence and economic empowerment programs are already running, launched by a young man named Godi who heard Kennedy's story and was inspired about what he might be able to do in his community. Young people from slums all over Nairobi have come looking for Kennedy, wanting to build SHOFCOs in their communities, driven by this spirit of grassroots change. One day we hope to help communities in Mombasa and Kisumu, all over the country, maybe even the continent, building empowered, healthy communities and an urban movement for change and justice—and the next generation of women leaders.

As Kennedy finishes his speech, I look around for Hillary—he's run off playing with Liz's daughter, Baby Jess. Liz is going to school to become a councillor, and Jess is a student at the Kibera School for Girls. A few weekends ago at the Java House over his favorite breakfast of a chicken quesadilla, Hillary talked to me about his current dream to become a scientist who researches cures for diseases like the ones people in Kibera face. At nine, he thought pensively, and said, "I think my beliefs are part Christian, part Jewish, and part scientist." I looked at him in amazement, this child who has become such a miraculous part of my and Kennedy's life together, and has parts of us both in him, yet is so uniquely himself.

A few weeks ago I was showing a group of our supporters around Kibera, and we visited one of the Newman's Own Foundation toilets SHOFCO has built in an area that never had a toilet before. An old man I'd never met followed me as I walked out and told my visitor, "You know she may not look like us, but she is one of us. She is married here."

Standing by the railway late at night, after another long day, sometimes I think that maybe this is enough. To be married to a place and a purpose and to the possibility of girls' schools in slums all over the country, connected to social services. I walk over to Kennedy where he stands in conversation with several parents and slide my hand into his. He grips it protectively. "Let's go home," I whisper to him.

"We already are," he whispers back.

To learn more and support the work of Shining Hope for Communities (SHOFCO), go to www.shofco.org.

Support like yours makes SHOFCO's work to transform the lives of tens of thousands living in urban poverty possible.

authors' note

Some of this book is based upon contemporaneous journals and shared oral histories, and for much of this book we have relied upon our own memories. As such, the dialogue is necessarily an approximation of what was actually said or relayed. For compression's sake, some characters are composites of people we have known and some events have been condensed and appear out of precise chronological order. For the sake of their privacy, the names of many characters have been changed.

acknowledgments

As Kennedy's mother would say, we have been so fortunate to encounter many "small gods" along our paths. We are forever grateful for the many who have supported, championed, and believed in us. May we continue to travel along this path with your continued love and support.

At Ecco, our editor, Hilary Redmon, always saw what this book had the potential to become, and her deft perceptiveness (along with her patience) shepherded it into this final form. Dan Halpern believed in this project, Craig Young devoted endless energy and friendship, Sonya Cheuse and Kate D'Esmond lent their publicity prowess—along with Tina Andreadis, who made us smile—and Emma Janaskie kept it all organized. Thank you all for bringing this story to life.

This project wouldn't exist without the diligence and fierce belief of our literary agent and friend, Stuart Krichevsky. From helping us bang out final drafts with chocolate at his kitchen table, to observing every little detail, Stuart always went above and beyond. We are thankful to our teacher, Anne Greene, for making this fortuitous introduction, and for her own influence and inspiration to our writing and to the evolution of SHOFCO.

Our dear friend Cynthia Ryan, who supported us deeply throughout this project and in so many other ways, introduced us to Ariane Conrad. Just when we thought we would never finish (after two years of working away!), Ariane showed us the way, held our hands, gave this book invaluable structure, added brilliant insight and editorial feedback, and ultimately helped us give birth to this book in its complete form. Thank you doesn't cover it. The MacDowell Colony gave us needed quiet and space to write, and the Ford Foundation and Rosemary Okello-Orlale made the completion of this project possible.

Deep thanks goes to Jordyn Wells; without her passion and dedication to SHOFCO none of this would have grown, and her friendship has meant so much to both of us along the way. We are also eternally grateful to George Okewa, who is the heart and soul of SHOFCO, an inspiring leader, and a dear friend. George, you truly make the impossible happen. To the incredibly dedicated and talented staff of SHOFCO, all 235 of them at this writing, your daily passion and dedication inspires, and it is our privilege to know and work with each of you. Thank you for being the change that drives the SHOFCO movement.

We have each been blessed to have friends and teachers who have supported and brought out the best in us. Wesleyan University, and the entire Wes community, have made so much possible for both of us—there is no place like it. Rob Rosenthal, it was a miracle that Kennedy was assigned to be your advisee. Our first board chair, dear friend, who even got ordained online to marry us—without you none of this would exist. To our teachers at Wesleyan—Alice Hadler, Ann duCille, Anne Greene, Jonathan Cutler and Renee Romano—you taught us to write and more, for which we are forever grateful. To Daphne Schmon, you first told Jess to go abroad and embraced Kennedy when he came to Wesleyan, and you have been along for the ride ever since. To

Elsa Chin and Peter Frank for friendship, website creation, movement building, and, most important, letting us have fun and laugh when we needed it the most—thank you for supporting this project and us.

Along the way, many amazing and generous people have stepped forward to guide us and to build SHOFCO into the movement it is today, pouring in endless time and energy. To all of our board members, past and present, we have learned much from you, and we've sure aggravated you—but mostly we've loved becoming your friends. Our board at present includes Todd Snyder (our current chair; we never thought his effusive hug after Kennedy's graduation speech would land him here, but we are so glad it did), Tim Dibble (our recovering board chair, incredible mentor, honorary Kibera elder, chief of the Dibblets), Abby Disney (first introduced to us by her daughter Chachi, Kennedy's writing tutor at Wes; her family has become our family, her friendship we count on for so much), Richard Cunningham (bwana mkubwa and more), Matt Chanoff (whose daughter Yael lived on Kennedy's hall, and who gave us our first individual contribution and so much more), Andy Snyder (who read about us in Nick's column, and dove in together with his family), Matt Sirovich (who bravely trekked across the world with his family to visit, and whose deep empathy and support always moves us), Bill Ford (for strategic insight and wisdom), Bob Patricelli (for being part of your family), Leslie Bluhm (for believing in women and girls), and David Luusa (Kennedy's very first Kenyan friend from outside of Kibera). The stories of how each of you became involved are precious to us. Not only do we love you, but we also love your families, which we have been grateful to be made part of.

To the SHOFCO Leadership Council, for helping us extend this movement to new places. Your energy, enthusiasm, and dedication allow us to bring more hope to girls around the world. Thank you for your many contributions.

SHOFCO got its first big push forward through the generosity of Newman's Own Foundation, which has believed in and supported our growth all along the way. Paul Newman always spoke about the power of luck, and the foundation's generosity enables us to create pockets of luck worlds away. We are grateful to the entire Newman's Own community. To Bob and Linda Forrester, your endless friendship and mentorship mean so much.

We have been fortunate to encounter incredible champions whose spotlights have been instrumental in growing our work. To Nicholas Kristof and Sheryl WuDunn—thank you for caring so deeply and shining such a hopeful light on what is possible. We want to thank everyone involved in both the *Half the Sky* and *A Path Appears* projects, especially the unstoppable Maro Chermayeff, and dear friends Mikaela Beardsley and Jamie Gordon, whose friendship means so much. Thank you to our champions who utilize their platforms to promote good. We are forever grateful for the support and involvement of Chelsea Clinton, President Bill Clinton, Mia and Ronan Farrow, Maria Menounos, Beyoncé, and Olivia Wilde.

There are several supporters and mentors who have been there for us along this journey, in particular early believers and friends David and Lisa Issroff; Amy Herskovitz, who saw potential from the start; Echoing Green (especially mentor Cheryl Dorsey); the Segal Family Foundation; the Cordes Foundation; Gucci's Chime for Change and Christophe de Pous; Marty and Arna Caplan for their educational expertise and more; the Chapin School; and Jodi Kahn and Fred Poust. Sincere gratitude to Debbie McLeod and Jay Sears, who have provided calm weekends to rejuvenate, as well as friendship and tireless support. To Reeta Roy, for her belief in us and for always anchoring us in what matters. Wendy Kopp, for paving the way. Bill Wetzel for always including us. Sarah Williams and Jeremy Mindich (and family), for advice and a deep belief in our work.

Finally, to our girls: you inspire, challenge, and make us believe in the power of dreams. We are deeply committed to seeing that you achieve yours! To all of the members of SHOFCO's communities in Kibera and Mathare—and in future locations—you are showing the world that change can come from the inside, and your resilience and determination to make tomorrow better for your community and children continues to drive this movement forward.

This book and our work would not have been possible without the support, love, and patience of our families. To our Hillary, we are thankful for your patience with the disease you have diagnosed us with—"TB" (too busy)—and for your spirit and generous heart. To Jess's family: David, Helen, Max, and Raphae, for their endless love and support, open arms, patience, and late-night edits. To Kennedy's family: Ajey, Jackie, Liz, Victor, Jasmine, Collins, and Shadrack, for embracing us both and for your inspiration to overcome. To the Studer family: Linda, Ray, Emily, Alyssa, and Maren, for creating a bond in a true leap of faith. To Kennedy's "American Dad" Bob Patricelli and his wife, Margaret, along with their gang—for always being there and for many firsts—including an education.

SHOFCO is truly a movement, and there are thousands of individuals and organizations that have made our growth possible, including all of our sponsors, donors, and volunteers. We are so grateful to every one of them. In particular, we would like to thank the following cornerstone supporters, without whose immense generosity we would not be where we are today: Colleen Abdoulah and Ruth Warren, Africa Direct and Elizabeth Bennett and Sarah Luther, Robert and Shirley Allen, Kojo Annan, Dorris J. Baker, Barclays Bank, John Bernstein, Bertha Foundation, Cornelia and Michael Bessie Foundation, Steffanie and Garvin Brown, Susan Buchsbaum and Karl Frieden, Arna and Marty Caplan, Lisa and Matt Chanoff, the Chapin School, Sharon and Mike Clayton, Child Relief International, the Clinton

Global Initiative, the Commonwealth Foundation, the Cordes Foundation, Richard and Roslyn Cunningham, Mark Currie, the Deerfield Foundation, Timothy and Maureen Dibble, Dining for Women, Abigail Disney and Pierre Hauser, the Roy and Patricia Disney Family Foundation, Tim Disney, Stephanie Dodson, Matthew Donohoe, James and Mary Donovan, DoSomething.org, ELMA Philanthropies, the Fine and Greenwald Foundation, Fins Family Foundation, Bill Ford, the Ford Foundation, the Kim Frank Family Fund, the Samuel Freeman Charitable Trust, Mark Gallogly, GE Foundation, Judith Gillespie, Give a Hand, the Global Fund for Children, Grant Me the Wisdom Foundation and Debbie McLeod and Jay Sears, the Greenbaum Foundation, Gucci's Chime for Change, Johnson Haefling Foundation, Hassenfeld Family Foundation, Leslie Bluhm and David Helfand, Conrad N. Hilton Foundation, Coppy Holzman, Amos and Barbara Hostetter, IDEO, Jewish Women's Foundation of New York (JWFNY) Isha Koach, Dan and Cathey Jinich, Moises and Ruth Jinich, the Kemmerer Family Foundation, Kimberly and Brad Keywell, Nicole Laceby and Dustin Gaspari, the Lefkofsky Family Foundation, the Lester Fund, Brad Lindenbaum and Jamie Gordon, Magpie Giving Circle, the MasterCard Foundation, Jack Meyer, Mobile Decision Africa (MoDe) and Julian Kyula, Blair Miller, Stephen Morgan, the Mother's Day Movement, the Morris Family Foundation, Newman's Own Foundation, Roxana Nikdjou, Tracy Nixon, the O'Reilly Foundation, Oak Foundation, Robert and Margaret Patricelli, Pentair Foundation, the Pershing Square Innovation Lab/the Pershing Square Foundation, Steven Phillips, Planned Parenthood Federation of America (and Cecile Richards), Josh Posner and Eileen Rudden, Propel Capital and the Mindich family, Sarah Rivlin, Kali Rosenblum and Kevin Smith, Mary Schorr, Scopia Capital, Segal Family Foundation, She's the First, SHOFCO Leadership Council, SHOFCO Wesleyan, Show of Force—Force Film Foundation, Matt Sirovich and Meredith Elson, Molly and Andrew Snyder, Phoebe Boyer and Todd Snyder, Starr International Foundation and Florence Davis, John Stellato, the Taft Foundation, Take Action Hollywood and Maria Menounos, TCI Consulting and Tilden Katz, Betsy Teutsch and family, Three Graces Foundation, Townsend Press, Adam Usdan, Christian Wait and family, Laith and Melanie Wark, Craig Wright, Nathan Yip Foundation, the Zimmerman Family Foundation and 100 Projects for Peace.

There are many important people who have been part of our life journey who we regret might not appear on this list, but they are in the list of our heart.

about the authors

kennedy odede is one of Africa's best-known community organizers and social entrepreneurs. He was raised in Kibera, where he experienced the devastating realities of life in extreme poverty, and started the Shining Hope for Communities (SHOFCO) movement. Driven by the innovation and entrepreneurial spirits of the people of Kibera, SHOFCO became the largest grassroots organization in the slum. Kennedy was named a "Forbes 30 Under 30" top social entrepreneur, is a recipient of the Muhammad Ali Humanitarian Award, a World Economic Forum Young Global Leader, and a trustee of Wesleyan University.

jessica posner is the cofounder of Shining Hope for Communities. She is a widely recognized social entrepreneur and activist. She graduated Phi Beta Kappa with honors in African American Studies from Wesleyan University. She won the 2010 Do Something Award and was named "America's top world-changer 25 and under" live on VH1. Jessica also received the prestigious Echoing Green Fellowship, and is the youngest alumna to receive the "Distinguished Alumni" award from Wesleyan University. Jessica speaks Swahili, and she splits her time between Nairobi and New York City with her husband, Kennedy.